NOTES

ON

POLITICAL ECONOMY

BY

JACOB N. CARDOZO

NOTES

ON

POLITICAL ECONOMY

BY

JACOB N. CARDOZO

WITH AN INTRODUCTORY ESSAY

J. N. CARDOZO AND AMERICAN ECONOMIC THOUGHT

BY JOSEPH DORFMAN

AND WITH SELECTIONS FROM

CARDOZO'S OTHER ECONOMIC WRITINGS

[1826]

AUGUSTUS M. KELLEY • PUBLISHERS

CLIFTON 1972

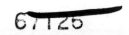

First Edition 1826

(Charleston: *Printed by* A. E. Miller, *4, Broad-Street*, 1826)

Reprinted 1960, 1972 by

Augustus M. Kelley Publishers

REPRINTS OF ECONOMIC CLASSICS

Clifton New Jersey 07012

I S B N *0 678 00860 4*

L C N *A63-72*

PRINTED IN THE UNITED STATES OF AMERICA
by SENTRY PRESS, NEW YORK, N. Y. 10013

TABLE OF CONTENTS

INTRODUCTION

APPENDIX I

APPENDIX II

APPENDIX III

APPENDIX IV

INTRODUCTION.

Jacob Nuñez Cardozo and American Economic Thought[1]

As the second quarter of the nineteenth century got under way, there was a world-wide movement to make the infant science of economics, or as it was then called, political economy, an instrument for promoting sound economic policy. To indicate the importance of this tendency, it is sufficient to recall the contemporary activity and influence of such famous British writers as Thomas Robert Malthus, David Ricardo, Nassau W. Senior, James Mill, John Stuart Mill and others of the school of philosophical radicals. Economics would dispel the ignorance of the citizenry and legislators.

Americans were prominent in this effort to devise useful doctrines and to elucidate previously obscure points. Southern writers were as active as Northern. Virginia, for example, offered at least two first rate minds: George Tucker, legislator, philosopher, historian, the first instructor in economics in Jefferson's University of Virginia, a pioneer in demography and an early advocate of regional central banks (an idea embodied in the Federal Reserve Act of 1913) ; and Charles Ellet Jr., engineer and pioneer in mathematical

[1] This is an elaboration of the introduction to the 1960 reprint of Cardozo's *Notes on Political Economy*. This edition is expanded by the inclusion of additional writings by Cardozo. For a detailed analysis of Cardozo's views see Joseph Dorfman, *The Economic Mind in American Civilization*, 5 vols. (1946-1959; Augustus M. Kelley Publishers, 1967-1969) II, 551, 566, 572-273, 847, 852-862, 939, 950, 985-987; III, 5, 11, 12, 80; see also, Alexander Brody, "Jacob Newton Cardozo, American Economist," *Historica Judaica*, October 1953, pp. 135-166; and Melvin M. Leiman, *Jacob N. Cardozo* (1966).

analysis, which he expounded in *An Essay on the Laws of Trade in reference to the Internal Works of Improvement in the United States* (1830). In Louisiana, there was James Dunwoody Brownson DeBow, the leading statistician of his day, superintendent of the Seventh Census of the United States from 1853 to 1855, and editor of the famous *DeBow's Review*, which was devoted "to commerce, agriculture, manufacture, internal improvements, education, political economy, general literature, etc."

South Carolina produced the most vigorous contingent. It was fast becoming the leading southern state, politically and intellectually. Thomas Cooper, first a professor and later president of South Carolina College and a leader in the formulation and popularization of the doctrine of nullification, was known throughout the United States and Europe for his *Lectures on the Elements of Political Economy* (1826; 2nd edition, 1829). The book was so persuasive in presenting the case for free trade that northern protectionists commissioned Friedrich List, fresh from Germany, to prepare an answer which appeared first in newspapers and then as *Outlines of American Political Economy* (1827).[2]

Of the galaxy of economists in South Carolina, the most distinguished intellectual figure was Jacob Nuñez Cardozo (1786-1873). His analytical gifts and his talent as a publicist made him widely influential in public affairs. He was one of those southerners who played an important role in their time, but whose fame was dimmed in the shadow of the Civil War. This would help to explain why so little is known about him. Like Ricardo and Senior, he descended from a Sephardic (Spanish-Portuguese) Jewish mercantile family. His father, David N. Cardozo, was a non-commissioned officer in the South Carolina militia in the Revolutionary War.[3]

---

[2] On his return to Germany, List later elaborated the *Outlines* into his famous *The National System of Political Economy*.

[3] The eminent jurist Benjamin N. Cardozo was descended from David's brother, Isaac.

David was one of the leaders in the gallant but ill-fated assault by the combined American and French forces on Savannah, Georgia, in 1779. Shortly thereafter he settled in Charleston, South Carolina, and there young Jacob Cardozo was reared and spent most of his life.

He left school at the age of twelve and was apprenticed to a trade, later becoming a lumber clerk. From his earliest years, he was an avid reader. He had the advantage of living in a center of learning, high level discussion clubs and influential journalism. He first came before the public in 1811 as a member of the Methulogic Society, with an address which was published as *An Oration on the Literary Character*. In 1816 he became a writer for the Charleston *Southern Patriot,* and began a career in journalism as contributor, editor and publisher that continued until his death in August 1873 in Savannah.[4]

Through his newspaper and magazine articles and his *Notes on Political Economy* (1826), Cardozo acquired a national reputation as a student of political economy, and in particular, the tariff, banking and commercial statistics. His editorials, especially in *The Southern Patriot,* were often reprinted in leading papers both in the North and the South. His introduction of "price quotations" of cotton in 1845 in the Charleston *Evening News* was soon imitated by other important newspapers. His successive statistical studies of the supply and consumption of cotton, largely in the Charleston *Courier* and *DeBow's Review,* were pioneer attempts at forecasting.

Leaders of his state and of the nation appreciated his talent as a one man "brain trust." He was a member of the committee that drew up the *Memorial of the Chamber of Commerce and the Citizens of Charleston against the Tariff on Woolen Goods, Proposed at the Second Session of the 19th Congress* (1827), which became a fundamental source for the southern case against the protective tariff system. He was also a mem-

---

[4] He had returned to the town of his birth for the last time in April.

ber of the various committees that drew up petitions for the promotion of the first extensive railroad in the United States, the South Carolina Railroad and Canal Company, which was chartered in 1827. He played a major role in the adoption of the Sub-Treasury system in President Van Buren's administration.[5] His series of articles, "Government and Banking," in *The Southern Patriot* in 1837, which was reprinted throughout the country, served to prepare the public for the eventual introduction of the system.

Cardozo's outlook was conservative. For example, while his younger brother Isaac was prominent in the first movement for reform Judaism in the United States, he remained staunchly orthodox. In the matter of the franchise, he was skeptical of the removal of the property qualification for voting, because he feared a struggle for spoils. He believed in state's rights, but he vigorously opposed the doctrine of nullification developed by his friends, John C. Calhoun and Thomas Cooper. The doctrine had arisen in protest against the "Tariff of Abominations" of 1828 and Cardozo was a powerful opponent of protective tariffs. But in the widely quoted *The Tariff: Its True Character and Effects Practically Illustrated* (1830), reprinted below, he observed that the tariff system with all its "attendant losses and prospective risks," was still a lesser evil than a separation of the states. "We should prefer making a large sacrifice even to the odious spirit of monopoly, sooner than break up and scatter, never to be reunited, the elements of this glorious scheme of Republican Federative Government." Though he supported slavery, he always opposed the proposal to reopen the African slave trade, and even declared that slave labor was, on the basis of "principles of universal operation, . . . far less effective than any other equal amount of voluntary service."

Cardozo was a strong believer in *laissez faire*, but

---

[5] Under the system, payments to and disbursements by the federal government were made exclusively in hard money through the Treasury and its branches (Sub-Treasuries).

this by no means precluded "the active fostering care of government" for economic expansion in a variety of areas. He advocated aid by the state of South Carolina for internal improvements, including railroad construction and the drainage of the swamp lands for the low country planters. He opposed federal aid for internal improvements on the ground that such aid was largely of sectional benefit, especially to the West at the expense of the rest of the country. At the same time, however, he favored federal subsidies for steamship lines to Europe and the West Indies. He stressed such aid on grounds both of national defense and of economic benefit. He even went so far as to protest in the Charleston *Evening News* in 1859 against cutting off the subsidy for American ships, because "it would seem as if our national legislature were alive to nothing more elevated than the saving of the 'almighty dollar.' Our system of economy has made us the laughing stock of all Europe and reduced our pretentions to rank among the nations of the earth to the smallest proportions."

Cardozo maintained that the improvement of labor's condition could not be achieved by direct legislative action. Rather it should be accomplished by "qualified reforms" such as the voluntary promotion of building and loan associations to encourage home ownership; and libraries and mechanics' institutes to provide lectures and publish appropriate tracts for the artisans.

Unlike most southerners, Cardozo was convinced that the South's reliance on cotton was a major economic weakness. As early as 1826, he pleaded for the South to diversify and engage in industrial development, especially cotton manufactures. The lead, he emphasized, must be taken by a few bold persevering innovators, whose example would overcome the timidity of the great mass of habit-bound cultivators. To stimulate industrial development, he urged the banks to ease loans for new industrial enterprises rather than foolishly to make advances to cotton dealers to withhold the staple for a "speculative price."

As early as the money panic of 1819, Cardozo began

a continuous discussion of what has since been called
"business cycles." He struck a modern note in empha-
sizing the world wide and cyclical character of these
"periods of stagnation and excitement." He wrote in
The Southern Patriot, in the midst of the panic of 1837,
that the current "revulsion" originated in one of "those
general and irresistible changes in human affairs which
follow in a cycle, alternating at periods irregular in
duration but powerful in action." In *Debow's Review*
in 1858, he commented that the country was "passing
through one of those commercial cycles with which we
are destined to be visited at about every decade."[6]

Unlike many economists, Cardozo did not believe that
the expansion of the circulating media, especially in the
form of bank notes, was the major or the originating
cause of the disturbances, but he did hold that the banking system was an aggravating factor. To a limited
extent, bank reform was feasible and desirable, particularly in connection with bank notes. From the stand-
point of the regulation of the currency he supported as
noted above the establishment of the Sub-Treasury
system. As an immediate relief measure, he proposed
during the panic of 1837 that the federal government
issue treasury notes to an amount limited to the absolutely necessary government expenditures and the
merchants' needs for domestic remittances.

During the Civil War, Cardozo used his influence in
the direction of restoring the value of the constantly
depreciating confederate currency. Through widely
read editorials in the Atlanta *Southern Confederacy* and
especially in the pamphlet, *A Plan of Financial Relief*
(1863), he deprecated price fixing, but called for some
reliance on taxation and more on gradual funding of
the paper currency into long term bonds. In the post
Civil War period, he noted in 1870 that the sectional
conflict had been accompanied "by a disarrangement of
labor without parallel in the history of the [cotton]
trade, and a disturbance of the relations between supply

---

[6] "Supply and Consumption of Cotton . . .," *DeBow's Review*,
May 1858, p. 396. Reprinted below as Appendix No. 4.

and consumption, of a magnitude that threatens its subversion."[7]

In articles in leading journals both North and South in 1869-1870, Cardozo proposed far reaching reforms of the currency and banking system of the nation.[8] In his modified form of the plan of "the late David Ricardo, distinguished author and legislator," he proposed the elimination of bank notes and the entrusting to a federal government board the exclusive power of issuing paper money. This would be convertible into specie on demand. Under his scheme, Cardozo said, the issue of paper money would be regulated "by a principle that adds to the currency in proportion to the increase of population, thus making the wants of the public the measure of issue." He argued that the Board would thus be bound to "follow a principle that would be self acting and unalterable; namely, the increase in the paper currency in the ratio of the increase of population."[9]

To cure the abuses of bank credit, that is, excessive credit, Cardozo proposed that the banks regulate themselves voluntarily. His suggestion later became a matter of "lively controversy" over central bank policy: a graduated rate of bank discount and a corresponding

[7] The quotation is from Cardozo's circular *Comparative Value of Hired and Purchased Labor in Producing Cotton.* I have been unable to locate a copy of the circular but a very brief summary including the above quotation appeared in the February 1870 issue of *The XIX Century.*

[8] "Essay on Banking and Currency," *Bankers' Magazine and Statistical Register,* March 1869, and "Systems of Banking and Currency," *The Southern Review,* April 1870. The latter, which is an elaborated version of the former, is reprinted below as Appendix No. 3.

[9] "Systems of Banking and Currency," *The Southern Review,* April 1870, pp. 372, 380, 400.

Cardozo's scheme had been advanced as early as 1851 by the New Yorker George Opdyke in *A Treatise on Political Economy.* Opdyke was a prominent business man and Civil War mayor of New York City. They both also proposed $10 *per capita* as the appropriate starting point for the experiment; Opdyke's proposal, however, differed in one fundamental respect from that of Cardozo. He proposed that the paper money should be legal tender and not redeemable in hard money. (On Opdyke, see Joseph Dorfman, *The Economic Mind in American Civilization,* II, 755-757, 968, 969; III, pp. 13, 16, viii).

term of credit. The rate would rise with every extension of the term of credit, and fall with every shortening of the term. The details should be arranged not by legislative regulation but by convention through a general meeting of the bank representatives in a central clearing city like New York. He suggested as a model the recent efforts of the insurance companies to obtain uniformity of practice. Threatened by the wiping out of their capital by "destructive fires in the different cities over the United States," they met at New York and set up a national board to supervise "the rates, or tariffs of insurance, and all other matters connected with or affecting the interest of underwriting." He thought that there should be "a similar board representing the interests of banks, . . . whose office it would be to watch the indications of a rise of the spirit of speculation in its earliest stages. Shall we surrender all chance of such improvement in the administration of banks as may prevent the periodical recurrence of speculation and overtrading attended by crises, revulsions, panics and bankruptcy, inflicting social evils which are an opprobrium of civilization?"[10]

Cardozo considered himself an arch critic of Ricardo and his "new school" but, as he said of the American Ricardian, Thomas Cooper, in *The Southern Patriot* in 1826, their differences were not over "practical conclusions," but over "the Metaphysics of the science"; in other words, over what would be called today value theory. Cardozo's value theory is presented in *Notes on Political Economy* and in his essay "Political Economy —Rent," in *The Southern Review* of February 1828, which are reprinted below. These works influenced such diverse figures as the free trader Cooper and the foremost theoretician of protectionism and industrialization in pre-Civil War America, Henry C. Carey.

They are quite suggestive for modern economic

---

[10] "Systems of Banking and Currency," *The Southern Review*, April 1870, pp. 389-390.

analysis. Among Cardozo's significant controversial discussions, in these two works, are the unconscious effect on the economist's thinking of prevailing institutions and laws, the impact of immediate practical problems on the development of economics, criticisms of the labor theory of value and the corollary of class conflict, the distinction between value and price, the use of the categories of production and consumption as correlatives of those of supply and demand, the recognition of the importance of demand or expenditure as well as supply or production in the maintenance and expansion of the economy, and his sophisticated treatment of "gluts," money, international trade and taxation.

Perhaps Cardozo's most important contribution is the emphasis on a continuous advance in technology or "inventive powers" in the development of the nation's "productive powers." This march of technology, he contended, held almost as much hope for agriculture as for industry. This germinal idea undercut the view then prevalent at home and abroad that the material progress of the United States was due primarily to the vast amount of wild, fertile land, and that the growth of population would eventually bring into play the "Ricardian" law of diminishing returns, with resulting misery and decay. For Cardozo, the progress of technology more than offset this threat in any dynamic or historical sense and would yield both labor and capital increasing returns; in fact, and this is an idea that Carey was to popularize, labor would gain both proportionately and absolutely, while capital gained in absolute amount. This was particularly true in the United States which, he declared in *Notes on Political Economy,* conformed more closely than the old world to "a natural state of the social system"; that is, "a country whose institutions and laws have done less to derange the natural order of things than where a vicious social organization has resulted either from military violence or a selfish policy."

Thus Cardozo emerges as a significant prophet of the future of America.

Let me add a word on this second edition of the reprint of the *Notes on Political Economy*. The 1960 reprint contained in addition to the *Notes*, the essay "Political Economy—Rent" as an appendix. The present edition includes three more items. These are drawn from his three major specialties outside the field of general theory: the tariff, banking and economic forecasting. The first is represented by *The Tariff: Its True Character and Effects Practically Illustrated* (1830), which originally appeared as a series of editorials in *The Southern Patriot* and then was brought out as a pamphlet. The second, "Systems of Banking," from *The Southern Review*, April 1870, was his most comprehensive as well as his last essay on monetary and banking policy. From the field of economic forecasting, I have chosen "Supply and Consumption of Cotton, with Tables Annexed of the Supply and Consumption for the Last Thirty Years" (*DeBow's Review*, May 1858). It evidences an effective blending of his talents as theorist, economic historian, statistician and journalist.

Columbia University
June 1971

Joseph Dorfman

NOTES

ON

POLITICAL ECONOMY.

BY J. N. CARDOZO.

CHARLESTON:

PRINTED BY A. E. MILLER,

4, Broad-Street.

1826.

TABLE OF CONTENTS.

———

PREFACE.

THE great abilities which have been brought to the investigation of the laws relating to the production, distribution and consumption of wealth, would seem to render any thing further on the subject unnecessary. But we have seen system succeed to system both in the practice of statesmen and in the works of the most profound and inventive minds, and the theorists are not more reconciled among themselves as to the true principles of public wealth, than are those who direct the destinies of states. This fact proves that truth makes its way much more slowly in those sciences that depend for their improvement on the true import and proper application of words than in those wherein precision of language can be more completely attained. The moral stand in contrast to the mathematical and physical sciences in this respect. Political Economy, of all subjects of analysis, seems peculiarly open to this disadvantage.

The spirit of system, it must be confessed, has also been among the most powerful of those circumstances which have caused endless disputes between those in whom the love of paradox and disputation has super-

seded a regard for truth and affection for mankind. The influence of paradox on the strongest minds is, indeed, every way remarkable. We know that the sect of the Economists exerted no small power over the opinions of many of their most enlightened contemporaries. Their minds were captivated by the novelty of an ingenious hypothesis—it has been long supplanted by others not less ingenious. In our day the love of novelty and refinement has given birth to one that is equally specious and captivating from the apparent simplicity of its results. or from the generalization it seems to offer of the complicated phenomena it professes to explain. It is however destined to perish in its turn. We allude to the theory of Mr. RICARDO *as developed in his work " On the Principles of Political Economy and Taxation." It is remarkable, in this instance also, that some of the most powerful intellects that were ever devoted to the investigation of such subjects have been seduced into admiration of this system, which exhibits in its developement specimens of rare analytical talents not only in the author, but his two principal supporters. It is only necessary to name the names of* MILL *and* M'CULLOCH *in England, to be convinced of this fact. They are destined to extend the reputation of this theory by the clearness of their style, and their admirable powers of illustration.*

A condensed view of this theory* has been lately presented to the American public by one of our public

---

Professors. Mr. M'V<small>ICKAR</small>, *of Columbia College, New-York, has edited this abridgment, and added to the text some valuable notes. Now it is the apprehension of the effect of that work (which is as far as it goes well calculated for a popular manual) that has induced the author of the following sheets to publish the results of some investigations on the subject which were originally intended for his private use. They are given to the Press with every respect for the talents of Mr.* R<small>ICARDO</small> *and those of his distinguished supporters. We are in fact well convinced that if the principles of this theory (which are founded on circumstances completely contrasted to those that are peculiar to our own country) should be adopted as texts for lectures in our Colleges and Universities, it will greatly retard the progress of this important science among us.*

In this country we feel assured that the laws which regulate Profits, Wages and Rent can be more successfully investigated than in the old world. The mind is naturally prone to argue from the fact *to the* right,* and this tendency has shown itself, in a remarkable manner, in all the systems framed by European Economists. True theory in investigations of this nature is founded on a comprehensive examination of phenomena as they are presented in a natural state of the social system. It is reasonable to suppose, therefore, that a country whose institutions and laws have done less to derange the natural order of things than where a vicious social organization has resulted either from military violence or a selfish*

---

* *This remark is made by Mr.* S<small>AY</small> *in the Introduction to his Treatise on Political Economy.*

policy, will present the fairest field for analysis and speculation into the causes of wealth. The results of such analysis should constitute the principles for the guidance of the statesmen of the new world. Systems framed by philosophers who have no influence in public affairs, generally perish with their authors; those devised by what are called practical statesmen survive in the policy of countries long after the names of their framers have been forgotten or have been consigned to oblivion. The Economical theory led to some important changes of public policy to the benefit of the agriculture and internal trade of France; but the theory being only partially true, soon perished. The Mercantile system, as it has been called, originating in the interested views of merchants and manufacturers, is likely long to influence the counsels of statesmen to the injury of the interests of mankind. Founded on the selfish and contracted principle, that the gain of one country in trade is the loss of some other, it is not only less just in its origin, but far less beneficent in its practical results than would have followed from the adoption of that of the Economists. It follows that we ought not to be implicitly guided by the results of investigations pursued by European writers into the sources of wealth without an examination of the circumstances on which their systems have been framed.

INTRODUCTION.

ALL theories of Political Economy that do not
admit the agency of Nature concurrently with the
labour and ingenuity of Man in the creation of value
must necessarily lead to erroneous conclusions. When
we speak of the agency of Nature in production, we
mean to use the expression in its most comprehensive
signification. The processes of fermentation and de-
composition carried on beneath the surface of the
earth, aid the labours of the husbandman as effectually as the wind, the water and the elasticity of steam
do those of the mariner, or as fire and the various
properties of the atmosphere do those of the manufacturer. The resources of chemistry and mechanical philosophy enable man hourly to multiply his
enjoyments by enlarging his dominion over nature.
Every new modification of matter that fits or prepares
it for consumption, is a fresh instance of the improvement of either skill or science in their connexion with

the arts that minister to our wants or our enjoyments.
In this respect there is no difference between Agriculture, Commerce and Manufactures. A new manure
that increases the productive powers of the soil consists merely in a better combination of the properties
or elementary parts of matter, according to an improved understanding of the law of nature or her
agency in production. In this view the earth itself,
independently of the manure employed upon it, is a
powerful natural agent, which assists the labours of
the cultivator equally with the air, the rain and th
sun. The balance of profit or advantage between
different employments depends on the admission of
the principle that Nature concurs with Man in each of
the arts of life, either conferring or giving additional
value to objects of use and exchange. The Economists inferred that as Landlords throughout Europe
derived a large share of the produce of the soil, in
the form of rent, that rent constituted a net surplus,
after the costs of cultivation were defrayed, peculiar
to Agriculture. The conclusion was natural and easy
from these premises, that this employment was more
productive and profitable than either Commerce or
Manufactures. The Economists went, however, further. They insisted that Agriculture was the *only*
profitable employment, thus allowing an influence to
the productive powers of Nature in giving value to the
produce of the land which is denied to her agency in
the fashioning of that produce for the uses of society.

and transporting it from where it is wanted less to where it is wanted more.

It is remarkable that Dr. SMITH, after employing a large portion of his valuable work in refuting the theory of the Economists, should have arrived at nearly the same conclusion. He never could have given the preference to the cultivation of the land as the source of higher relative profit unless the agency of Nature in Commerce and Manufactures had been overlooked by him. The ingenious founder of the new school has adopted an error the reverse of Dr. SMITH's. Whilst the latter attributed nothing to the agency of Nature in Manufactures and Commerce, Mr. RICARDO leads the mind, by his reasoning, to the irresistable inference that she does nothing for man, aided by his science and skill, in Agriculture. The system of the latter conducts us finally, therefore, to the conclusion that Commerce and Manufactures are more beneficial employments than the cultivation of the land. It was natural in this system that labour should have had a disproportionate influence attributed to it in the formation of value. It is not quite so evident, however, why it should have been made the *only* element, and, as a consequence, the regulator of value. There is no period of society in which capital does not constitute one of its ingredients. The materials of the weapons of the savage possess value in their rude state, however small, and which do not cease to be a component part of the value which the

weapon acquires after being fashioned for the purposes intended. Nor is it different after capital has
been accumulated in every variety of form for the
uses of civilized society. It is under all shapes, merely another name for those natural substances, which as
soon as they are appropriated, and there is a demand
for them, become of value, and receive an increase of
value with every new modification they undergo from
the combined action of labour and natural agents on
them. The notion, therefore, that capital is nothing
but accumulated labour, is as erroneous as the idea
that labour is the sole element and only regulator of
value ; or, that the agency of Nature does not add to
value in exchange, which, in fact, is what Mr. RICARDO
has positively asserted.* Natural agents *in themselves*
possess only *value in use;* they cannot be appropriated,
but *possession* alone cannot confer exchangeable value
on any object whatever. Natural agents possess the
power of *adding to* value, and no more can be said
of either labour or capital until there is a demand for
them. Of what value would be the industry of man
if the substances it is instrumental in modifying, with
the assistance of Nature, for the purposes of society,
could not be exchanged for other objects which have
undergone a similar modification ? Of what value
would land as well as labour be, if there was no market for the produce they created ? Natural agents,

* Principles of Political Economy and Taxation, first American Edition,
chap. 18. p. 293.

and natural substances, which take the name of capital, are, therefore, as much as labour among the elements of value, and every system of Political Economy that omits either of these constituents must be imperfect.

Mr. RICARDO, thus setting out from the principle, that labour is the sole element and regulator of value, and taking for granted that the level of profit between Agriculture and other employments is still maintained, notwithstanding the increase of expense in raising raw produce, was bound to conclude, *assuming population at the same time to augment*, that there was a proportional advance in the price of the products of the land, which made an addition to Rent, Such a system leads to theoretical results, precisely similar to what occurs in fact, from laws which confer advantages on some classes of society to the injury of other classes. Thus, when labour is made the sole constituent and regulator of value, it is impossible to avoid the conclusion that, as a greater quantity of it, or which is the same thing, an increased sum in wages, is made necessary to an augmentation of raw produce, which leads, finally, to an advance of rent, the balance of advantage must be on the side of Agriculture compared with other employments. Rent will, on such a system, be higher than it ought naturally to be, and every addition made to it, must be at the expense of the other classes of society. Now, exactly the same result is produced when some advantage is given by law to one portion of the community at the expense of some other portion, which must destroy the equality of benefit between different employments.

On this theory it is then assumed, that profits will continue on a level, on the supposition that a given quantity of capital employed in Agriculture *necessarily* yields a smaller return of produce, or its value, than the same quantity if employed in either Commerce or Manufactures, or, what is equivalent to this assertion, that, from a *Law of Nature*, raw products are raised at a greater comparative expense than is necessary to fabricate manufactured produce. The rate of Agricultural profit must, then, on this system, *regulate* the rate of profit in both Commerce and Manufactures. But it is impossible, if this doctrine be admitted with all its consequences, to avoid the following results :—

First, That Agriculture, including the amount which the Landlord is supposed on this system to receive, is the most beneficial of all employments.

Secondly, That Rent must absorb the gains of the Capitalist, beyond a certain amount, as fast as they are made ; and thus limit the increase of both wages and profits ; and

Thirdly, That population must come to a stop, and capital cease to accumulate at no very distant period.

It is impossible, however, to admit that profits will *continue on a level*, on the supposition that raw produce is, *from the nature of things*, raised at a comparatively greater expense than that which is manufactured, *whilst the population at the same time increases.*

If we suppose population to come to a stop, profits will fall to a level; but if the condition of an increase of population be an additional expense in raising food to support it, without a proportionate return in its quantity, the level of profit between different employments is necessarily destroyed. There will, on such a supposition, be a lower rate of profit in Agriculture than in Commerce and Manufactures. This is however precisely the same result as that to which the mercantile system in fact led. It encouraged by law, Manufactures and Commerce to the injury of Agriculture, and by the inequality of profit between the two former employments and the latter, prevented the formation of capital on the land. The new theory would seem therefore to be the revival in part of that system in another form.

Mr. RICARDO, pursuing this new theory to one of its more immediate results, has been induced to say, that as raw produce is raised with increased difficulty, and the food of the labourer rises, more must be expended on wages, and that this increase of wages is a deduction from profit.* The same principle has compelled him to assert, also, that there is no advantage to a state from a large population,† for if wages encroach on profits as the necessity increases of cultivating inferior soils, or, if what is gained by the labourer is lost to the capitalist, and *vice versa*, the labouring classes can

* Principles of Political Economy and Taxation, chap. 5, p. 86.
† Idem, chap. 24, pp. 374, 375.

contribute nothing to the real wealth of society—they
merely replace the necessary expenses of their maintenance. On such a supposition, the support of a
large population, if a smaller will produce as great a
value in amount, must be at the expense of the net
revenue of all other classes except labourers, and the
aggregate riches of society will remain without either
increase or diminution. But in thus assuming that
the labouring classes do not reproduce a greater value
than they consume, the radical error of the Economists, which vitiated their whole system, is revived.*
Or taking for granted that there is the same amount
of productive power with a smaller as with a larger
number of producers, it follows that production is not
co-extensive with consumption, and the natural balance
between them is thence destroyed.

It is from the same principle that saving in expenditure is made identical in its effects with an increase
of productive power on the riches of society,† thus
confounding the increase of individual with that of
general wealth.

It flows from the same principle that capital is said
by Mr. RICARDO to augment as well from increased revenue as diminished expenditure,‡ meaning by increased revenue, not that addition to profit derived from enlarged powers of production, but that which is gained
from the rise in the price of one or more commodities,

---

* The Economists made an exception, however, with regard to Agricultural
labours.
† Principles of Political Economy and Taxation, chap. 6, p. 111.
‡ Idem. chap. 6, pp. 110. 111.

which must be attended by a proportionate fall in others, thus again neglecting to distinguish a partial from a general increase of wealth, or making the benefit of one class of society to the correspondent injury of some other, the criterion of a general augmentation of riches. What is this but alleging that that which is true under some circumstances only, is true under all, making *price* and *value in exchange* identical at all times, when, in fact, they are so only when some derangement has occurred in the due proportion between demand and supply. Thus if they are examined, in almost every one of the series of deductions drawn by Mr. RICARDO, will be seen the influence of the principle that labour is the sole constituent and regulator of value.

Mr. MALTHUS, in his last work entitled "Principles of Political Economy," sets out from the identical principle of Rent from which Mr. RICARDO has deduced this series of results, and arrives nearly at the same ultimate conclusion, but by a different process. He also omits all consideration of the influence of skill and science in turning the powers of Nature to a more productive account in Agriculture, or, in other words, in augmenting the quantity of raw produce with a proportionally smaller expense; and he infers a fall of profit also, but from a totally different cause to that assigned by Mr. RICARDO for this effect. It is the *increase of capital* and not *difficulty of production* to which Mr. MALTHUS attributes the fall of profit. It

was natural, on the supposition that the competition
of capitalists reduces the rate of profit, that Mr. MAL-
THUS should dread the too rapid accumulation of
capital, more especially from the effects he had witnessed for the last forty years in Great Britain of an
increase in the powers of production apparently too
great for consumption.   Dr. SMITH, the author of this
principle, that competition influences the rate of profit,
did not draw any such inference from it; for the increase in his day of productive power was much more
gradual; whilst Mr. RICARDO, by allowing more than
full effect to the opposite principle, seems to have
had an apprehension that finally it would become too
strong for the principle of improvement.   Thus it has
happened that economy in expenditure, or rather the
privation of enjoyment, is made necessary to the accumulation of wealth in the system of Mr. RICARDO,
whilst Mr. MALTHUS is the advocate of expenditure,
and seems afraid that production will so far outrun
consumption that the world will have more wealth
that it can well employ.   It is for this reason that a
body of unproductive consumers is said by him to be
necessary to a state.*

---

* How could Mr. MALTHUS contend, as he has done, in his last work, for the
necessity of unproductive consumers to maintain the balance between produce
and consumption, when the effect of every increase of unproductive consumption is to destroy such balance   How could he say that the augmentation of
wealth rests upon the proper distribution of produce, and at the same time
contend that such augmentation also depends on maintaining a body of unproductive consumers? effects absolutely incompatible.   The discussions which

Thus, however widely they may diverge in their conclusions, are the two leading Economists of the age agreed in the primary principle of the new theory of Rent, to wit, that the necessity of resorting to inferior soils to raise the additional food to support an increasing population, is attended with an augmentation of expense without a proportionate return in the quantity of agricultural produce. We have endeavoured to show that this principle is deduced from overlooking the effect of science and skill in procuring the more effectual co-operation of Nature in Agriculture as in Commerce and Manufactures.

It is true that the cultivation of soils naturally very inferior may be forced, and the additional produce raised at such an increased expense as by augmenting its price must elevate Rent; but this is not *necessarily* followed by a less return compared with the expendi-

---

have, in fact, taken place as to the proper limit to individual expenditure and accumulation, can never lead to any practical result, if they have not been Idle. The self interest of individuals fixes the limit here as in every other case where the arrangements of society do not interfere to disturb the regular action of this principle and weaken its natural influence. These arrangements give sometimes too great a stimulus to the wish or propensity to spend in individuals, and by generating habits of extravagance, which sometimes endure for a considerable period, destroy the natural balance between production in the gross and expenditure. If Economists would confine themselves to au inquiry into the causes which produce this disturbance, they would confer a greater value on their labours in this branch of the science, than by discussing the question in the abstract, whether accumulation or expenditure contributes most to the increase of the wealth of society. Among those circumstances which give too great a stimulus to individual consumption, it will be found, perhaps, that the paper system has been the most efficient and universal

ture. An unusual stimulus applied to the land, combined with restrictions on the foreign trade in corn,
may produce effects very similar on Rent to what
follows in a more natural and wholesome state of things.
It therefore does not result that in any instance of a
resort to naturally inferior soils, to support an additional population, the increased food can be obtained
in no other way than by an increased expenditure
without a proportionate return. But in the regular
progress of wealth and population there is always
room for the employment of fresh capital on the land
with increasing profit, because with every addition to
the quantity and consequent fall of the price of produce, whether rude or manufactured, the demand for
it is extended. The increased return is the fund which
pays not only increased profit, but increased wages.

Is it not evident, unless this view be admitted, that
a near limit, as we have before remarked, must be
placed to the increase of both capital and population ?
for if land of a still decreasing fertility, which lessens
the proportional quantity of food produced, is successively taken into cultivation, as profits will be
reduced with every step in this progress, the funds for
the maintenance of labour must be diminished in proportion. The increase of population and consequent
augmented demand for food are, therefore, evidently
assumed in this theory. Its authors were compelled
to raise up the additional population to give the in-

creased price of raw produce, as a motive to extend cultivation to inferior soils.

Thus we cannot but perceive that on every additional outlay the returns of capital laid out on the land must be augmented, if the skill and ingenuity of cultivators with the resources of science are sufficient to overcome the failing powers of the soil.* The proof that they are so is to be found in the augmentation of population whilst fresh capital is continually applied to the land. During the continuance of the last general war in Europe, the quantity of inferior land taken into cultivation in Great Britain was very great, and the effect on profits must have been disastrous, according to the new theory, unless it had been counteracted

---

* It is the constant end of improvements in the science and art of Agriculture to equalize the relative disadvantages of different soils and situations. The resources of Agricultural Chemistry have not yet afforded the principles by which this can be completely effected; but who is able to say that a more perfect analysis may not instruct us in the mode by which the processes of Nature may be more completely imitated? Who can place the limit to discovery and skill in this branch of Art any more than to improvements in Mechanical Philosophy and the application of its inventions, in other departments of industry, to the multiplication of the conveniences and enjoyments of life? Can any one pronounce that fallows may not be superseded by a more economical and less tedious method? or that a more complete knowledge of the Laws of Chemistry in their operation on soils, may not enable us so to combine the properties of matter, in the preparation of manures, as to save the necessity of alternate crops? If this should be finally established, what a splendid triumph would be afforded to the science of Agriculture? In the application of the proper methods of irrigation and draining, according to the diversity of soils and situations, what a vast field is yet open to improvement! Not to speak of the Machinery used on the land, that may enable the Agriculturist to increase the quantity of his produce at a much smaller comparative expense.

by an opposite principle of superior efficacy. This principle was, of course, as we have already remarked, the improvements in Agriculture, which prevented the fall of profits. The population went on increasing, and was supported by a constantly increasing fund, to wit, constantly increasing revenue. But it is necessary to subject this new theory of Rent to a more detailed examination.

NOTES

ON

POLITICAL ECONOMY.

———

CHAPTER I.

RENT.

THE rent of land has been variously defined by Mr. Ricardo in different parts of his work on the Principles of Political Economy and Taxation. It is defined, first, to be "that portion of the produce of the earth, which is paid to the Landlord for the use of the original and indestructible powers of the soil."* Rent, according to this definition, is made to depend on *natural* fertility. But the definition given of Rent by Mr. Malthus, to wit, that "excess of price above the costs of production at which raw produce sells in the market," is sanctioned by Mr. Ricardo.† This definition is, however, essentially different from the other, and confounds that Rent " which is paid for the use of the original and indestructible powers of

---

* Principles of Political Economy and Taxation, chap. 2, p. 35.
† Idem, chap. 29, p. 423.

the soil," with that paid in consequence of the advance in the price of raw produce from restrictions on the trade in corn, and the monopoly which in some countries is connected with the possession of land.

The *origin* of rent is described in the following manner by Mr. Ricardo. " It is then only because land is of different qualities with respect to its productive powers, and because in the progress of population, land, of an inferior quality, or less advantageously situated, is called into cultivation, that Rent is *ever* paid for the use of it."* Rent is accounted for in this description from *relative* fertility. But relative fertility, in this theory, not only *accounts* for rent, or is meant to be descriptive of its *origin*,† but its *progress* and *amount* are made to depend on the same

---

* Principles of Political Economy and Taxation, chap 2, p. 38.

† Mr. Malthus defines rent as we have stated above (vide Principles of Political Economy, considered with a view to their practical application, chap 3, p. 106) to be " the excess of price above the costs at which raw produce sells in the market;" but his reasonings on this subject mainly refer to the other definition given by Mr. Ricardo, although not formally stated, to wit, the *absolute* fertility of land. Mr. Malthus' statement of the *origin* of rent is, however, less consistent than that given by Mr. Ricardo, as he accounts for it from both absolute *and* relative fertility. " The causes (he observes, chap. 3, p. 110) of the excess of price of raw produce above the costs of production, may be stated to the three—

" First, and mainly, that quality of the earth, by which it can be made to yield a greater portion of the necessaries of life than is required for the maintenance of the persons employed on the land.

" Secondly, that quality peculiar to the necessaries of life of being able, when properly distributed, to create their own demand, or to raise up a number of demanders in proportion to the quantity of necessaries produced.

" And, thirdly, the *comparative* scarcity of fertile land, either natural or artificial."

Now, it is obvious, on the least attention to this statement, that the first cause accounts for rent from *absolute* fertility, and the third cause from *relative* fertility—in other words, rent is made to depend upon both *difficulty* and *facility* of production—on both *abundance* and *scarcity* Mr. Malthus' reasonings however are, as we have before remarked, founded *principally* on the absolute or positive fertility of land, but in part also, on its relative fertility, whilst Mr. Ricardo's are *exclusively* based on the latter.

circumstance. Rent, according to Mr. RICARDO, never *begins* on the first quality of land until the second quality is taken into cultivation, and rent never *rises* until the third quality is cultivated; it then *commences* on the second and *rises* on the first quality. Now *relative* fertility can only account for the *inequality* of rent, it can neither explain its *origin* nor its *increase*. If rent be " that portion of the produce which is paid for the use of the original and indestructible powers of the soil," its amount must be in proportion to those powers, and can be increased only as they increase, or diminished as they diminish. But when inferior land is taken into cultivation, those powers are not altered—they remain as to absolute fertility as they originally were. If the productive powers of the land are increased, this is owing to acquired fertility— to the additional productiveness of the soil from the skill, capital and ingenuity of the cultivators. The " original and indestructible powers of the soil," as they do not admit of diminution, cannot admit of increase. Land of *different* degrees of fertility will yield *different* rents. Relative fertility will therefore account for *relative* rent, and nothing more.

It is the opinion of Mr. RICARDO that " it is when inferior lands are required to feed an augmenting population, that both the landlord's *share* of the whole produce, and the *value* he receives progressively increase."* Now we would ask what is to *entitle* the landlord to an *increased share* of the whole produce, if an increase of the whole has been effected by the skill and capital of the cultivators? If the landlord has furnished any of the capital by which this increase has been obtained, his share will be in proportion to his investment—if he

* Principles of Political Economy and Taxation, chap. 29, p. 424,

gets a greater share, it will be a transfer of a portion of that to which the farmers are entitled from *their* capital and skill. As extended cultivation, therefore, if it has been effected by cultivators without any aid from landlords, is the result of their own improvements, the *whole* of the increased produce arising from this extension of cultivation, is their exclusive property. There can, therefore, of *right*, be no increase of rent from the increased quantity of produce. If the soil has been exhausted by the farmer, he must place it in the situation, as to productive power, in which he found it, or allow the landlord such a sum as will compensate him for the degree of exhaustion which it has undergone. This, therefore, can make no difference in the amount of rent derived from land in proportion to its natural fertility.

Nor can the landlord *in fact* obtain an increase of rent from an increased quantity of raw produce, under any circumstances whatever, *in addition* to its increased *value* or *price*. The landlord obtains in all cases a rent in proportion to the price at which raw produce sells in the market*—that price depends again on the proportion between the demand and the supply of such produce ; but to say that the price or value of any commodity has increased, is precisely equivalent to one or the other of the following assertions: First, that the quantity which the consumer is able to command of such commodity, for the same money amount, is diminished ; or, secondly, that the quantity which he is able to command, for a larger amount of money,

---

* When it is said that rent depends upon the price at which raw produce sells, it is not meant to refer to very short periods, but to that state of the demand and supply which affects the price of landed products during the currency of a lease—one or two bad harvests, or a temporary increase of the demand, can have no effect on rent,

is the same. In the first case there is a diminution of supply—in the second case an increase of demand. If the demand for raw produce has augmented, without an increase of the supply in an equal degree, the landlord will receive a larger proportional money amount than before, or, in other words, the consumer will receive the same quantity of raw produce for a greater amount of money ; or, if the supply of such produce has diminished, without a correspondent increase of the demand, the landlord will also, in this case, receive a larger proportional amount of money than before, or, which is the same thing, the consumer will receive a smaller quantity of such produce for the same amount of money. When Mr. RICARDO, therefore, speaks of an increased *quantity* of raw produce falling to the share of the landlord, *in addition* to its increased *price* or *value*, and of the landlord being in consequence *doubly benefitted* by difficulty of production, the idea is inconceivable. The *money* rent of the landlord is of course plainly distinguishable from his *corn* rent—but they must, under all circumstances, rise and fall in an inverse ratio. His money rent is governed by the proportion which the demand bears to the supply of raw produce—so also is his corn rent. A part of what he gains in the one way he loses in the other. Rent is therefore never in proportion to the greater or less difficulty of production—that is, it does not increase from a Law of Nature as the quantity of food diminishes, and diminish as the quantity of food increases : but is governed in its amount by those circumstances that keep the market, for any length of time, understocked with the produce of the land. There can then be no increase of rent from an increased *quantity* of raw produce in addition to its

increased *price*, in any state of things; nor can the
landlord acquire any such increase of rent from an
additional price of raw produce, connected with the
"original and indestructible powers of the soil," for,
as under all circumstances, these powers remain the
same, the landlord can never derive any addition to
his rent for the use of these powers.

We are now led to consider *in what manner* the
increased *value* of produce leads, in the new system,
to an increase of rent. Mr. RICARDO has this passage.
"In speaking of the rent of the landlord, we have
rather considered it as the proportion of the whole
produce, without any reference to its *exchangeable
value;* but since the same cause, the difficulty of production, *raises* the *exchangeable value* of raw produce,
and raises also the *proportion* of raw produce paid to
the landlord for rent, it is obvious that the landlord is
doubly benefitted by difficulty of production. First,
he obtains a *greater share*, and, secondly, the commodity in which he is paid is of *greater value*."* The
new theory teaches besides, that the whole of the increased price of raw produce raised on the worst land
goes to the cultivator to defray the additional expenses
of cultivation, and the whole of the increased price of
that raised on the best land, to the landlord in the
form of additional rent. The increased price, however, cannot take place under the circumstances supposed. It is founded on an *assumption*, as we have
already remarked, of an increased demand and an
increased population—it is taken for *granted* that population is augmenting whilst capital is diminishing.
The additional price cannot therefore be *given*. The
authors of the new theory of rent have in fact involved themselves in inconsistency. They make the rise

---

* Principles of Political Economy and Taxation, chap. 2, p. 54.

of raw produce to *follow* from difficulty of production, and yet they state that the demand for additional produce *precedes*, as it must, the cultivation of inferior land, which is, in fact, saying that the increase of price is both *cause* and *effect*. The price of raw produce rises, say they, *because* the cost of obtaining an additional quantity is increased, and yet this additional quantity is produced *in consequence* of the demand augmenting and the price rising. This is making the increase of the price the effect of additional demand, and, also, the effect of additional expenditure.

How then, it may be asked, can that increase in the price of raw produce which obviously goes to augment rent be accounted for? The excess of the price of the products of the land caused by monopoly, above that price for which they might be obtained if the monopoly did not exist, is the source of increase of rent. The augmentation of rent arises, under all circumstances, from whatever cause prevents the supply of food from being proportioned to the demand. Deficient harvests, as they are accidental in their occurrence, and their effects well known, need not be taken into view. Every other limitation of the supply of raw produce is either immediately or remotely connected with monopoly. Perhaps the term monopoly is not strictly accurate in the sense we employ it,* but,

---

* There are various senses in which this term is employed. It is most frequently used with the meaning I have just attributed to it, but surely it does not convey the same idea, in this sense, as when it is meant to be descriptive of what is called *natural* monopoly, or that scarcity arising from a limited quantity of peculiar products in the market, as in the case of certain wines, the produce only of particular soils. This species of monopoly *does* result from a *law of nature* : but the monopoly connected with rent arises out of certain *social arrangements*. In this case what is gained by one class of the community, which these arrangements favour, is lost to another class—in the instance of rent, what is gained by landlords is lost to the rest of the society.

as it has always been used to express that state of
things by which room is not permitted for the full
influence and effect of competition, we have adopted
it as the most convenient for our purpose. It is agreeable to every principle of supply and demand to conclude that as land is locked up in the hands of large
proprietors, rents and raw produce should proportionally advance.

The original division of land, and the state of law
consequent on that division, have a most important
influence on rents, profits and wages. If the sovereign (as is the case in some of the Eastern Monar-
chies) should be the sole proprietor of the soil, and
exact an undue portion of its produce as rent, it is in
principle the same as the appropriation of land in large
portions by an aristocracy who have fenced their possessions and prevented their free alienation by the
barriers of law. If land cannot be brought freely
into market for sale or mortgage, it will not be pretended that it will sell or rent at a competition price,
or that price which is in proportion to its natural fertility. This is the true criterion of the real value of
rent. All that is obtained as rent, (in the absence of
commercial restrictions,) above the power of land in
a natural state, to yield the necessaries of life, is attributable to the peculiarity of its division, and to the
laws by which its alienation by devise or its transfer
by purchase is clogged.

If we suppose on the settlement of a new country
that land is of easy acquisition, and that division prevails which is most conducive to the increase of capital
and population, in such a case land being obtainable
at the price of free competition, its rent can never exceed
its productive powers derived from nature. This is

on the supposition that capital and population are in due proportion, and that no obstacles exist to a free commercial intercourse with other countries. If land, under these circumstances, is purchased to hire, its rent must continue invariable in amount, and must be governed by the same law which regulates the interest on a loan of capital to be employed productively by the borrower. The amount of rent can never vary—can never increase nor diminish, because the natural fertility of the land—its " original and indestructible powers," are always supposed to be the same. It is the use of these powers for which rent is paid, and whatever value the proprietor sets on them, or what they have cost him, must determine, on the principle of an ordinary loan, the amount of value annually paid for their use—in other words, the amount of rent. The price of food raised on such land, the price of the land itself, and its rent, will all be at fair competition rates—which we may call the natural price and rent of land.

Let us now suppose the settlement of a country where the land is appropriated by persons who become the proprietors of large tracts. Let us further suppose that its alienation is prevented, on the demise of the owners, by the law of descent—that its transfer by mortgage and sale is trammelled from the difficulty of ascertaining title, and by the complexity of the forms by which its transmission is regulated. The value of land, in such a state of things, must be higher than where, as in the other case, it can be brought into market without restrictions on its transfer or alienation. A relatively higher price of land, a relatively higher rent, and relatively higher price of raw produce, must be the consequences. All that portion of price and rent obtained above what would have been obtained if land had been subject in its rent and price to the principle of unrestrained competition, may be denominated monopoly rent and monopoly price, in contradistinction to natural price and natural rent.

The price and rent of land, in such circumstances, are prevented from falling as low as they would fall if the competition of proprietors to sell or landlords to hire was as great as the competition of capitalists to purchase and of farmers to lease. If we pursue this parallel, and suppose these countries to have equal taxation, equal natural fertility of soil, and equal improvements in agriculture, the excess of the price of raw produce, in the country subject to the disadvantages mentioned, above the price at which it could be imported would exactly measure the extent of the monopoly, and it would be undersold in its own markets by the country more favourably circumstanced. In such a case, unless a duty were laid on the imported corn in proportion to the difference of the price, the whole supply must come from abroad, and no land could be cultivated in the country suffering under this species of monopoly, however fertile and convenient to market. This case is put on the supposition that there are no duties, or equal ones, laid on the raw produce of either country by the other. It follows that the consumers of corn in the country whose land is tied up by the law of descent, and its transfer clogged by legal forms, must pay a higher price for food than the consumers of corn in the country which permits land to come freely into market for sale or rent. The saving which the labourer would have made in that part of his wages applied to the purchase of food, and those articles of his consumption of which raw produce forms a part, is prevented; the addition which the capitalist would have made to his revenue by a similar saving, is also prevented. In this view it is that an increase of rent, arising from a higher price of food than would have existed under a different state of things, is a transfer from profits and wages to rent. If those to whom the profits and wages rightfully belong, were permitted to derive the whole benefit of their skill and exertions, it would form a stimulus to the further increase of capital and population, or it would enable the existing population to subsist in greater comfort. Being spent as revenue and unproductively, it prevents as rapid an increase in national wealth as prevails in countries where the whole of the difference between the costs of cultivation and the price at which raw produce sells, is divided between the labourer and capitalist, allowing the rent of land, in its natural state, as among these costs. If, in addition to this cause of the higher price of food, is added restrictions on the trade in corn, the effect is the same in *kind*, and only different in *degree*. It is an aggravation of the evil from an extension of the monopoly. These restrictions may be temporary, but the faulty or unequal division of land, and the institutions to which it gives rise, to preserve the influence of a landed aristocracy, may endure for centuries. As long as such a state of things exists, the price of landed products is prevented from falling to that level which unlimited competition would effect. The inferences from this review are these—

First, that the rent of land has its *origin* in natural fertility, or those " original and indestructible powers of the soil" by which it is made to yield a surplus above the profits of the capital and the wages of the labour employed in its cultivation:

Secondly, that the *increase* of rent is owing to those circumstances which limit the supply of raw produce, either from restrictions on commercial intercourse, or from a faulty division of the land and the laws by which its free transfer and alienation are prevented, or from both circumstances united:

Thirdly, that no increase in the *quantity* of raw products can augment rent, and that no increase in the *price* of those products, which in fact goes to augment rent, can take place unless the supply is prevented from being proportioned to the demand.

The *commencement* of rent, according to the new doctrine, is delayed until land of a decreasing fertility is taken into cultivation. The best land and the worst are put on the same level in this respect, until a certain period of time has elapsed. But rent, pursuant to one of Mr. RICARDO's definitions, (being " for the use of the original and indestructible powers of the soil,") should commence as soon as those powers are made available for the purposes of cultivation. It should, consistently with this definition, have its beginning from the moment those powers are brought into profitable use. Suppose land on the first settlement of a country purchased as an investment, the proprietor preferring hiring to cultivating it, will not rent be derived from the instant it can be made to yield a sufficient quantity of produce to pay rent in addition to wages and profits? The authors of the new theory would not contend that the cultivation by the proprietor himself would make any difference in this respect. If he prefers to cultivate rather than to hire, he must receive an interest on his capital, which is only an-

other name for rent.   He must obtain such a quantity
of produce, or its value, as will pay him an annual
sum in the ratio of his investment, in addition to what
he derives, as cultivator, for profit.

Mr. RICARDO lays much stress on the circumstance
that, in new countries, land is abundant and cheap,
but it does not follow that because land is abundant
that it can be obtained for nothing.   No one, says
he, " would pay for the use of land when there was
an abundant quantity not yet appropriated, and therefore at the disposal of whosoever might choose to
cultivate it."*   This is, however, assuming what does
not exist; it is taking for granted that land is not
generally appropriated where it is most fertile and
abundant, and that any cultivator who chooses may
convert it to his benefit without paying any thing for
its use.   " On the common principles of supply and
demand," says he again, " no rent could be paid for
such land, (he is speaking of the fertile land of a new
country,) for the reason stated why nothing is given for
the use of air and water, or for any other of the gifts of
Nature, which exist in boundless quantity."†   Now it
is not true that land exists any where in such boundless quantity as to be without price or value when
available for profit to a cultivator; nor is it correct to
compare land to air and water, which, in themselves,
have a value in *use*, but no value in *exchange*.   Land
is capable of appropriation—air and water are not.
Land, from its abundance, may be of *little* value, and
some land, on account of its distance from markets,
may lie waste from the want of purchasers or lessees,
but the real question is this : when land can be mad

* Principles of Political Economy and Taxation, chap. 2, p. 37.
† Idem. chap. 2, p. 37.

to yield more than the ordinary profits of stock and
wages of labour, will any one be suffered to appropriate or occupy it without price or rent?

It is not presenting the question in its true aspect,
therefore, to consider land without reference to *demand*. Mere *quantity* without *demand*, can determine
nothing in relation to *exchangeable value*. The worst
lands of an old country, or the best lands of a new
one, may remain on the same footing as to value. The
great distance of the most fertile tracts from markets,
may produce the absorption of the whole price of
their products in the costs of transportation, as the
sterility of a portion of the territory of an old country may prevent such returns as will pay the costs of
cultivation. The demand and the price may, however, increase so as to permit the cultivation, with both
profit to the cultivator and rent to the landlord, of
land too far distant from markets or too sterile to be
cultivated under ordinary circumstances. If the demand for and the price of raw produce should augment to this extent, land which before could command
neither purchaser nor lessee, will yield some rent to
the landlord, otherwise, if cultivated the addition to
the price will go into the pockets of the cultivators and
disturb the level of profit between agriculture and
other employments. If the price of necessaries is
forced up by a high stimulus to population, and difficulties are thrown in the way of importation, land,
which in ordinary circumstances might lie waste,
would pay nothing, after cultivation, for original or
natural fertility. Its power of paying rent has its
origin in a forced state of things. It is the effect of
the application of excessive stimuli, which, when withdrawn, will throw the land which has felt its influ-

ence again out of cultivation. It would appear, therefore, that, under all circumstances imaginable, whenever or wherever land is cultivated, whether it be more
or less fertile, near or distant to markets, it pays rent,
and it seems neither agreeable to fact nor just theory,
to say that rent does not commence before the natural
power of the soil to produce food begins to diminish.

It is not a little singular that the discrepancy between this opinion and the definition given of rent by
Mr. RICARDO did not occur to him. He considers the
fertility of the land the foundation of rent, for it is
" that portion of the produce of the earth which is
paid to the landlord for the use of the original and
indestructible powers of the soil." Yet the new theory
teaches that when the productiveness of these powers
begins to lessen, that rent commences and increases
with every step in the descending scale of fertility.
Mr. MALTHUS has strongly insisted on the advantages
of *absolute* or *natural* fertility. He considers it as a
gift of Heaven to man of the highest value : he views
it as the source of the greatest social improvements :
he explains it to be the origin, by the relief from labour
it affords, of arts, sciences, &c.* yet this great gift is
never rendered available until the lapse of a certain
period of time ; these inestimable powers of the soil
are never made to yield that surplus, in the form of
rent, which is described as the peculiar attribute of
the land above every other natural agent, until they
begin to diminish in productive energy—until natural
fertility lessens. From the view of the subject we
have taken, we consider rent, therefore, to commence
from the moment land is taken into cultivation, and
that its *amount* will be regulated by the surplus which

* Principles of Political Economy, chap. 2, sec. 10, p. 179.

it will yield after the replacement of the capital of the cultivator with the average rate of profits and wages.

In a state of society in which neither taxation, commercial restrictions, nor a vicious division of the land, prevents the labourer and capitalist from receiving as large a share of its produce as they are entitled to from their skill and exertions, rent will never exceed, as I have endeavoured to show, the originally productive powers of the soil. It follows that as population increases and fresh land must be cultivated to raise the additional food required, the rent paid for the use of land of decreasing fertility will be relatively less than that already in cultivation by the difference in its naturally productive power. The rent received for land of this comparative inferiority will then be in proportion to the surplus it can be made to yield, after the deduction of all the expenses of cultivation, including, of course, average profits and wages, as in the instance of the land first cultivated. On every descent made in the scale of fertility, the same principle will apply. Let us adopt the illustration of Mr. RICARDO, although for a different purpose.* Thus, suppose land No. 1, 2 and 3 to yield, with the employment of an equal quantity of capital and labour, 100 90 and 80 quarters of corn respectively, and suppose 60 quarters to be the net return on each quality. The surplus on No. 1, which would constitute rent, would be 40 quarters, on No. 2, 30 quarters, and on No. 3, 20 quarters. These portions would exactly measure the originally productive power of these different qualities of land. Now, as the population increased, so as to make a resort to No. 2 necessary, the increase of skill and science in Agriculture that had taken

---

* Principles of Political Economy and Taxation, chap 2, p. 39.

place, would permit capital to be employed on No. 2, with increased returns. Whether it were employed on No. 2 or No. 1, would make no difference as to profit—the capital applied to No. 2 would be equally productive with that applied to No. 1, with proportionally less rent. No. 2 is resorted to, however, because land is of limited extent, and constant additions to the quantity of raw produce cannot be made on the same surface. No. 2 would not then be cultivated unless it could be made as productive and profitable with the same outlay as No. 1, and unless the landlord consented to receive a relatively less rent than the owner of No. 1, in the ratio of the difference in their productive powers. If improvements in agriculture had not taken place so as to yield as large returns, with an equal amount of capital, on No. 2 as on No. 1, no additional quantity of food could be provided, and population would come to a stop. It is only necessary to extend the same principle to No. 3, and so on. The increase of population, therefore, depends on the extent of the improvements in agriculture, and inferior land is laid down in tillage exactly in proportion as these improvements extend. This is the reverse of the new theory which connects the augmentation of population and produce with the increased difficulty instead of the increased facility of production. This is only an extension, however, of the principle with whose wonderful results in Manufactures we are familiar.

Why should a different law prevail in one of the great departments of production to that which governs in the others? Is it not consonant to the general analogy of Nature to conclude that a provision is made in the skill and inventive powers of man for the

decay, or rather the inequality, of those natural resources which minister to his necessary wants? What
evidence is there, that skill, science and ingenuity are
not, in all stages in the progress of society, able to
overcome that natural inferiority of soil which refuses
to yield, without the co-operation of these powerful
human aids, an increase of the means of subsistence?
The results of skill and science in Manufactures are
visible to all—they are embodied in machinery. But
in Agriculture they become a part of the soil, or are
blended with it and cannot be distinguished from it.
We are therefore urging no novel principle in insisting
that in Agriculture the inventive powers of producers
will be as efficacious from the same causes as in Manufactures.   That they will be *equally* efficacious is
necessary to the level of profit or to an equality of
benefit between Agriculture and other employments.

From the view, then, which I have taken of the
subject of rent, it may be supposed that I do not acqui-
esce in the conclusions drawn by those writers who
consider rent, *under all circumstances*, in the nature of
a monopoly.   The price paid for the hire of land,
supposing it cultivated exclusively by the capital of
the farmer, or, in other words, the sum given annually
for the use of its " original and indestructible powers,"
cannot be considered as connected with monopoly of
any kind.   This is, as I have already remarked, the
natural rent of land, whether it is cultivated by the
proprietor or any other person as lessee.   It is almost
unnecessary to add that the higher rent, *under any
circumstances*, paid to the landlord, is connected, as we
have endeavoured to show, with monopoly, either arising out of the possession of land in the manner already described, or with restrictions on the trade in corn.

Mr. MALTHUS insists that rent is not governed by the laws of monopoly under any circumstances whatever. Mr. SISMONDI, in his work *de la Richesse Commerciale*,* views rent under all circumstances as of the character of an ordinary monopoly. Mr. BUCHANAN, in his edition of the Wealth of Nations,† entertains the same idea. But this is confounding the rent paid for the " original and indestructible powers of the soil" with that arising from the price at which raw produce sells above what it would bring, if restraints on importation and the monopoly connected with the possession of land in many countries, of which I have already spoken, did not exist. As the former is natural rent, it is governed by the laws which regulate a loan of capital, and not by those which monopolized commodities obey. It does appear singular, as asserted by Mr. MALTHUS, that Mr. RICARDO should, holding the opinions he has expressed, coincide with Mr. SISMONDI and Mr. BUCHANAN in these views on the subject of rent. Surely, if rent, according to Mr. RICARDO, arises out of the *necessity* of resorting to inferior soils, it is the deduction of a fact from a Law of Nature. There is, therefore, an evident inconsistency between this idea and the notion of an ordinary monopoly—that which is deduced from a *Law of Nature* cannot possibly partake of the character of monopoly in the sense of this term when Mr. RICARDO considers it as leading to a transfer from profits and wages to rent.

From these principles it appears necessarily to follow that rent must be a component part of price.

---

* Vol. 1. p 49.

† Vol 4, p. 134 · These references to the opinions of Mr. SISMONDI and Mr. BUCHANAN are taken from Mr. MALTHUS' work already quoted.

No land, as I have endeavoured to show, that will yield a quantity of produce above the expenses of cultivation, will be suffered to be cultivated by any one but the proprietor, unless something is paid for its use. The surplus is his property, and no one will be allowed either to appropriate or use it without an equivalent. The payment of this surplus, or of a value equal to it, must be as much one of the conditions of the supply of raw produce as the other expenses of cultivation.

It would then appear from this view, that the argument of those who consider Agriculture the most productive employment, is founded on the misconception that, because land can be made to yield, in certain parts of the world, a high rent, this is additional value or a net surplus peculiar to land.

The large portion of the produce of the soil transferred, in the form of rent, in consequence of the social arrangements that have taken effect throughout Europe, has given rise to the idea of a net surplus peculiar to Agriculture. But we perceive that where more natural arrangements prevail, there is no surplus for rent, in the sense of this term as it is generally understood. The proprietor of land in a new and fertile country, as in the United States for example, if he is the cultivator himself, derives, as we have shown, an amount, in addition to the profit on the capital employed in cultivation, in proportion to his investment in the purchase of the land itself, and we may call this rent or not as we please; yet we would find, if we could make the comparison, that this amount is much less than that received as rent on the same quality of land, all other circumstances being equal, in any part of Europe.

CHAPTER II.

PROFITS AND WAGES.

IT is scarcely possible, nor is it necessary, to separate Profits from Wages in investigating the principles by which their increase and decline are regulated. The laws which they obey are strikingly similar, and they lead to results in the progress of national improvement, nearly identical. In our reasonings concerning wages and profits we must distinguish between what is received in *money amount* from what the amount derived will command either of labour or commodities. Money profit is the quantity of money received by the capitalist as the return from his investment—real profit is the quantity of produce, whether destined for unproductive or productive consumption, for which this money will exchange.

Money wages are the quantity of money received by the labourer for his labour—real wages the quantity of the conveniences and necessaries of life his money wages will command. The *rate* of profit must therefore be in proportion to the difference between the outlay and the returns, not in money, but in what that money will purchase. The *rate* of wages is in proportion to the difference between the money received by the labourer and what that money will command of the commodities necessary to his subsistence.

In the progress of society money wages fall, in a natural state of things, and real wages rise. Real wages rise, because the price of necessaries falls, and the labourer's command of them is increased. Money wages fall, because the labourer, from the rise of his real wages, is induced to marry and multiply, by which the number of labourers is increased in the market. But real wages will rise in a higher proportion than money wages fall, or the condition of the labourer would not be improved, and he would not be induced to marry and increase.

Money profits do not fall in the progress of society, for although the prices of all commodities decline, their quantity increases in an equal proportion, and the capitalist receives as large a money amount as before the decline. Real profits rise, for they depend on the amount of the returns *in produce* compared with the amount of the expenditure, and as the quantity of productions in the progress of society is multiplied, the real gains of the capitalist must increase.

We thus see how well these principles harmonize with those laid down on the subject of rent and the increase of the produce of the land. There can be no addition, in the first instance, to raw products unless the productive powers of the soil are increased. The additional produce is brought within the reach of a greater number of consumers from the fall of its price. The number of consumers is increased in proportion to the addition made to the means of subsistence, on the principle that as quantity augments, price is reduced and consumption enlarged. The labourers, in the ratio of their increase, are compelled to receive less wages, which enables the capitalist, with the same money amount, to employ an additional number of labourers, or an additional quantity of labour, which is the same thing, and which, as we see, has been already provided. Thus is capital made not more instrumental to the increase of population than population to the increase of capital—thus is the ratio of their increase precisely equal. Wages do not encroach on profits nor profits on wages. All that is necessary to the final results is, that science and skill should be able to overcome the difficulty of production on land of a decreasing fertility.

The effect of an augmentation of the quantity of raw produce, from the diminished difficulty of production, must give such a stimulus to population as will reduce money wages. There is the cost of producing labourers as well as the cost of producing the labourer's subsistence. The cost of production with regard to the labourer, is the price of that food and those necessaries which are essential to the continuance of the race of labourers, and ensure a sufficient supply of them. And as the consequence of an addition to supply, is a decline in price, money wages must inevitably fall, on the same principle that raw or manufactured products are reduced in price from increased facility of production. But if the cultivator will be able to command an increased quantity of labour, in consequence of a fall in money wages, (labour being the most costly of the instruments of production,) it will further stimulate production on the land, promoted, as it must be, by additional skill and science. Raw produce must again augment in quantity, its price must again fall. and by enabling the labourers to command more food and necessaries, induce them further to increase, which will again add to the supply of labour in the market. Thus the same series of effects is always recurring and never interrupted but by the folly or selfishness of those who are entrusted with power.

The reader will not fail to see the importance of the principle, that the reduction of money wages enables the capitalist to command an increased quantity of labour for the same money amount, or the same quantity for a smaller money amount. His interest will prompt him to increase the number of his labourers, for every additional fall in the price of his commodity, as it is increased in quantity, extends the demand for it. This principle, so important and necessary to explain the phenomena of production, seems to have been entirely overlooked by the school of Mr. RICARDO, who never view the increased *quantity* of labour necessary to an augmentation of produce in connexion with a fall in its *price*, or conceive the possibility of such a reduction of money wages as will enable the capitalist to employ an additional number of labourers or greater quantity of labour, to obtain an augmentation of produce, without a proportional increase of expenditure.

How much more consonant with what we may suppose the arrangements of Nature thus to infer that population and capital are permitted to increase together. According to the new theory they are alternately checked in their increase, each by the other, at repeated intervals. Profits cannot fall below certain limit, for the capitalist can have no motive to accumulate, if the accumulation is to be absorbed by wages as soon as made. But the fall of wages has its limit also. The population must decline if the labourer's wages are so reduced as greatly to lessen his command of the means of subsistence.

The authors of the new theory, perceiving to what results it led, were compelled to place the limit to a fall of profits and wages when the capitalist would have no further motive to accumulate, and the labourer no additional inducement to marry and increase, for, unless this had been conceded, the landlord must have absorbed, in constantly increasing rent, all the profits and all the wages—*á reductio ad absurdum*. What then must be supposed to take place on the new system? Wages rise until they can rise no higher, from the inability of the capitalist to pay any more for labour. They then must begin a retrograde course— they begin to fall, to allow the capitalist the power to increase his capital by an increase of profit, for, on this system, it is as wages fall that profits rise; but as soon as the capitalist's profits are augmented to a certain point, wages will again rise and soon overtake the increase of capital. During the period between the fall and the rise of wages, the condition of the labourer must be miserable, for not only is he made to receive a smaller money amount for his labour, but this sum commands, from the rise of raw produce, fewer of the necessaries and conveniencies of life. To such inconsistent results does the new theory lead. This course is retarded but for very short periods by improvements in Agriculture, pursuant to this theory, for it teaches that, by a Law of Nature, raw produce is raised with increased difficulty, or that the costs of cultivation are augmented in the progress of wealth and population without a proportional increase of produce.

" With the progress of society (says Mr. RICARDO)
the natural price of labour has always a tendency to
rise, because one of the principal commodities by
which its price is regulated, has a tendency to become
dearer, from the greater difficulty of producing it. As,
however, the improvements in Agriculture, the discovery of new markets, whence provisions may be imported, may, *for a time*, counteract the tendency to a
rise in the price of necessaries, and may even occasion their natural price to fall, so, also, the same causes
produce the correspondent effects on the natural price
of labour."*   Again : " The natural price of all commodities, *excepting raw produce* and *labour*, has a tendency to fall in the progress of wealth and population."†

Mr. MALTHUS also admits the effect of improvements
in Agriculture in lowering the price of raw products,
but he states the difficulty of production, as the most
efficient cause, and capable in the end of overpower-
ing the principle of improvement.‡

But it may be said that the doctrine we have been
contending for is contradicted by the state of things
that took place in Great Britain during the last general
war, when the price of raw produce rose at the same
time that both money wages and profits increased.
According to the principles we have laid down, the
prices of labour and raw produce ought to have fallen
if profits advanced. Instead then of there being a
reduction of money and a rise of real wages, these
fell, or, which is the same thing, the price of raw produce rose, and money wages increased. But in this

* Principles of Political Economy and Taxation, chap. 5, p. 67.
† Idem chap. 5, p. 68.
‡ Principles of Political Economy, &c. chap. 5, pp. 233, 234

case, although the effects were reversed, the principle for which we contend is sustained.

It will be recollected that it is the *difference* between real wages and money wages that forms the true reward of labour. This difference may be caused as well by a rise of money wages as by a rise of real wages. If, whilst real wages fall, money wages rise in a higher proportion, a difference is created as well as when these effects are reversed. The causes that produced the advance in the price of labour, in the period and country above referred to, are very obvious. The demand for labour rose faster than the supply could be furnished. The population increased very rapidly, but the demand, for the whole period in question, was in advance of the increase. The war employed unusual numbers of the people, and the effect, in consequence of this circumstance, was that the market, for the entire period of the war, was understocked with labour, which advanced money wages in a higher proportion than it depressed real wages.

But the great reward, or high wages of labour, as well as the high profits of capital, kept up also the price of raw produce, for the labourer and capitalist had an increasing money amount to devote to the purchase of the necessaries of life. The supply of raw products was augmented, but it was not increased in proportion to the additional wants or additional demand of the increasing population. The demand was always therefore in advance of the supply of necessaries, which augmented their price. We see, then, that the price of labour rose instead of falling, and, by increasing the costs of production, must have, apparently, on the principles we have been explaining, proportionally reduced profits. But although that portion of the cultivator's expense, consisting of wages, increased with the other parts of his outlay, still the quantity of produce obtained far exceeded this increase of expenditure.

It will be recollected that the stimulus to the inventive powers of producers was of an uncommon kind, and that the inducements to improve machinery employed on the land, to save in animal power generally, as well as to increase the productive powers of the soil, from the more skilful use of manures, cannot be judged of from what takes place in ordinary circumstances. The wages of labour, it should also be borne in mind, were prevented from rising to the height they would have reached from the effect of the legal assessment for the relief of the poor. The labourers, from an unnatural competition among themselves, were thence precluded from receiving as large a recompense as they were entitled to, from the increased demand among employers. Wages, therefore, did not rise in an equal ratio to the increase of capital and of work to be done, although the condition of the working classes was universally much improved.

If these opinions be correct, the doctrine of a general glut, (if by this is meant a glut in a particular country,) which has excited so much controversy, must be sustained. A glut of certain commodities is the consequence of production exceeding demand in certain quarters, or of a faulty distribution of capital, and the principle admits of an extension to the whole of the commodities produced by a country, if the productive powers of such country had been previously stimulated in an uncommon degree by an unusual foreign demand. In the instance we have been considering, what occurred? In Great Britain profits fell, after the cessation of the foreign demand, not in one or a few employments, but in all. Wages fell too universally. Rents fell also, and the whole in the order they had risen—manufacturing and commercial profits and wages first, and agricultural profits and wages last. In the United States, the same effects were also experienced in all employments as the foreign demand ceased. In both countries commodities were produced in excess compared to the demand, and their prices fell because the former demanders supplied again their own wants ; they became, when their habits of industry had been resumed, producers as well as consumers.

It is an admitted doctrine, that if there is excess of commodities and capital in one or more employments, there must be a relative deficiency in others ; but, allowing the accuracy of this principle, it is inapplicable to the cases in view. There was no evidence of the defective or unequal distribution of capital in either country ; and the best proof that a general glut existed in both, was to be found in the fall universally in both, not only of profits but wages.

But if by the expression general glut is meant a glut in all countries, such a consequence is inconceivable. The different states of the great commercial commonwealth are in this view like the different districts of the same country, or like the various employments carried on within it. If from any cause capital or population should be in relative excess in a particular district, it must flow to that or those districts in which there is a relative deficiency, until the equilibrium is restored. If higher relative profits or wages are derived by those who follow certain employments, they will attract capital or labour, in the same manner, until the level is brought about. We have only to apply the same principle to the different states composing the great commercial republic, and if any circumstance has happened to produce a different distribution of capital between them to what ordinarily prevails, the same effects, on a more extended scale, will follow.

It is true, as Mr. SAY has asserted, that productions are bought finally with productions*—in other words, when no unusual circumstances cause a derangement in the ordinary relations of commerce between countries, there is as much produced on one side as on the other ; or in a trade of barter, equal value is given for equal value received. These are the natural arrangements established through the self interest of individuals. But wars, especially if they are general and long protracted, disturb these natural arrangements, and by stimulating excessively on one side, whilst they stop the powers of production on some other, disturb in a more than ordinary degree the natural state of prices between countries.

But the effects will be felt long after the causes of the disturbance have ceased to act. The equilibrium of prices between countries, like that between different districts of the same country, or between different employments carried on within it, must be finally restored, and those countries which have had their powers of production excited in the greatest degree, will have to endure, when the re-action occurs, the longest period of suffering.† In the unnatural state of things which leads to these results, those countries whose powers of production have been suspended, will have no increase

---

* Treatise on Political Economy, chap. 15, p. 87.

† Mr. MALTHUS makes a similar remark. See his Principles of Political Economy, p. 387.

of produce to exchange with states, for the time, more favourably circumstanced. As their revenue does not augment, a part of their capital must be encroached upon to supply their necessary wants. The conclusion from this view is, therefore, that the rise in the general rate of profits and wages, in the United States and Great Britain, during the hostilities in Europe, and their subsequent fall, were the effects of an unnatural state of things. The general change on the continent of Europe from the arts of peace to the pursuits of war, and then back again to the occupations of peace, caused so great a derangement in the ordinary relations between prices and demand, that the phenomena were as unlooked for as they were difficult of explanation.

It is necessary then to distinguish between a general rise of profits and wages in a particular country, produced by an excessive stimulus, and that general rise which is the effect of its regular progress in wealth and population, and to distinguish between a fall of the same nature, when the stimulus is withdrawn, from that fall which occurs from circumstances, such as heavy taxes, war expenditure, &c. that impede the acquisition of riches and the augmentation of population.

When the advance or decline of profits and wages is general, all capitalists or labourers gain or lose in an equal proportion. But when the advance or decline takes place in particular employments, it is to the benefit or disadvantage of those who pursue those employments to the loss or gain of others in the society. The equilibrium between these employments and the others will be finally adjusted by the operation of the principle of competition.

The limit to a fall of profits from heavy taxation is not very remote. The rise of profits from increased facility of production is without limit. We have explained the circumstances that determine the *natural* increase in the rate of profit. We have also endeavoured to show that when it increases in a higher ratio, it is the effect of unusual excitement, which must, sooner or later, be succeeded by a re-action and stagnation, which proportionally reduce it. To the point then, of natural increase in their rate, profits always converge, however they may occasionally rise above or fall below it. The principle of competition can have no influence on the progress of either profits or wages, in a natural state of things. Profits and wages advance inevitably in the regular progress of society, as has been shown.

It is not a little singular that Mr. MALTHUS should so much underrate the importance of the principle, that an increase of capital is necessary to provide both employment and maintenance for additional population. If the capitalist regularly augments the difference between his outlay and his returns, he proportionally enlarges the sphere for the employment of the whole of what he saves from his necessary expenditure, not only with undiminished but constantly incraesing revenue. The uninterrupted progress of the cotton manufacture of Great Britain during the last forty years, notwithstanding the fall in the price of the goods, affords a striking illustration of this general fact. The accumulation of capital, therefore, which Mr. MALTHUS constantly supposes will be followed by declining profits, may go on to an indefinite extent without any such decline, if room can be found for the employment of the successive additions made to it. That such room

will be found if trade is left unobstructed by restrictions and by wars, I have no doubt. The old channels
of commerce are constantly enlarged and others created with every increase of capital, if the inventive
powers of producers and the various resources of
states are properly developed. The diversity of soil,
situation, products and wants, opens sources of mutual
and increasing gains to countries whose governments
are wise enough to profit by this diversity. There can
then be no *assignable limit* to the employment of additional capital, for the experiment of a general and
free commercial intercourse between countries has
never been fully tried. Where, in fact, can we place
the limit to human ingenuity in inventions to increase
the powers of production? At what point can we
say Nature must fail to supply the variety of objects
that enlarges the commercial intercourse between
states, and by affording the means of additional gra-
tification, stimulate producers to new exertions? Mr.
MALTHUS' theory of profits, therefore, (which is in
substance Dr. SMITH's,) would appear to be no better
founded in fact than that of Mr. RICARDO—the former
placing the limits to an increase of profit in the redundancy of capital, and the latter in the necessity of
resorting to inferior soils to obtain additional produce.

In the view presented in the foregoing pages, of
the natural progress of wealth and population, it may
be objected that it places no limit to the fall in the prices
of labour and produce. It is no doubt true that the
point of their ultimate declension will be when the
earth can be made, with the utmost improvements in
science and by the increase of skill, to yield no more
produce. Whenever the entire globe is cultivated to
the utmost extent of its capacity to produce, and the

population which it is capable of maintaining on its
surface is fully up to the measure of that capacity, both
population and produce must come to a stop.   Both
will then remain stationary.   But this does not invalidate the principle that they are capable of an increase
up to this point.   The period is very remote indeed
at which they will have reached it, if rulers are
wise enough to profit by the various resources which
Nature places at their command for the benefit of
those they govern.   So distant indeed that we may
not trouble ourselves about the consequences when
that desirable consummation shall have been attained.
The rate of increase, we must recollect, is slow, when
things are left to take their natural course.   We must
not be deceived by the rapidity of the rate at which
some countries occasionally augment in capital and
population—in such cases it is a partial and not a general advance—an advance of one or more countries at
the expense of others—an advantage that is temporary
and is sure to be finally followed, when the re-action
occurs, by a measure of suffering fully equal to the
former impulse of prosperity received.

CHAPTER III.

MACHINERY.

IF the opinions expressed in the preceding chapters be correct, Mr. RICARDO's conclusion " that in proportion to the quantity and the durability of the fixed capital employed in any kind of production, the relative prices of those commodities on which such capital is employed will vary inversely as wages;"* cannot be sustained. That doctrine is the inevitable inference from the writer's premises, in order to maintain the level of profit. We have endeavoured to show that in the natural progress of wealth and population, money wages fall as profits advance, and, if this be the correct view, Mr. RICARDO's inference that the fall in the price of goods produced by machinery or fixed capital, takes place in consequence of a rise in money wages or an advance in the price of labour, must be erroneous. If profits always fell as the price of labour rose, Mr. RICARDO's doctrine would seem to be necessary, as we have said, to the equilibrium of profit; but during a state of things the most favourable to his hypothesis, during the last general war in

---

* Principles of Political Economy and Taxation, chap. 1, p. 29.

Europe, money wages and profits advanced together
in England, and the fall of goods arose, as it does in
every such case, from additions made to fixed capital,
or improvements in machinery.   But on other considerations the doctrine is untenable.   If the prices of
manufactured commodities fall as the price of labour
rises, then the prices of such commodities must rise as
labour falls in price.   Thus we have goods to advance
in price while machinery is improving.

The only way to avoid this dilemma is to insist that
in a natural state of things, the price of labour rises
and never falls.   Let us admit this, and see how the
principle will work on this supposition.   It is in proportion as fixed capital or machinery increases that the
prices of goods manufactured by its agency are reduced ; but wages, in the new theory, encroach on profits
as rapidly as they are increased, and any permanent
addition to capital from revenue is in consequence prevented.   How then is machinery to be increased, and
how are the prices of goods to fall ?   It cannot be
meant that the addition to fixed capital is made from
circulating capital, because, on such a supposition, the
means of employing labour are diminishing, whilst
wages are at the same time made to advance.   In fact,
it is precisely, in the natural progress of wealth, as
wages fall and machinery is improved, that circulating
capital increases, and in the same proportion with
fixed capital.   The proportions never vary, in a
wholesome state of things, in any employment.

It is not to save labour, if *quantity* be meant, that
machinery is improved—it is to save in the *price* or
wages of labour that the machine is made.   The effect
of machinery, were it to displace labour, or make a
less quantity necessary to production, would be an evi

instead of a benefit. It would check the increase of population, for population augments in proportion as the prices of manufactured as well as agricultural products decline, and it is as money wages are reduced, and the revenue devoted to the payment of labour increases, that the prices of all commodities, in a natural state of things, fall. Circulating capital is not, therefore, more nor less necessary to fixed than fixed is to circulating capital. With every augmentation of the one description there is a proportional increase of the other in all employments. If we could suppose that they increased irregularly, or in varying proportions, whether machinery improved as labour was displaced, or labour was more fully employed as machinery was thrown out of use—on either supposition the progress of a country in wealth and population would be retarded.

The popular prejudice against machinery has in a great measure given way, because it is plainly seen that, with every increase of its powers, more labour is employed—with every additional reduction of wages is there a demand for an additional quantity of labour, or an additional number of labourers. It would appear, then, that fixed and circulating capital never vary in their proportions to each other. It is not meant by this that these two kinds of capital are always equal in quantity in the same employment. Some employments require a larger and others a less portion of the one or of the other.

It requires no reasoning to prove that the capital which is consumed and reproduced at short periods, and that which is replaced at long periods, is employed in the manufacture of products that must sell at such relative prices as will preserve the level of

profit ; for if goods manufactured exclusively by labour, or partly by labour and partly by machinery,
sold at such rates as would not put the manufacturer
of them on the same footing as to profit with the
capitalist who used fixed capital solely, or in a different proportion, no commodities could be manufactured
at all by labour.   The proposition is so obvious that
it requires no reasoning to prove it.

If the view taken above of the effect of machinery
be correct, the whole of the labour disposable in consequence of the improvement in its powers, will be
required to obtain an increase of produce.   But without an additional quantity of labour, in a still higher
proportion than this, the augmentation of produce will
not be as great as the wants of society will require.
If there was not such additional quantity employed,
it would be giving as great a rate of increase to machinery as to population, which is impossible.   The
extension of markets, both foreign and domestic, demands more produce than can be supplied unless all
the labour which it is possible to obtain is employed.
Thus, if we suppose a manufacturer of cloth to increase
the powers of his machinery, in any given time, ten per
cent. and consequently able to employ, from the fall
in its price, the whole quantity of labour rendered
disposable to the extent of this increase, he will not
be able to meet the wants of consumers should the
demand for cloth have augmented in a higher ratio.
It must, however, augment in a higher ratio, for *the
increase in the powers of machinery is limited by the
faculties of the mind,* and *the demand for additional
produce is determined by the procreative principle, or
faculty,* which is far more active.

It is impossible to assign the relative rate of increase in the case of machinery and population. But if we suppose the increase of the former to be, in a given period, ten and the latter twenty per cent. if the manufacturer of cloth formerly employed 100 men and his improvements in machinery enabled him to manufacture an additional quantity of this commodity with the same number of labourers, he would be compelled to employ 110 men to produce as much cloth as the demand will take off; but he will obtain these 110 men at reduced wages, not merely in the proportion of the increase in the powers of his machinery, but in the higher proportion of the increase of population, otherwise he would make no addition to his profits by employing ten additional men. The rate of wages follows the rate of increase of labourers—as their number is augmented the price of their services must fall. And as we have seen that labour increases with every decline in the prices of raw and manufactured products, the labourers themselves are fully as much interested in improvements in machinery as the master producers. They obtain an increased quantity of the necessaries and conveniences of life from the fall in their price, and as the market for these products is extended, proportionally, so also is the market for labour. Thus is the actual population not more necessary to the actual produce than the latter to the former—without the actual numbers, the same quantity could neither be produced nor consumed. This appears to be the only rational explanation of the fact, that every invention that reduces the price of labour, has the effect of giving employment to an additional quantity—not only is there none displaced but more is demanded.

Mr. Ricardo attributes too much power to machinery. "If (says he) five millions of men could produce as much food and clothing as was necessary for ten millions, food and clothing for five millions would be the net revenue."* It is true that *if* five millions of men *could* produce as much food and clothing as was necessary for ten millions, this additional population would be at the expense of the net revenue. But if, when the population is five millions, fifty per cent. measures, in any given period, the rate of increase in the powers of machinery, or should it have improved so as to provide food and clothing for seven and a half millions, and the population has augmented, during such period, to ten millions, five millions with this additional power of production acquired by machinery, would be inadequate to that increase of produce required for the consumption of ten millions. To suppose any thing else is to give as great a rate of increase to machinery as to population.

The explanations that have been given by different writers of the effects of machinery on the labouring classes, appear to me to have been eminently unsatisfactory. Thus Mr. Say says " whenever a new machine or a new and more expeditious process is *substituted* in the place of human labour previously in activity, *part* of the industrious human agents, whose services are thus ingeniously *dispensed with,* must needs be *thrown out of employ.*" " In as much (he continues) as machinery produces that *evil,* it is clearly objectionable." Again—" New machines are slowly constructed, and still more slowly brought into use ; so as to give time for those who are interested to

---

* Principles of Political Economy and Taxation. chap. Gross and Net Revenue, p. 374

take their measures, and for the public administration to provide a remedy."* And, in a note, Mr. SAY has the following remarks. " Without having recourse to local or temporary restrictions on the use of new methods or machinery, which are invasions of the property of the inventors or fabricators, a benevolent administration can *make provision for the employment of supplanted or in active labour in the construction of works of public utility* at the public expense; as of canals, roads, churches, or the like; *in extended colonization; in the transfer of population from one spot to another.* Employment is the more readily found for the hands thrown out of work by machinery, because they are commonly already inured to labour." Now this explanation leaves the mind at a loss to conceive how the population accommodates itself to those changes which are natural to an improved state of society, in consequence not only of mechanical inventions that augment the quantity of manufactured products but of those discoveries in natural science which increase the produce of the land. It is obvious that room must be found *in the same occupation* for all the labour formerly employed in it, without occasioning even temporary distress, or the public admistration being under the necessity of employing labour in the construction of works of public utility.

If there was not some principle, by which every change of this kind finds those who are to benefit by it, prepared to receive its full effect or influence, nothing but derangement between different employments would be the consequence. Every such change is slow and gradual, and time is allowed for its accommodation to existing circumstances or to the interests

* Treatise on Political Economy, pp. 30. 31.

of all classes. Whenever any portion of the labour
of society is employed in public works, it can only be
done by its abstraction from private employments, and
whenever it is so employed without any such abstraction, some derangement must previously have occurred by which the market was overstocked with labour.
Even in the instance of a change of fashion, by the
caprices of which it sometimes happens that distress is
produced among a small part of the operatives, it happens that they find in the variety of employments of
a wealthy society, a resource against want. In the
case, however, of an improvement in machinery, there
is no necessity for such a resource, or of a change
from one employment to another similar to it, for this
would be attended with some loss or inconvenience to
the labourer. All such transitions, therefore, are so
gradual that a provision is made in those arrangements which take place, *independently of all human
interference*, in the natural progress of things, and no
evil is ever experienced from the utmost extent to
which such improvements can be carried, unless by
the intermeddling of those who pretend to *regulate*
the order of society. It would be an impeachment
of the wisdom of Providence to suppose that the
powers of human invention (in whatever mode these
powers are displayed) are conferred that they may
not be improved for the benefit of the human race
to the fullest extent of their possible improvement,
without occasioning any such derangement as must
follow the displacement of a part of the labouring
population from its regular and accustomed employments. Even in the invention of the art of printing,
the most striking instance of a total change in the
nature of the employment, who can pronounce that

the copyists were not prepared for the change, and did not find the transition easy and natural, and not sudden and abrupt?

We quote the following passage from Mr. SAY as an instance of very unphilosophical explanation on this subject and in obvious contradiction to all sound principles. " It may be allowable to add that viewing human labour and machinery in the aggregate, in the supposition of the extreme case, viz. *that machinery should be brought to supersede human labour altogether, yet the numbers of mankind would not be thinned, for the sum total of products would be the same,* and there would probably be *less suffering to the poor and labouring classes to be apprehended;* for in that case the momentary fluctuations that distress the different branches of industry would *principally affect machinery,* which, and *not human labour,* would be paralyzed ; and machinery cannot die of hunger : it can only cease to yield profit to its employers, who are generally farther removed from want than mere labourers."*

The supposition made by Mr. SAY, in the above passage, is so extravagant that if it were possible to see it realized, the greatest disorder in the natural proportions between fixed and circulating capital, and even between capital in the aggregate and population would be the consequence. How could Mr. SAY conceive that " the numbers of mankind would not be thinned and the sum total of products would be the same" if " machinery should be brought to supersede human labour altogether ?" Is not this at once destroying the ordinary proportions between fixed and circulating capital, or giving a rate of increase to the

* Treatise on Political Economy, p. 32.

former far more rapid than to the latter, or, which is still nearer the truth, allowing the one description of capital to augment to the entire destruction of the other? To contend that the amount of produce would be as great without as with labour, is giving an effect to machinery which it never can have—it is making population less necessary to production than to consumption and thence destroying the balance between them. Every increase of produce, unless the population has concurred in this increase with machinery, must subtract from profits, and in this proportion put a stop to any further improvement in machinery. Can Mr. Say imagine a case in which there would be " less suffering to the poor and labouring classes" on " machinery being brought to supersede human labour altogether," than when both are used in their due proportions; and how can he suppose " the momentary fluctuations that distress the different branches of industry would principally affect *machinery* and not *human labour?*" The error of Mr. Say is substantially the same as that which affects the labouring class itself, who invariably attribute a disproportionate influence to machinery.

CHAPTER IV.

VALUE AND PRICE.

IT were to be wished that writers on Political Economy had kept invariably in view the meaning they attach to the word *value*. If this had been done many of the points which have been made debateable in this science would have been determined with little or no difficulty. By almost all writers it has been considered as identical, under all circumstances, with price—whilst with very few has it been viewed as equivalent in meaning to *wealth* or *quantity*. Mr. Ricardo regards value as essentially different from riches, " for," says he, " value depends not on abundance, but on the *difficulty* or *facility* of production."* According to this definition, considered literally, value depends both on abundance *and* scarcity, for commodities are abundant as they are produced with facility, and scarce when produced with difficulty. If value depends on facility of production, then there is no difference between it and riches, for nations are rich in proportion as they produce with facility. If value depends on difficulty of production, then there is an obvious distinction between it and riches, for countries

* Principles of Political Economy and Taxation, chap 18. p. 282

are poor which have to purchase their enjoyments by a great sacrifice of toil or exertion. According to one view of value, in the above definition, productions become valuable as they become scarce—according to the other view they become valuable as they become abundant.

But I suppose that the meaning of Mr. RICARDO is that value depends on the *greater* or *less* difficulty or facility of production. Value, then, pursuant to this opinion, must diminish as the quantity of productions increases, or as they are produced with facility, and value must increase with the scarcity of productions, or as they are produced with difficulty—in other words, *value* is made, under all circumstances, equivalent in meaning to *price*, and Mr. RICARDO consequently employs *relative* and *exchangeable* value, as if they were always convertible terms. Value and price differ, however, when demand is properly proportioned to supply, or when produce is distributed exactly according to the wants of consumers, or, which is the same thing, price is, under such circumstances, in an inverse proportion to quantity.

In the regular and natural progress of wealth, there is an increase in the quantity of all commodities, including labour; the whole augments in an equal ratio, and the exchangeable value of every part increases. The quantity of produce or of labour which each producer is able to command, is equal to the quantity parted with by every other producer. It is increased quantity exchanged against increased quantity; but it is precisely because quantity is increased universally, that prices fall universally, and in every quarter. But in such case, whilst exchangeable value has risen, relative value remains the same. Suppose that a ma-

manufacturer of hats exchanges this year 1000 hats for 1000 pair of shoes, but by an increase of skill he is able to make the following year 1200 hats, and the manufacturer of shoes increases his commodity in the same proportion, the value of hats, according to Mr. RICARDO, will have fallen, as well as the value of shoes ; but it is their *price* only which will have been reduced. The exchangeable value of both shoes and hats will have increased, for each commodity exchanges for a greater quantity of the other. Here, then, the relation of these commodities to each other, as to their prices, is unaltered, or their relative value continues as before, but their value when exchanged for each other has varied—it has increased.

This is no longer the case, however, when demand is not properly proportioned to supply, or when produce is not distributed according to the wants of those who are to consume it. In this state of things price and exchangeable value are identical, but the relation to each other, as to prices, of the commodities affected by the change, is altered. The prices of some rise, under these circumstances, and their exchangeable value is augmented, but the prices of others for which they are exchanged, must proportionally fall—in other words their value in exchange lessens. Suppose, to continue the illustration just employed, the shoes should not have increased in proportion to the hats ; in this case the exchangeable value of the hats and their price will have fallen, if the demand continues as before for both commodities, for in exchanging hats for shoes a greater quantity of the former must be parted with to obtain the same quantity as before of the latter. Thus suppose the difference in the increase to be twenty per cent.—in these circumstances 1200 hats must be

exchanged for 1000 pair of shoes instead of 1200 pair
as before. The price and exchangeable value of shoes
will have risen, and the exchangeable value and price
of hats will have proportionally fallen.

If we now take the opposite supposition, and imagine that the quantity of hats has lessened whilst the
quantity of shoes and the demand for both commodities continue as before—in this case the effects will
be reversed, the exchangeable value and price of hats
will have advanced whilst the price and exchangeable
value of shoes will have been lowered, for instead of
1000 pair of shoes exchanging, as in the former instance, for 1200 hats, 1200 pair of the former must be
parted with to obtain 1000 of the latter. In these cases
it is supposed that the demand for each commodity is
neither lessened nor increased, but this is not necessary to prove that price and exchangeable value are
identical when demand and supply are not in exact
or natural proportion to each other. The manufacturer of shoes (of which the quantity we have supposed not to have either increased or diminished) may
augment his consumption of hats in proportion to their
increased quantity. In this case the demand for hats
will have risen, and their price and exchangeable value
would be unaltered. If the manufacturer of shoes
lessens his consumption of hats in the ratio of their
increased quantity, the price as well as exchangeable
value of hats must fall both from additional supply
and diminished demand, and they will fall in a
higher proportion, of course, than if the supply had
merely increased. In this case 1400 hats must be exchanged for 1000 pair of shoes. These distinctions
are not vain and unnecessary—they are essential to a
clear understanding of the principles of the science.

The identification of *price* and *value in exchange*, UN-
DER ALL CIRCUMSTANCES, is, I am convinced, at the
foundation of some of the peculiar views entertained
by the school of Mr. RICARDO. The following para-
graph will show how entirely this writer has confounded price with value in exchange.

" For if an improved piece of machinery should
enable us to make two pair of stockings instead of one,
without additional labour, double the quantity would
be given in exchange for a yard of cloth. If a similar improvement be made in the manufacture of cloth,
stockings and cloth will be exchanged in the same
proportions as before, but they both would have fallen
in value, for in exchanging them for hats, for gold, or
for other commodities in general, twice the quantity
must be given. Extend the improvement to the production of gold and every other commodity, and they
will all regain their former proportions. There will
be double the quantity of commodities annually produced in the country, and therefore the wealth of the
country will be doubled, but this wealth will not have
increased in value."* The wealth will not have increased in *value*, if by value *price* be meant. The
productions of which this wealth consisted will have
fallen in price, and if this is meant by the expression
" the wealth will not have increased in value," the
remark is correct—it will have fallen in value. But
Mr. RICARDO has said that " if a similar improvement
be made in the manufacture of cloth to what is made
in the manufacture of stockings, they will have fallen
in value ; for in exchanging them for hats, for gold,
or other commodities in general, twice the former
quantity must be given." Now it is precisely because

* Principles of Political Economy and Taxation, chap. 18, p. 288.

double the quantity of cloth and stockings is given for double the quantity of hats and gold and other commodities to which the improvement has extended, that the cloth and stockings have increased in exchangeable value equally with the hats and gold. They will, therefore, if value in exchange be meant, have augmented in value, in consequence of an additional quantity of the two former commodities being given for an additional quantity of the two latter. Not only will the wealth of the country be doubled, but that wealth will have derived twice its former value in exchange. Again :

" Although," says Mr. RICARDO, " ADAM SMITH has given the correct description of riches, which I have more than once noticed, he afterwards explains them differently, and says ' that a man must be rich or poor according to the quantity of labour which he can afford to purchase.' Now," continues Mr. RICARDO, " this description differs essentially from the other, and is certainly incorrect ; for suppose the mines were to become more productive, so that gold and silver fell in value [price] from the greater facility of their production ; or that velvets were to be manufactured with so much less labour than before, that they fell to half their former value, [price,] the riches of all those who purchased those commodites would be increased : one man might increase the quantity of his plate, another might buy double the quantity of velvet : but with the possession of this additional plate and velvet they could employ no more additional labour than before ; because as the *exchangeable value* of velvet and plate *would be lowered*, they must part with proportionally more of these species of riches to purchase a day's labour. Riches then cannot be esti-

mated by the quantity of labour which they can purchase."*

Now if it were true that the quantity of labour is
not increased proportionally with the quantity of commodities, and its price did not fall also in proportion
to the fall in these, Mr. RICARDO's conclusions would
be inevitable.   But the supposition of a rise in the
price of labour with the increase of its supply, which
he takes for granted in all his reasonings, cannot, as
we have endeavoured to show, be admitted.   Mr.
RICARDO, therefore, evidently views labour erroneous-
ly when he considers it as not subject to the same laws
that regulate the increase and the prices of commodities in general.   It is obvious that without this condition of a constant and equal augmentation in the
supply of labour with capital, and a proportionate fall
of its price with the price of productions generally,
that both the power and the will to accumulate would
cease on the part of producers.   The power to accumulate is founded on the reduced wages of labour ;
for it is by savings in these that capital is made available for an increase of population, and it is by the
consequent addition to the number of working producers that productions are multiplied and profits still
further augmented.

To suppose the quantity of labour not to increase
equally with the quantity of commodities, is to give
greater efficiency to fixed than to circulating capital.
But we know that more labour, in every period of
society from the most rude to the most refined, is rendered as necessary to the increase of produce, equal
to the wants of the population, as this increase is to
provide for its maintenance and employment.   What

* Principles of Political Economy and Taxation, chap. 18, p. 289.

possible inducement could the capitalist have to save in the expenses of production if he could not command more labour at a reduced price, or for the same amount in money.

How could the fact be reconciled of the extended market for labour, unless on the supposition that the quantity of commodities is by this means multiplied, and the market for them extended also. Mr. RICARDO has then laboured under a palpable error in saying that "A certain quantity of clothes and provisions will maintain and employ the same number of men, and will therefore procure the same quantity of work to be done, whether they be produced by the labour of 100 or 200 men ;"* for it is obvious that without the 200 men the same quantity of work will not be done, or such a quantity of clothes and provisions provided as will maintain and employ the 200. Neither the power nor the inducement to provide clothes and provisions for 200 men could possibly, under such circumstances, exist. Dr. SMITH is then correct in saying " that a man must be rich or poor according to the quantity of labour which he can afford to purchase." It is only another form of expression, in describing an equivalent effect, to assert that a man must be rich or poor according to the quantity of *labour* instead of the quantity of *commodities* which he can afford to purchase, for these quantities are equal when demand is exactly equal to supply, as regards both labour and commodities.

It follows, from this view of the subject, that if, according to Mr. RICARDO, the *quantity* of labour expended on commodities governs their price, when market and natural prices correspond, it can have no

* Principles of Political Economy and Taxation, chap. 18, p. 290.

influence on their *exchangeable value;* for then value
in exchange and prices rise and fall in an inverse ratio.
But neither can the *quantity* of labour govern the
prices of commodities, in such a state of things, for
we have shown that prices decrease as the quantity of
labour increases, or they advance and lessen also in an
inverse ratio. But it is the *price* of labour that governs
the prices of commodities, for they rise and fall together. The price of labour does not, however, regulate the prices of commodities more than the prices
of these do the price of labour. They have a mutual
influence and fall in regular and equal proportion.

It cannot be pretended that the quantity of labour
bestowed on productions has any influence on their
prices, as these prices vary from natural prices, for as
in such case commodities are not increased but their
distribution only altered, there can be no increased
quantity of labour employed. There is an increase
of produce in some quarters, but attended, of course,
by a proportional diminution in others.

The following passage affords a further proof that
Mr. RICARDO has attached to exchangeable value a
meaning that belongs only to price in the circumstances
supposed. " In contradiction to the opinion of ADAM
SMITH, Mr. SAY, in the 4th chapter of his work, speaks
of the value which is given to commodities by natural
agents, such as the sun, the air, the pressure of the
atmosphere, &c. which are sometimes substituted for
the labour of man, and sometimes concur with him
in producing. But these natural agents, though they
add greatly to *value in use,* NEVER ADD EXCHANGEABLE
VALUE, of which Mr. SAY is speaking, to any commodity ; as soon as by the aid of machinery, or by the
knowledge of natural philosophy, you oblige natural

agents to do the work which was before done by man, the *exchangeable value* of such work *falls* accordingly."*

Mr. SAY is no doubt correct when he states, that natural agents and machinery add to the exchangeable value of the productions which by their aid have been increased in quantity, and in the ratio of this increase have fallen in price, provided that they are not produced in excess. If the demand will not take off the whole quantity supplied, we have shown that the fall in price and exchangeable value are coincident. If the distinction between the cases is not observed, the partial increase of wealth—or its increase in some quarters, (attended by its diminution in others,) will be mistaken for that general increase in which all producers participate, when prices vary inversely to value in exchange. It will be found, in a wholesome state of things, that the augmentation of the quantity of a commodity is always accompanied by the augmentation of others for which it is exchanged, or that the motive or the will to add to the powers of production, operates equally on all producers, so as to cause an increase in the quantity of all the objects of consumption, as well as of the labour by which they are to be obtained.

Nor is the principle that determines the exchangeable value of commodities different in a rude from an improved state of society. Dr. SMITH, has said, " that in that early and rude state of society that precedes the accumulation of capital and the appropriation of land, the proportion between the quantities of labour necessary for acquiring different objects seems to be the only circumstance which can afford any rule for

* Principles of Political Economy and Taxation, chap 18, p. 293.

exchanging them for one another.."* Now if this principle be true, in its application to one period of society, it must be true in its application to all. We have shown that the exchangeable value of commodities in an improved period, is determined by the degree of skill and science to which society has attained—it is the same thing, when by the address and sagacity of the savage, he can either with the aid of natural agents, or by the improvement of his rude weapons or implements, acquire in less time a greater quantity of those objects which he usually exchanges for others. A fisherman to take twenty salmon employs a day's labour, but, by his ingenuity, discovers means of taking, within the same time, forty salmon. Now will it be contended that this additional quantity of salmon will exchange for an additional quantity of game, unless the same improvement has been extended to this commodity also? If the hunter has been able to effect the same increase by equal address and skill, both parties to the exchange will gain in an equal proportion. Whether the fisherman will continue to catch twenty salmon or forty, will depend of course upon the demand of the hunter for salmon or the supply of his commodity. If the consumption of the fish has increased, as it will most probably be, the hunter will have been able to increase his commodity to render the exchange advantageous to both parties. But this is precisely the principle that regulates the exchange of commodities in an improved period of society. If we suppose the existence of a market for labour in the ruder period, it would be found that it had fallen in price as well as game and salmon. These

* Wealth of Nations, book 1, chap. 5.

productions would more nearly measure the value of each other and of labour in the rude than in the improved period, for then there are fewer causes in action to disturb the natural proportion between demand and supply.

CHAPTER V.

MONEY.

WE have endeavoured to show that in the natural progress of society all commodities as well as labour fall in price. But money, or the material of money, is a commodity subject to the same laws and therefore to the same changes in exchangeable value as other commodities. It has its natural as well as its market price. In the regular progress of wealth and population, it must rise in exchangeable value,* or exchange for a greater quantity of produce, as its quantity increases, or as improvements are made in the machinery by which it is produced. An increased quantity of commodities requires an increased quantity of money to circulate them, for the number of exchanges is proportionally augmented, and it is precisely equivalent to say that labour with agricultural and manufactured products increase in quantity or rise in exchangeable value, as to assert that money or its material increases in quantity or rises in exchangeable value. Each commodity would be a measure of value

* I allude of course to the whole mass, and not to any particular portion of money.

of every other, if market prices always corresponded
with natural prices. Equal quantities of labour in
one employment, would exchange for equal quantities
in every other employment, allowing for their comparative disadvantages.

But although this supposition of a perfect correspondence between natural and market prices is necessary
to a settlement of first principles, the disturbing influence of taxation, restrictions on trade, &c. which
perpetually change the natural proportions between demand and supply, have a correspondent influence on
prices—either elevating market prices above or reducing them below natural prices. Whenever market
prices rise above or fall below natural prices, it always
terminates in a proportional decrease or increase of
the relative value of money. Whilst, therefore, we
are investigating the effects of taxation, restrictions on
commerce, &c. on the relative value of money, we are
at the same time investigating the effects of these circumstances on the value of those commodities for
which it is exchanged.

We have seen that an increase in the quantity, whether of labour or commodities, reduces their price—
a diminished quantity must therefore elevate their
price. Taxation diminishes the quantity of a country's
productions, in proportion to the amount of the taxes
imposed ; they must then proportionally diminish the
quantity of money in that country, for the quantity of
money must bear a relative proportion to the quantity
of commodities and labour it has to circulate, or to
the number of exchanges it has to effect, as its value
must bear the same proportion to the demand for it
as a medium of circulation. Taxation is, however,
constantly and happily counteracted in its effects by

an increase of productive power. Were this not the case, population and capital would decline to that point at which the amount of taxation would permit them to remain. They are opposite forces, if we can so express it, in the economical world, and as the one or the other prevails is a country in the enjoyment of wealth or suffering from poverty. It is necessary, however, for the proper elucidation of the subject, that we should first consider the results of taxation separately from the consequences of an increase of productive power, and afterwards in their combination.

Let us then commence with the effects of taxation on the value of money. Let us suppose a tax imposed on income and the government to export the money in payment of a subsidy. The *first* effect of such a tax would be to diminish demand for labour and produce. The persons who contribute to the payment of the tax will have a smaller money amount to devote to the purchase of commodities than before the imposition of the tax. Commodities could not possibly bear the same proportion as before to the medium of circulation. The excess would be exported in exchange for money which had risen in relative value. The effect would be the restoration of the former proportions between money and commodities and the value of both would come to a level. The quantity which each consumer could command of both would be lessened. As the prices of commodities had fallen, in the first instance, from diminished demand, so they ultimately rise from diminished supply, and as the value of money had risen in consequence of its exportation, its return in exchange for the excess of the commodities exported, will be in proportion only to this excess. It will have fallen ultimately in exchangeable value exactly in the ratio that commodities will have fallen, because its quantity has been reduced in the same ratio.

If we suppose the tax to have been collected in kind—in corn, for instance, the final effects would be precisely the same. In such case, if the government export the corn to feed its troops abroad, or for any other purpose, money would be in excess compared with commodities, and instead of its being the *first* it would be the *last* exported. It would be profitable to send it abroad in exchange for commodities which had risen at home, as in the other case it was profitable to send commodities abroad in exchange for money which had risen at home. In both cases the quantity of both will have been equally diminished and the exchangeable value of both ultimately and equally reduced.

This deduction of effects is founded, however, on the idea that the tax reduces consumption equally and at the same time of commodities of every kind; but this supposition, although it has been adopted to simplify the explanation, and is theoretically true, never occurs in fact. The imposition of a tax is attended, in the great majority of cases, by a reduction of expenditure on certain objects with the same expenditure on others—with a diminished consumption of luxuries that the wants of consumers may be satisfied for articles of more necessary consumption. In such case the price of necessaries will not *at first* fall, for the demand continues as before, but the price of luxuries will be reduced as the consumption of them has been diminished. But the producers of luxuries are also the consumers of necessaries—the decline in the de-

mand for the commodities they produce, will compel
them to lessen their consumption of other productions.
The producers of necessaries will obtain for a short
period higher relative prices and profits than the producers of luxuries, but the level of prices, and of
course of profits, will soon be adjusted, and all commodities, whether luxuries or necessaries, will settle
at a higher price than before. The whole quantity of
commodities, money included, will be reduced in proportion to the tax, and every man's portion, or power
to command the former portion, is finally diminished.

If money was not altered in value—if as large a
quantity could be obtained in exchange for the same
quantity of commodities as before, these results would
not take place. But as the principle cannot admit of
dispute, that money lessens as the quantity of productions it has to circulate diminishes, or, which is the
same thing, that it is subtracted from the circulation
as the number of exchanges it has to perform is reduced—it follows necessarily that the command of
money, whether by rich or poor consumers, is abridged
with the progress of taxation ; they must make a
greater sacrifice, if they wish to obtain the same
amount of the conveniences or luxuries of life as
before the tax was imposed. It will be recollected
that we are considering the consequences of taxation
on the value of money and produce generally, without any countervailing effect from an increase of productive power. Restrictions on trade produce precisely the same effects on the value of money as
taxation. They prevent the market from being as
fully supplied as it would be with commodities if the
restrictions did not exist. They, therefore, compel
the exportation of the money of the country, in which

they are adopted, exactly to the extent of the relative excess of the whole quantity of the currency to the whole quantity of productions it has to circulate. Restrictions, however, and the same may be said of bounties, whether on production or exportation, are only of temporary advantage to those whose interests they appear to favour. It is merely whilst capital and labour are shifting from the employments which do not to those which do benefit by those restrictions that higher profits are derived by the capitalists who are thus favoured. Profits soon come to a level, for competition must adjust them to the general rate. The prices of all commodities are prevented from falling as low as they would have been reduced to, if the restrictions had not existed. They therefore eventually re-act on those in whose favour they are passed, unless the duty or bounty is increased as soon as the equilibrium of profit is restored.

Another cause that affects the value of money is the issue of paper, as a medium of circulation, by the state, or when such issue takes the form of a loan from banking institutions to the government, which is in effect the same thing. Such loan or issue is only another name for a tax or taxes—it is taxation in disguise and like the foreign duties, blend the tax with the prices of commodities. The same results follow precisely as when taxes are *directly* imposed. The metallic money, which is the standard, is exported, in proportion as the whole quantity of currency exceeds the whole quantity of productions to be circulated, or number of exchanges to be performed, and the *value in exchange* of the whole produce with that of money, finally settles at a lower point than previous to the loan or emission, or, which is the same

thing, prices are prevented falling to their just and
natural level. The issues of banks to individuals also
cause the exportation of a part of the gold or silver
employed in the circulation, precisely in the ratio also
of the excess, and the same results are produced.

We have thus seen the effects on the value of money
from those circumstances which disturb the natural
progress of wealth and population, or which produce
a variation between natural and market prices. In
all these cases we have been supposing taxation, restrictions, bounties, &c. to operate without check or
restraint.

An increase in the powers of production may, however, as I before remarked, counteract the consequences of an increase of taxation, although considerable ;
the quantity of commodities thrown into the market
by producers may exceed the quantity taken out by
government, and the tendency to a decline in national
wealth from taxes, restrictions, &c. may be counteracted by an opposite tendency still stronger. If the
effects from these opposing causes balance each other,
countries subject to their influence would of course be
stationary in wealth and population. If no disturbing
influence were to take place in the due equilibrium
between money and the commodities it has to circulate,
the level of prices would be unaltered, and money or
the material of money would be imported during the
progress of improvement, for an additional quantity
would be wanted for the increasing business of society.
If countries continued in a stationary condition, money
would be neither imported nor exported. But, according to the principles we have been explaining, any
degree of taxation whatever must produce a correspondent effect on the level between money and the

produce it is employed to circulate. The same may be said of bounties, restrictions, &c.

It may be supposed, however, that an extraordinary stimulus being given to the industr, and commerce of a particular country, the demand for additional currency may increase more rapidly than the supply of the precious metals could be augmented from abroad, and that in such case an issue of paper, supposing the currency to consist entirely of one or the other of the precious metals, might take place without producing disturbance, provided that the issue was no greater than in proportion to the increase of produce. But these are erroneous conclusions: For

First, The increased powers of production of one or more countries, in such case, is no more than equal to the diminution of the productive powers of other nations of the commercial world. If the country receiving an unusual stimulus requires an additional quantity of money in a shorter period than bullion can be produced at the mines, those countries whose progress in improvement must have been necessarily retarded, will have a redundancy of the precious metals which they would be ready and willing to exchange for the commodities which their wants or habits made necessary to them. Thus the nations of the continent of Europe, during the long contest into which Buonaparte's domination drove them, must have suspended in great part their powers of production and encroached on their capitals. They had therefore a surplus of the precious metals which would have been imported into Great Britain and the United States in payment for the manufactures and colonial produce of the former and the raw produce of the latter, if the circulation of both countries had not been for a great part of the time surcharged with paper. Instead of specie finding its way into the United States and Great Britain, therefore, in proportion to their increased want of money, it was excluded by their paper issues, and was even driven abroad to countries where it went to increase the prices of those foreign commodities which were necessary to their consumption. But

Secondly, Neither is it possible to introduce even the smallest amount of paper into the circulation without producing disturbance of prices, although it should not exceed the quantity of gold or silver that would have circulated in place of it. If it were possible to add paper to the circulating medium *in the same manner* that the precious metals are added to it, in the regular progress of improvement, no derangement could occur. If this be true, paper money cannot be productive of national advantage, as by leading to a disturbance of prices it must alter the level of profits between different employments, and terminate in much individual loss and distress. The currency which a contrary opinion has so long obtained, is truly surprising. Dr. SMITH's views on the subject of money in general, and paper money in particular, have assisted in giving an extensive and lasting influence to error in this branch of Political Economy.

His misconception in this matter consisted in viewing the expense of procuring and supporting the precious metals for the purposes of money as a deduction from the net revenue of society. But if it can be made to appear that the amount of population and produce would have been greater, in any given period, with than without the use of the precious metals as money, Dr. SMITH must be condemned on his own principles. He has very properly considered the maintenance of the actual population as no deduction from the net revenue of society, because the productive classes reproduce a greater value than they consume during their maintenance. It was on this principle that he successfully overthrew the theory of the Economists. But if this be correct, and it can be shown that the produce and population of a country would be less in any given period with than without the use of paper as the instrument of circulation, the contradiction between Dr. SMITH's opinions in regard to money generally, and those he has expressed in relation to the Economical theory, will be made out. This it will be our purpose now to show.

If it were correct, that on the substitution of paper for the precious metals as money, *an equal rise in the prices of all commodities* took place, the consequences which have been deduced from this principle could not fail to occur. But I am satisfied that its too ready admission has been the origin of the various disputes that have occurred in regard to money and exchange.

It must always be borne in mind, that there can be no variation in prices unless the due proportion has been altered between demand and supply, and whether the alteration has its origin in the quantity of circulating medium exchanged for the commodities which have varied in price or in the quantity of commodities themselves, the effects on price are identical. Setting out from this principle, it can be made to appear that whenever a rise of prices takes place on an issue of paper, it is *partial* and not *general*, and that the rise is only in certain articles for which the demand will have increased, accompanied by an equivalent fall in the prices of other articles which will have experienced, in the same degree, diminished demand. Let us trace the consequences of an emission of paper which displaces an equal amount of one or the other of the precious metals from the circulation. The demand *for those particular commodities* of which additional competition will have augmented the price, in consequence of the issue, will be, of course, in proportion to the increased quantity of circulating medium for which they are exchanged.

We have said that this will be accompanied by an equivalent fall in the prices *of other commodities* for which the demand will in an equal degree have diminished, or, which is the same thing, which will have been exchanged for a smaller quantity of circulating medium. The point of inquiry then is, what portion of the national produce is it for which the demand will in this manner have lessened and the price been reduced? The answer is obvious—that portion which it was usual to send abroad in exchange for bullion. Thus, suppose, to confine ourselves to a single commodity, that we may simplify the explanation, that it had been usual to export cloth to purchase bullion in some country possessed of mines of the precious metals. If the amount of paper issued in one year be one million of dollars, and the value of cloth which would, in the same year, have been exported to [be exchanged for bullion abroad, have been five millions, the price of cloth will fall in the foreign market to which it had been customary to send it, one fifth.

It will be obvious, on the smallest reflection, that the diminution in the demand for bullion, to be converted into money, in the country employing paper, will compel the producers abroad of bullion to lessen their demand in an equal degree for cloth, and that the value of the exports of the country which employs paper will fall precisely in proportion to this reduced demand. The value of the cloth exported will be therefore *four* millions instead of *five*. This will turn the balance of payments against the country suffering under this disadvantage, and compel it to export some other commodity, of the value of one million, to restore the balance or to bring the exchange to par should it have been previously at par. This commodity will be money, for money when in that state that renders it fit for exportation, is to be viewed as subject to the same laws as commodities in general. It is precisely that portion and no other of the metallic money, to the amount of one million, of the country the value of whose exports has thus lessened, that had been previously applied to the purchase and transmission of cloth to be exchanged abroad for bullion, and which, being no longer applicable to this purpose, is exported to pay a balance of debt created by an emission of paper to the same amount, in the manner above described.

The producers of cloth will necessarily experience a fall of profit in proportion to the diminished demand for that commodity, and will have to remove a portion of their capital to some other employment. A part of their gains will be transferred to the producers of the commodity or commodities of which the issue of paper had in the first instance raised the price. This class of capitalists will have a larger money amount to devote to the purchase of articles either of necessity or enjoyment than those whose productions have fallen in price. The wages of the labourers in the employments thus favoured, must increase to the correspondent diminution of the wages of those who were engaged in the preparation for the foreign market of that portion of produce for which the demand has lessened.

Thus, we have seen, that if one million of dollars in specie be exported from the introduction of paper to the same amount, and this sum bear the proportion in value of one fifth to that of the produce it circulated. this portion of produce will unavoidably fall in value from *five* to *four* millions in consequence of diminished demand. There being no market abroad for one fifth part of it, except at a reduced price, its production will be discontinued in this proportion. Now, if we suppose that fifty millions of dollars constitute the amount of the precious metals that would have circulated in a particular country, in any given period, if paper had not been introduced into its circulation, it is obvious that such country, if it adopts paper to an equal amount as a medium of exchange, will, at the end of such period, have a less value in produce by fifty millions of dollars than if it had employed one or the other of the precious metals for money. The amount of its population would, at the end of the same period, be also less in the ratio of the numbers which would have been required to raise or manufacture the value of these fifty millions. It is in this manner we conceive that every issue of paper will discourage production and population to the extent of such issue. But if the power of a country is to be estimated by the amount of its wealth and population together, the conclusion that it will not be as powerful with the use of paper as with the use of either of the precious metals, as the instrument of circulation, seems inevitable.

It is evident also that the effect on the value of the exports which have been deduced from an issue of paper, must follow from whatever circumstance deranges prices, whether it be an alteration of the standard, a deterioration of the coin in any mode or degree, an increase of the taxes, or restrictions on commercial intercourse. Each of these causes leads to the exportation of a less value than would have gone abroad if it had not exerted a disturbing influence on prices—or, in other words, the balance of payments is turned against the country subject to either of these disadvantages. In every case, therefore, of an undue increase of the circulating medium, when it is said that a commodity is in consequence raised in price, it is merely a different form of expression, but the same in substance, as if it were asserted that it exchanges for a greater quantity of money. In the same manner, when it is said that a commodity has fallen in price, unless it is from excess in the supply, it is identical with the assertion that it exchanges for a smaller quantity of money, and the rise in the one case and the fall in the other, are both consequences of the same cause of disturbance. The idea, then, of a *general* fall in the value of money, as regards a particular country, or, which is the same thing, a *general* rise in the prices of its commodities, under the circumstances supposed, cannot be correct.

The question as to the origin of high or low prices resolves itself, therefore, in every instance, into a single point, whether the alteration is in the demand or supply of the article or articles for which money is exchanged. If the terms depreciation or fall in value, as regards money, are meant to convey the meaning that the quantity of currency given in exchange for articles which are high in price is greater than when their price is less, the proposition cannot admit of dispute. In this sense the idea of a fall in value or depreciation of money, if confined to that portion only which is exchanged for such articles, is sufficiently intelligible. But the fall in the value of money in such case, is the same thing as the rise in value of the articles for which it is exchanged. In this sense, also, the quantity of money which is given in exchange for articles which have fallen in price, may be said to be less than when their price is higher, or, in other words, that portion of the currency exchanged for articles which have been reduced in value, must have risen in value relatively to those articles.

If we are correct in these views, the opinion of modern Economists, that by the use of paper money the quantity of the precious metals displaced is a clear addition to national wealth, by the value of the returns received for it abroad, must be erroneous. We have, we think, shown that the specie exported in such case is not replaced by an equivalent value imported, but on the contrary by a less value.* We thus see that the dispute whether the exportation of the precious metals has its origin in a balance of debt, or what is sometimes called a balance of trade, or in an alteration of the value of the circulating medium, has been vain and illusory.

It also results from these views, that as the balance between produce and consumption is always disturbed from whatever cause alters that natural distribution of

---

* Dr. SMITH, although correct in saying that by the substitution of paper there was an equal amount of the metallic money exported, did not perceive that this was to pay a balance of debt, or to make up for the deficiency in the value of the exports caused by this substitution of paper, and that the fall in the price of certain portions of the produce in an equal degree that the price of other portions had risen, is the only mode of relieving the circulation of the superfluous quantity of circulating medium.

capital which takes place when prices are not deranged, the use of paper money has the same effect on the progress of wealth as taxation and restrictions on commercial intercourse. And we find, accordingly, that nations become more thriftless in proportion as they depart from the use of a medium of circulation possessed of intrinsic value. It would seem essential to maintain the level between production and expenditure (should taxation even not exist) that the instrument of exchange should not be too cheaply acquired either by governments or individuals.

I am satisfied that if the resources of Political Economy were such as to allow us to ascertain the truth of the position that paper has been instead of a cheap a very costly instrument of circulation. If it has given an extraordinary stimulus to the productive powers of nations which have adopted it, in certain employments, it has been followed, if not accompanied, by a proportional relaxation in others ; by a more than corresponding expenditure on the part of that class of producers who have derived great relative gains, and by all who have obtained so cheap an instrument without any present sacrifice or exertion.

We do not by any means admit then the position, that if nations could substitute paper for the whole or any part of the precious metals as money, without causing, at frequent periods, a derangement of prices, such a result would be desirable, as it must render, as we have shown, the amount of population and produce less with than without its employment. But when we look at the impossibility of devising a check that will operate with uniform effect on the issuers— when we witness the tremendous abuses of this power which have distinguished our day—at the revolutions of property, the violations of private and public faith, the relaxation of morals generally which it has occasioned, we do not believe that the world has ever been afflicted with a moral evil, under the disguise of a public benefit, more pestilent and dreadful. Whatever discovery of a cheaper medium of commerce than gold or silver may hereafter be made, I conceive that, in addition to its other qualities, to fit it for this purpose, it must possess intrinsic value. It must be obtained by a certain quantity of labour or personal exertion equal in value to that parted with. To discover such an instrument would produce the same effect on the progress of wealth as an increase in the powers of production, it would reduce prices generally. But the real cheapness of such an instrument will be found, we apprehend, not in substituting that which possesses no value intrinsically—which costs no expense of labour or capital, except what employs the makers and signers of notes, but in procuring the additional quantity of the precious metals required for the increasing wants of commerce and industry at a relatively less expenditure—by improving the processes of extracting and refining the ores now in use.

The causes enumerated in the course of this chapter are the only ones, we believe, that disturb prices and thence alter the equilibrium of the money of countries. This, however, does not appear to be Mr. RICARDO's opinion. He has stated "that the *improvement of a manufacture* tends to alter the distribution of the precious metals amongst the nations of the world."* And, in the next page, the following remark occurs. " In the former part of this work we have assumed, for the purpose of argument, that money always continued

* Principles of Political Economy and Taxation, chap 6, p. 122.

of the same value ; we are now endeavouring to show
that besides the ordinary variations' in the value of
money, and those which are common to the whole
commercial world, there are also partial variations to
which money is subject in particular countries ; and,
in fact, that the value of money is never the same in
any two countries, depending as it does on relative
taxation on *manufacturing skill*, on *the advantages of
climate*, natural productions, and many other causes."

How could Mr. RICARDO conceive that any " advantage of climate" or of " manufacturing skill"
could occasion an alteration of the distribution of the
precious metals ?   Do nations possessing either a natural or artificial advantage improve it so as to adapt
the products they raise or manufacture for foreign
markets, unless they can obtain *by a trade of barter*
an equivalent quantity of foreign commodities better
suited to their necessities or enjoyments ? Or will any
country improve its manufacturing skill or its natural
advantages, unless such improvement is met by a correspondent improvement of another kind, in some
other quarter of the world with which it has commercial intercourse ?   The motive to make every such
improvement is reciprocal, and the advantages received must be also reciprocal, or it never would be made.
But in such a state of things, although money or the
material of money may be imported, it can never be
exported—we mean that the level is never altered
when no disturbing influence exists which compels
nations to receive or part with a greater quantity of
money than is required for their natural or regular
wants.

Each country of the commercial world imports an
increased quantity of bullion, or money, in conse-

quence of its improvements in agriculture and manufactures. The case put by Mr. RICARDO cannot be supposed to exist. Admit its existence and countries would cease to trade on equal terms. Grant that money ebbs and flows as one country is favoured by nature more than another for raising a certain species of produce, or as one nation manufactures certain goods with greater comparative skill than another, and we at once confound the distinction between that increase of wealth in which all countries permanently participate, from the improvement of their peculiar advantages either from nature or art, with that partial and temporary augmentation of riches, which is, for the time it lasts, altogether on one side—in which what is gained by one of the parties to the intercourse is lost by the other. It is in fact carrying us back to the leading principle of the Mercantile system.

Instead, then, of viewing that variation in the equilibrium of money between countries which leads to its exportation and importation as the effect of derangement, it is attributed by Mr. RICARDO to causes that tend to prevent or counteract such derangement, and keep the money of countries at rest, instead of that state of movement which alters their proper distribution among the nations of the commercial world. The comparative value of the precious metals between countries is not to be determined by the comparative quantity in each, but by the proportion which the amount in each bears to its wants both for the purposes of money and ordinary manufacture. Rich nations have an abundance of these metals because they require an abundance both for circulation and other uses. Their large powers of production demand a greater quantity than countries whose productive powers are more limited. The value of money in different countries may therefore be very unequal—it may exchange in one nation for a smaller and in another for a greater quantity of commodities, and this inequality of value may continue or may increase without causing disturbance in the equilibrium of the precious metals, and altering their distribution among nations.

It will be recollected that the distribution of these metals is not varied, although one nation should export coined metal and another receive it in exchange for its productions, provided that the country exporting the coined metal employs its capital in coining money for the supply of other countries, for this is in fact a species of manufacture, the raw material of which may have been purchased from countries possessed of the mines. It is still a trade of barter, for the nation importing the coined money pays the price of the raw material as well as the workmanship added to it by the coinage, by the export of a portion of its produce. When England exchanges her manufactures for the gold bullion or dollars of Mexico, it occasions no more disturbance in the due proportion between her currency and the business it has to perform, than if she had given her goods in exchange for the corn of Poland. It appears to us, then, that Mr. Ricardo has confounded two circumstances which are entirely distinct, namely, the import of money, or its material, from countries which produce the precious metals, or manufacture them into coin, with their importation from countries which neither produce nor manufacture them, but are sometimes under the necessity of sending them abroad to discharge a balance of debt or to restore the proportion which has been lost between their currency and the number of exchanges it has to effect.

Nor is the relative value of money and its equilibrium altered from the greater or less distance from the mines of countries trading together. This is a circumstance which gives a higher exchangeable value to the precious metals in some countries than in others. Nations at a great distance from the mines have to part with a greater quantity of the produce of their industry in exchange for gold and silver than countries more near, but as this does not alter the proportion between their money and the quantity of produce it has to circulate, no derangement of prices can take place, and no variation consequently in comparative value with the money of countries more fortunately situated. Under every aspect, therefore, that we can view the subject, it is impossible to conceive the existence of any other causes that will disturb prices and the equilibrium of the precious metals between countries, than those we have enumerated.

CHAPTER VI.

EXCHANGE.

If the reasoning be accurate in the preceding chapter, the distinction between the *real* and the *nominal* exchange falls at once to the ground.   The numerous and prolonged controversies to which this subject has given rise in England, consequent on the restriction of cash payments there, turn out then to have been merely verbal. Every variation in the exchange is reducible to a *single* principle, to wit, an alteration in the due proportion between the demand and the supply of bills, or, which is the same thing, to an increase or diminution in the value of the exports.   The various causes which produce an alteration in the value of the exports may exert a combined influence, and to assign to each its share in producing the whole effect, is plainly impossible.   An increase of the taxes may be made at the very moment of a large issue of paper, and these causes may be united with restrictions on commercial intercourse that did not exist before.   If at such period an unfavourable harvest should occur, the value of the exports relatively to the imports would be still further lessened, and the fall in the exchange proportionally increased.

In the case of a failure of the harvest or of a war expenditure abroad which compels the export of bullion, there will be an increased quantity of the circulating medium applied to the purchase of this article for exportation, which will be equivalent to the diminished quantity applied to the purchase of other articles, which from their consequent fall of price will be exported to pay a balance. But whether the exportation of the precious metals be a *cause* or a *consequence* of an unfavourable balance, it can make no difference in the value of the exports and in the state of the exchange. If the disturbing cause is of equal influence, the encouragement to export will be also equal, and the balance will be restored in an equal period of time. If money or bullion is exported, in the first instance, commodities will be subsequently sent abroad to discharge an unfavourable balance. When it is said, therefore, that an unfavourable exchange increases the exports, the expression is not less applicable to the export of money when the balance is to be discharged by sending *it* abroad, as by sending *commodities* abroad when there arises a necessity of first exporting money.

If the usual level of prices between countries is not disturbed by war, a highly unfavourable exchange will soon be rectified, but if a particular country is in the the receipt of great profits from war demand abroad, or from the suspension of the powers of production of those countries which consume unproductively, it is impossible to prescribe the limit either to the degree or the duration of an unfavourable exchange, as long at least as the profits of such country are proportionally high. It must always be recollected that the *real* limit to an unfavourable exchange consists in the inability of the country subject to this disadvantage to consume any longer at high prices. Every increase in the premium of exchange is an additional tax on consumption. Unless, therefore, the country subject to a high tax in this shape is more than usually stimulated in its powers of production—unless it is in the enjoyment of monopoly profits, the limit to an unfavourable exchange will very soon be reached. The principles or tests, therefore, that apply on ordinary occasions in regard to this subject, are inapplicable in other periods when wars unexampled in extent and duration occur, which derange all the ordinary relations of commerce. It was this circumstance that produced so anomalous a state of the exchange in England during the latter period of the war in which she was engaged, and rendered the phenomena so inexplicable on the ordinary principles. The limit to an unfavourable exchange in the ordinary state of things, is unquestionably the expense of transmitting money from the debtor to the creditor country in payment of a balance. It would consequently be impossible, when the usual level of prices between countries is not for a considerable period disturbed, for banking establishments to suspend payments in specie and continue the suspension, unless the country in which they were situated was deriving very high profits from its foreign commerce. The natural limitation of mercantile profit, and of the disposition to borrow with a view to such profit, is the check given to consumption by an unfavourable exchange of too long continuance. Every inequality of this nature is speedily corrected, if the high prices of the imports are not counterbalanced by the proportionally high prices abroad of the exports.

In determining the question, whether the unfavourable exchange in England arose from an increase of the government expenditure or the undue issues of the Bank of England, it is indifferent to the point at issue, if this expenditure were defrayed by loans, in what mode these loans were effected. The two circumstances of an increased public expenditure and enlarged issues, were in necessary connexion. If the government by means of its loans diminished the amount of capital which would have been otherwise employed in commerce, the Bank by replacing the capital which was withdrawn for public expenditure, did not issue more paper perhaps than was necessary for the *due wants of trade*, but its issues did add to the whole quantity of circulating medium above what was required *for the wants of the country at large*, in proportion to the amount of capital borrowed by government. The heavy public expenditure, therefore, was the *origin* of an issue of paper by the Bank of England, not probably beyond the fair demands of commerce, but certainly beyond what could be added to the circulation without producing considerable disturbance of prices, and leading to an exportation of specie equal to the excess of the whole quantity of currency compared with the number of exchanges to be effected. In one sense, then, the circulating medium may be said to have been redundant, whilst in another sense, it may be asserted to have been in its due quantity, or in fair proportion to the business it had to perform. If this view of the subject be correct, the difference of opinion as to the origin of the unfavourable exchange in England, in the period already referred to, is reconcileable.

We find that the facts correspond with this explanation. The exchange was at par in England from the period of the Bank restriction until t e very heavy expenditure required to maintain the British armies in the Peninsula arose in 1808. As this expense increased, the exchange became proportionally unfavourable. The great exportation of coin and bullion that almost immediately took place, in consequence, was partly, perhaps, the *cause*, first, and then the *effect* of the unfavourable exchange. They were exported, in the early period of this expense, on public account, in addition to the sums required for the pay of the forces, on the same principle that their export takes place on the *necessity* of an immediate import of corn from a failure of the harvest. The *subsistence* as well as *pay* of the troops in the Peninsula required an immediate and a direct remittance in specie, to purchase a portion of the bread stuffs with which they were at that time supplied by neutral nations. A circuitous remittance by bills is too slow an operation in such pressing circumstances, as is the export of goods in payment for such necessary supplies. The greater the quantity of gold exported, however, on public account, necessarily lessened the quantity sent abroad on private account. But if individuals sold to the government, it must have been at a price which was equivalent to the profit they would have derived if they had disposed of their bullion in any other mode. The premium on exchange would of course measure this profit, for by exporting bullion and drawing a bill against it, the possessor of this article would gain a sum, deducting the expense of transportation, equal to what he would have derived by selling his bullion to government, or to the profit he would have made in the home market on the commodities he would have obtained in exchange for it in foreign markets.

But although the advance in the price of bullion in the first year of the great public expenditure in the Peninsula, may be thus entirely accounted for, from the government demand, this cannot explain its continued high price, until the end of the war. After time had been allowed to provide, in other modes, for this expense, a very small part of it would be defrayed by the exportation of coin or bullion. The only satisfactory explanation of the continuance of the high price of the precious metals until the close of the war, is to be found, therefore, in the increased individual demand that took place, for the purposes both of hoarding and of profit to be made by exportation, in addition to the more limited demand, at the same period, by the government itself.

I have before observed that the causes which affect the price of bills are various. It is therefore obvious that these causes may act all in the same direction or in opposite directions—or, in other words, the exchange will become proportionally unfavourable to a particular country if all those circumstances by which it may be affected co-operate. The *computed* exchange will then express the *sum* of their *united* influence; whilst if the various causes by which it may be affected are of *equal* influence in *different* countries trading together, the value of their exports will be equally diminished, and the exchange between them will not vary. Thus, if the exchange between two countries having commercial intercourse together, is at par, and a deficient harvest should occur in one of them, the value of its exports will lessen proportionally, but if the country from which the supply of corn is purchased shall have issued a quantity of paper, by which it lessened the value of its exports in an equal degree, the exchange between them would continue at par; or if one country increases its taxes to the same extent that another enlarges its paper issues or alters its standard, the value of their exports would, in the same manner, be reciprocally and equally reduced, and the exchange between them would not vary. But if whilst a particular country is compelled to import a portion of its corn, it, at the same time, increases its taxes and enlarges its issues of paper, or alters its standard, its exchange with another, the value of whose exports is not affected by either of these circumstances, will become unfavourable to the degree of the combined influence of all these causes.

CHAPTER VII.

COMMERCE.

THE intercourse between countries is more or less a trade of barter as the market prices of the commodities they respectively export and import agree with or differ from their natural prices.   All other circumstances being equal, both parties gain in proportion to their skill, capital and natural resources. But this is no longer true when taxes, restriction no the free circulation of capital, &c. in a particular country, so diminish the relative value of its productions as to compel it to exchange the same quantity of them for a less quantity of those commodities it is in the habit of importing. This is attended by an immediate loss to one of the parties and an eventual loss to the other, for the nation which obtains a higher price for its products than usual, by such an unequal interchange, proportionally restricts their market and consumption.   The intercourse between the countries so circumstanced ceases, at such time, to be purely a trade of barter. The level between the quantity of money and the quantity of commodities it has to circulate of the country whose trade is subjected to this disturbing influence, is necessarily altered, and the profits of its merchants are partly derived from the exportation of its circulating medium. The commerce between different countries is in its nature and final results like that between the different districts of the same country. The diminution of profit in one quarter must be accompanied or followed by diminished demand and reduced profit in some other, and although the reaction is not so quickly communicated from country to country as from one district or employment to another in the same country, still it much sooner takes place, I believe, than is commonly imagined.

There would appear to be no difficulty in determining in what manner mercantile profit is derived, and to point out the sources of that mutual gain which states enjoy in exchanging what they want less for what they want more. It is a familiar principle, that every reduction in the prices of commodities, when demand is properly proportioned to supply, gives extension to the foreign as well as domestic market, and that states are reciprocally benefitted by this reduction of prices when general, or, which is the same thing, by an equal augmentation on both sides of the quantity of consumable products. But although it has been admitted that an increase in the *quantity* of commodities is the consequence of an extension of foreign trade, it has been denied that an increased *value in amount* is derived from such extension. Mr. RICARDO is the author of this new theory of commerce.* It seems a necessary consequence of his peculiar view of value in other parts of his work, as distinguishable, under all circumstances, from wealth.

---

* Principles of Political Economy and Taxation, chap. 6, p. 107.

Mr. RICARDO invariably assumes that what is gained in value by one class of the community is lost to some other. This doctrine is an unavoidable inference again from the principle, that the value of commodities is determined, from first to last, by the quantity of labour which they have cost, and that as more or less is paid for wages and rent, more or less remains for profit, and *vice versa*. As Mr. RICARDO had thus determined that profits could not increase unless wages and rent diminished, or profits diminish unless wages and rent increased, he was bound to follow out this principle to its consequences, and to insist, that, as profits, wages and rent together always continued of the same value, however they may be divided, no greater value in amount could be derived from the importation of a larger than a smaller quantity of commodities. On the same principle, as nothing can increase profit but a diminution of wages, he was bound to conclude that as wages are not lowered, unless the commodity imported constitute the subsistence of the labourer, the gains of the merchant are not increased, any more than those of the producer, by any extension, however great, of the foreign market ; but, according to this principle, the profit of the merchant must be always of the *same money value*, which leads inevitably to the conclusion that Mercantile profit is stationary, whilst the profit of the other productive classes is increasing.

Now, although, as commodities increase in quantity, or, which is the same thing, fall in price, the profits of their producers continue always of the *same money value*, this is not true of the profits of the merchant. It will be recollected that the merchant's gains are always received as well as estimated in money, and,

although his real profit is in proportion, as in every
other case, to what money will purchase, the quantity
of both money and real profit is always equal in his
case, unless some disturbance of prices has occurred.
But in the case of the *producer* his money and his real
profit are always unequal, if no such disturbance of
prices has taken place. We have endeavoured to
show that there is the same money profit, or value in
money amount, received by him when his commodity
is at a *less* as when it is at a *greater* price, if its quantity has at the same time proportionally increased.
But no increase of mercantile profit can take place
(if relative prices are not altered by some disturbing
influence) without an augmentation in the quantity of
money obtained in exchange for an increase of commodities.

Suppose a manufacturer of cloth was to produce
this year 1000 yards and to obtain one dollar per yard
for it, should he the next year augment the quantity
25 per cent. he must submit to a reduction of price in
this proportion—he must accept of 80 cents per yard
when its quantity is increased in the above ratio ; for
1250 yards at 80 cents per yard will bring the same
amount of money as 1000 yards at one dollar per
yard.   This is the situation of the *producer ;* but the
case is different with regard to the merchant whose
business it is to export cloth in exchange for some other
commodity.   He must receive a larger money amount
for a greater than a smaller quantity of commodities,
or his profits will be below the general level.   Thus,
if we suppose him to export 1000 yards of cloth when
its price is one dollar per yard, and to derive 25 per
cent. profit, he must sell the commodity he imports for
$1250 ; but when he invests this amount in the pur-

chase of cloth, the quantity having proportionally increased, he must obtain $1562 50, for the goods he
imports in return ; for as the gain of the manufacturer
of cloth is 25 per cent. when its quantity, or, which
is the same thing, the quantity of other goods he obtains for it has increased in this ratio, the possession
of the above sum is necessary by the trader in this
article to put him on the same footing in regard to profit.   Unless it be admitted that the merchant receives
a larger money amount for a greater than a smaller
quantity of imported commodities, his profit will continue *stationary* whilst that of the manufacturer or
producer will *increase*.   Accordingly, we find that
this is the precise conclusion to which Mr. RICARDO's
reasoning leads.

" If," says he, " by the purchase of English goods
to the amount of £1000 a merchant can obtain a
quantity of foreign goods, which he can sell in the
English market for £1200, he will obtain 20 per cent.
profit by such an employment of his capital ; but
*neither his gains nor the value of the commodities im-
ported* will be *increased* or diminished by the greater
or smaller quantity of foreign goods obtained.   Whether, for example, he imports 25 or 50 pipes of wine,
his interest can be no way affected, if at one time the
25 pipes and at another the 50 pipes equally sell for
£1200.   In either case his profit will be limited to
£200, or 20 per cent. on his capital, and, in either case,
the same value will be imported into England."*

But if the manufacturer or producer of goods parted
with in exchange for wine obtains 50 pipes or the value
of 50 pipes at one time and 25 pipes or their value at

---

* Principles of Political Economy and Taxation, chap. 6, pp. 107, 108.

another, how can the conclusion be resisted that his
profit is 80 per cent. above that of the importer of wine,
for the absolute increase of the manufacturer's or producer's profit in this case is 100 per cent. as the quantity
of wine he has obtained in exchange for his goods
has doubled; but if the importer of this article gets
no more than £1200 when 50 pipes as when 25 pipes
are imported, he obtains no part of this increase—in
other words, his profit remains stationary, whilst that
of the producer or manufacturer has doubled.

Taking Mr. RICARDO's own criterion of value, or regulator of price, to wit, the quantity of labour which
a commodity from first to last has cost, surely an increased quantity of such commodity cannot be transported from the place of production to that of consumption, without an additional quantity of labour to
what has been employed in the transportation of a
smaller quantity of such commodity. The value
must in such case proportionally augment. But not
only must the sum expended for the labour employed both in the production and transportation of
an increased quantity of commodities, be replaced
by the additional value for which they sell abroad, the
capital, with the usual profit, employed, must be, from
first to last, also replaced, or the requisite quantity of
produce could not come to market. How under these
circumstances can it be said " no extension of the
foreign market will *either increase the gains of the importer or the value in amount of the goods imported?*"

But it is not mercantile profit merely that is kept
stationary, according to this theory, whilst markets
are on every side extending and products increasing—
profits generally are made subject to the same law,
namely, that the quantity of labour which commodities

have cost regulates their value. It is not in consequence," says Mr. Ricardo, " of the extension of the
market that the rate of profit is raised, although such
extension may be equally efficacious in increasing the
mass of commodities, and may thereby enable us to
augment the funds destined for the maintenance of
labour and the materials on which labour is employed."*

But it is by increasing the mass of commodities that
the general rate of profit is augmented, and from no
other cause. To increase the mass of commodities—
to augment the powers of production—to lower the
prices of products generally, are all terms expressive
of equivalent effects. What do we intend to assert
when we say that capital is augmented, by an increase
in the rate of profit, if it is not meant that the mass
of commodities is increased?

But Mr. Ricardo makes an exception to this principle, as the following passage will show. " It has
been my endeavour to show throughout this work,
that the rate of profits can never be increased but by
a fall in wages, and that there can be no permanent
fall of wages but in consequence of a fall of the necessaries on which wages are expended. If, therefore,
by the extension of foreign trade, or by improvements
in machinery, the food and necessaries of the labourer
can be brought to market at a reduced price, *profits
will rise.* If, instead of growing our own corn, or
manufacturing the clothing and other necessaries of
the labourer, we discover a new market from which
we can supply ourselves with these commodities at a
cheaper price, wages will fall and profits rise; but if

* Principles of Political Economy and Taxation, chap. 6, p. 112

the commodities obtained at a cheaper rate, by the
extension of foreign commerce, or by the improvement of machinery, be exclusively the commodities
consumed by the rich, no alteration will take place in
the rate of profit.   The rate of wages would not be
affected, although wine, velvet, silks, and other expensive commodities, should fall 50 per cent. and consequently profits would continue unaltered."*

This limitation of the principle, that no extension
of foreign trade can increase the rate of profit, was
necessary from Mr. RICARDO's peculiar view of labour
as the regulator of the price of raw products, and
through them of the rate of wages and profits.   But
it requires the concession that the manufacturers of articles of necessity, or those consumed by the poor, are
in the enjoyment of higher profits than the manufacturers of articles of mere luxury, or those consumed
exclusively by the rich.   It requires the further concession that the importers of necessaries are also deriving higher profits than the importers of luxuries.
How would luxuries be either produced or imported
on such a supposition, or how is the level of profit to
be maintained under such circumstances?   What motive could the manufacturer of articles of luxury have
in increasing the quantity of his goods by machinery,
if he is tasking his ingenuity constantly for the advantage of others in lowering the prices of his products?
or what inducement could exist for the importer of
such articles, in enlarging the bounds of his enterprize,
to discover new markets whence they may be bought
at cheaper rates, if this is to redound to the exclusive
benefit of their consumers?

* Principles of Political Economy and Taxation, chap. 6, pp. 112, 113.

Let us, however, for a moment, admit the principle that the quantity of labour employed in raising raw products is the sole regulator of their price, and through them of the rate of wages and profits, and behold the consequence that follows. The consumers of cheap commodities, whether manufactured at home or procured from abroad, will be soon in the condition of persons who have accumulated from savings until their accumulations have ceased to be of any value. What is it that gives value to capital? Is it not that it may be employed by its owners or borrowers in increasing the enjoyments of a different portion of society to themselves, who are at the same time adding to the enjoyments of some other portion? Demand insures demand, and unless it is co-extensive with supply, of what use is the greatest sum of the necessaries and conveniencies of life? Of what value is the greatest multiplication of commodities and the reduction in their prices, if what is in consequence saved and added to capital cannot be made available, under all circumstances, to an increase of profit?

Mr. Ricardo always speaks of reduced expenditure or the diminished consumption of necessaries and conveniencies as an equivalent effect with the increase of revenue, or as equally contributing with such increase to an augmentation of capital. " There are two ways," says he, " in which capital may be accumulated; it may be saved either in consequence of *increased revenue* or of *diminished consumption.* If my profits are raised from £1000 to £1200 while my expenditure continues the same, I accumulate annually £200 more than I did before. If I save £200 out of my expenditure while my profits continue the same, the same effect will be produced ; £200 per annum will be added to my capital."*

But profits cannot continue the same in one quarter while expenditure is reduced in another, or increased in one quarter while expenditure continues the same in another, for expenditure must keep an equal progress with profit, if all classes of producers are to benefit by an interchange of their respective productions. It is not individual profit but profit generally—not temporary but permanent effects, to which Mr. Ricardo alludes, we presume, in the above passage. Profit may be temporarily raised in one employment compared with another, from causes which disturb the proper distribution of capital and in consequence alter relative prices ; but no general or permanent increase of profit can take place unless consumption in one quarter keeps an equal progress with production in some other—unless, in short, demand, whether for the necessaries and conveniencies of life, or for articles of productive investment, is equal to the supply of the whole mass of commodities of every kind. It follows that profits cannot continue the same if expenditure be reduced, or raised if expenditure continue the same, without destroying the balance between produce and consumption. Commodities would cease to be produced if they were not consumed.

" The merchant," says Mr. Ricardo, " who imported wine after profits had been raised from 20 per cent. to 40 per cent. instead of purchasing his English goods for £1000, must purchase them for £857, 2s. 10d. still selling the wine he imports in return for these goods for £1200 ; or if he continued to purchase his

---

English goods for £1000, must raise the price of his wine to £1400 : he would thus obtain 40 instead of 20 per cent. profit on his capital, but if in consequence of the cheapness of all commodities on which his revenue was expended, he and other consumers could save the value of £200 out of every £1000 they before expended, they would more effectually add to the real wealth of the country ; in one case the savings would be made in consequence of an increase of revenue, in the other in consequence of diminished expenditure."*

If Mr. Ricardo distinguishes between individual and general gain, there is a *more* effectual addition to the real wealth of a country from the cheapness of all commodities than from the increase of revenue of one or a few of its inhabitants ; but if he does not intend a distinction of this kind, there is a *less* effectual addition to the real wealth of a country from the increase of profit of one or a few of its inhabitants, than from the cheapness of all commodities. The rise in the price of wine cannot at all add to the real wealth of the society, for it must be followed by an abstraction of demand in some other quarter—it is simply a temporary advantage obtained by one class or portion of the community at the expense of some other class or portion. " If," says he again, " by the introduction of machinery the generality of the commodities on which revenue was expended fell 20 per cent. in value, I should be enabled to save *as effectually* as if my revenue *had been raised* 20 per cent. ; but in the one case the rate of profit is stationary, in the other it is raised 20 per cent. If by the introduction of cheap

* Principles of Political Economy and Taxation, chap. 6, p. 111

foreign goods, I can save 20 per cent. from my expenditure, the effect will be precisely the same as if by machinery I had lowered the expense of their production, but profits would not be raised."[*]

Mr. RICARDO is perfectly correct if he refers to *individual* profit when he says, that savings are made with as much effect by the cheapness of commodities as by the rise of revenue, making the rise of revenue in such case to proceed from the advance in price of one or more commodities ; but if he refers to permanent and general effects, it is impossible to conceive a difference between a rise of revenue and the general cheapness of commodities in their effects on the wealth of society.

But Mr. RICARDO makes the rate of profit stationary in the one case and raises it in the other. It is stationary when the quantity of commodities is increased—when the greatest stimulus is in action to add to the quantity—when their prices have fallen and consumers are able to purchase a larger quantity than before for the same money amount, and it is permanently raised when the rise has occurred from accidental causes—from a disturbing influence which must soon cease to act.

[*] Principles of Political Economy and Taxation, chap. 6, pp. 111, 112.

CHAPTER VIII.

TAXATION.

IF the principles laid down in the preceding chapters be correct, the final equalization of taxes results unavoidably from those principles. Whether they are laid on wages or profits, on necessaries or luxuries, on income or capital, the burthen must fall eventually on all classes of producers. It must always be borne in mind that every alteration of prices from taxation must be either accompanied or followed by a change in the due proportion between demand and supply. On this principle there can be no doubt that all classes of producers are finally affected, in an equal degree, by every variation in the state of the demand and supply caused by taxation. The time that it takes to shift capital from those employments that yield relatively lower to those that yield relatively higher profits, will determine how much longer a period one class of producers will have to sustain the burthen than another. If there are no restrictions on internal intercourse—if capital and labour can freely circulate between different employments, the period that the tax will be unequally borne will be very short. The tendency to an equilibrium of burthens as well as benefits in society is too strong to be resisted by any but the most powerful circumstances. I will then first trace the consequences of a tax on *wages.*

A tax on wages will lessen the labourer's command of the necessaries of life, for he will have a smaller money amount than before to devote to the purchase of necessaries, unless he should increase the quantity of his personal exertion in proportion to the amount of the tax. Such a tax will not raise the price of labour, for that depends on the proportion between the demand and the supply of labour, which is not affected by the tax. The quantity of labour in the market is not reduced, nor is the ability of the capitalists increased to employ a greater quantity than before. It will be recollected that we are speaking of the immediate effects of such a tax. But such a tax, if it lessen the quantity of money which the labourer can command, will operate on profits. It will immediately diminish the demand for necessaries, in proportion as it takes from the labourer the power of purchasing them, unless, as before remarked, he increase proportionally his personal exertion, or, which is the same thing, he is both able and willing to consume a greater quantity of food. If he is unwilling or unable to do this, the cultivator's profits must be reduced. This effect on the profit of the cultivator must be to diminish his demand for other commodities. The profits of all producers must come to a level, and the prices of all commodities, after the equilibrium is restored, will be prevented, by the tax, from falling to that point to which they would have been reduced if the tax had not been imposed.

The consequences, however, will not stop here on the above supposition. The fall of profit will lessen the demand for labour, and the labourer will be affected, by the operation of the tax, in lowering his money wages below that point to which they ought naturally to fall. As he will be unable to shift the tax from himself to others, it will proportionally diminish his comforts. If the tax augments so much as to operate as a restraint on the increase of the lower orders, it will operate in an equal degree to prevent the increase of capital. Population and the means of employing and supporting it, must, in a natural state of things, come to a level, quantity for quantity.

The effect of a tax on *profits* would not be different. It would finally reach the labourer by lessening the demand for labour, and thence reducing his money wages below their natural limit. The price of necessaries, as in the case of a tax on wages, will fall from the inability of the labourer to purchase as large a quantity as when his wages were higher, unless, as in that case, he increase his personal exertion in proportion to the tax. The cultivator's profit must of course be still further lessened, in the ratio of the reduced power of the labourer to purchase food, on the supposition, as before stated, that he is neither able nor willing to make any further sacrifice to obtain it. But this reduced consumption of necessaries will operate to lessen the demand for the objects of consumption of the cultivator also, until by the cessation of demand proportionally in every quarter, the tax will be finally equalized in its effects.

A tax on necessaries would be followed by the same ultimate consequences. It would occasion a fall in the profits of their producers, should the demand have been proportionally diminished, and it must be diminished, unless the consumers increase in the same proportion, their personal exertion, if labourers, and lessen their consumption of other things, if capitalists. But this fall of the profits of the producers of necessaries will, by lessening their demand for other commodities, reduce the profits of their producers also, in connexion with the wages of labour. The prices of the whole mass of commodities will finally settle at a higher than their natural level.

A tax on luxuries would not be different in its final effects. It would, by reducing the demand for them, affect their producers, and as the producers of luxuries are the consumers of necessaries, it would eventually act on these also. According, then, to this explanation, whatever commodity is selected to be taxed, the effect will be finally felt on the producers of all other productions, and it will be delayed in proportion to the greater or less facility of removing capital from the least to the most beneficial employment. A tax, whether laid on revenue or capital, if this view be correct, would be attended by similar results. If the tax is imposed on revenue, and the capitalist saves from his expenditure, in proportion to the tax, in order that he should not diminish his capital, he will necessarily lessen demand for the commodities of some other producer, and this will finally react on himself. The same consequence precisely would follow if he had deducted the amount of his tax from his capital.

It is the increase of productive power that adds to capital and not savings from ordinary expenditure—not reducing consumption, for it is constantly increased consumption that gives the most effective stimulus to the inventive powers and industrious efforts of producers. The actual consumption is necessary to the actual production. It is not more injurious, therefore, to impose a tax on capital than on revenue. This is contrary to Mr. RICARDO's opinion, who thinks the effect will be the same if the capitalist pays the tax either by reducing his expenditure or by an increase of his productive powers; but the diminution of consumption and the general multiplication of products at the same time, are incompatible effects. The additions that are made to capital from revenue result from enlarging the market, both domestic and foreign—from inducing an increase of consumption generally, by an augmentation of the quantity of commodities and a proportionate reduction of their prices. It is, therefore, not the same thing should additional taxes be met by a diminished consumption as by an increased production, as stated by Mr. RICARDO. What is saved from revenue, in consequence of taxation, is attended by diminished demand exactly in the same degree as if it had been deducted from capital.

The general inference from the above view is, that the price of a taxed commodity will not *necessarily* rise.* If the consumption diminishes of this particular commodity, in proportion to the amount of the tax, the producer will be unable to reimburse himself, in

---

* When the demand for any commodity is increased, the supply remaining the same, there is an increased quantity of money given in exchange for the same quantity of such commodity; but when the supply of any commodity is diminished, the demand remaining the same, there is the same quantity of money given in exchange for a less quantity of such commodity—in both cases the price rises. In taxation, however, here may be a rise of price without any increase of demand or diminution of supply—all that is necessary to produce such a rise is, that the demand for the taxed commodity should not diminish, but the demand for some other commodity must fall, in proportion as the quantity of money given in exchange for it is less than the quantity given in exchange for the taxed commodity is greater than before.

the increased price of his commodity, and to throw any share of the burthen of the tax on the consumer. But whether the price of a taxed commodity rise or not, relative prices will be altered. If the consumer should not lessen his demand for this commodity, he must for some other, which, by reducing its price, in proportion as the taxed commodity has risen, will necessarily alter their former relation to each other as to prices and demand, and by causing the flow of capital from the production of that which has fallen to that which has risen, restore the equilibrium of prices and profits between the disturbed employments. If the price of the taxed commodity should not rise, from diminished demand, the power of purchasing other commodities by the producers of the taxed commodity, will be reduced in proportion to the tax. The prices of those other commodities will fall, therefore, and relative prices will alter. The level will be restored by the abstraction of capital from those employments which derive relatively lower and its removal to those which enjoy relatively higher profits.

We are aware that some of the above conclusions militate against the received doctrines of taxation. The opinion that the labourer pays no portion of that contribution, in the form of taxes, which society exacts from the rest of its productive classes, has received an almost universal assent; but it is clear to my mind that the labourer pays his fair proportion* of the taxes,

* I am doubtful whether the labouring classes do not pay *more* than their fair proportion of the taxes, for they cannot reduce their numbers as the taxes increase with the same facility that supply is proportioned to demand in other cases. The effect is that the competition for employment always tends to keep their money wages below their natural limit, whilst the proportionate demand for food also tends to keep their real wages below that point to which they ought properly to fall.

either in an increase of personal exertion or in a diminution of his comforts and enjoyments. It is true
that there is a point below which the labourer cannot
suffer from additional taxation, for the increase of population will be arrested if a certain limit be passed.
But where shall we place that limit? We see in the
case of Ireland that its population is excessive, whilst
its standard of enjoyments has fallen far below that
of any civilized people with which history has made
us acquainted, with the same advantages from situation for commerce, fertility of soil, &c.

We cannot fail to see also, that the heavy taxation,
in every variety of mode, to which the English people
are compelled to submit, although it has not proportionally reduced *their* comforts, still those comforts are
purchased by a correspondent increase of personal
exertion—by tasking the powers of the body in a
higher degree than is exhibited in the case of any
people, ancient or modern, with the same measure of
freedom and the same extent of general wealth. The
principle, then, that wages rise whenever a tax is imposed on them, or on the labourer's subsistence, must
be received with the limitations I have given to it.

It must also be recollected, that, with the present arrangements of society in almost every part of the world,
although an increased command of comforts will be
invariably followed by an augmentation of population, it does not result that the *proper check* operates
with the same efficacy and uniformity AGAINST as the
stimulus TO an increase of numbers. Mr. MALTHUS
has admirably explained and illustrated, from the past
and present condition of mankind, the *tendency* of
population to multiply faster than food can be provided for it. All the institutions of society give the

fullest play to the principle of increase, whilst there is scarcely any room allowed for the influence of that check which Mr. MALTHUS has well denominated *moral restraint*. It results, however, from this view, that the price of labour is *not* a correct barometer of the wants of society with regard to population, as asserted by this writer,* for the *same* numbers may subsist on a much smaller quantity of food at one period than at another, or the same quantity may be purchased by a greater sacrifice of toil. There is, therefore, no certain or invariable standard of enjoyments for the labouring class. The amount of their comforts is not only very different in different countries, but very different in different periods in the same country.

If Mr. MALTHUS had stated the principle of popu-tion with the qualification, that the price of labour is a correct criterion of the wants of society with regard to it, or as expressing the relation between the supply of provisions and the demand for them, where the *proper preventive check* operates with the same efficacy and uniformity AGAINST as the *stimulants* TO an increase of numbers, there are none who could dispute the proposition. He has, to be sure, spoken of the price of labour, as expressing the wants of society respecting it, when that price is left to find *its natural level*, but this expression is obviously used in reference to those particular institutions which disturb the proper proportion between the demand and the supply of labour, such, for instance, as assessments for the relief of the poor, and not to the entire structure of the social system, in connexion with the whole body of laws and the habits

* See his able work on Population, first American Edition, vol. 2, pp. 164, 165.

superinduced on them.   The error of Mr. MALTHUS
consists, then, I think, in stating that *positively* as a
Law of Nature, which, for what we know to the contrary, may be the result of an imperfect social organization.

It is certainly possible to imagine the existence of a
state of society in which the *proper preventive check* in
regard to population may be in full activity, whilst every
possible developement being given to the capacities of
the earth for the production of subsistence, the *stimulus* TO should not be more active than this *check* AGAINST
an increase of numbers.   The respective ratios of the
augmentation of food and population might, in such
a state of society, vary materially from those exhibited
in any period past or present.   The rate of production would, on this supposition, probably increase, whilst
the rate of population would probably diminish, and
the relative rate of increase might by equal, or, which
is the same thing, the absolute rate of either might
never exceed that of the other.

Without indulging, therefore, in dreams of perfecti-
bility, it is not venturing on visionary speculations of
unattainable or impossible improvement to infer, that
if the institution of primogeniture were abolished
wherever it prevails, with every species of monopoly,
supposing the security of person and property complete, and the public burthens moderate, the rate of
increase in the production of food might greatly augment; whilst the more ample leisure for instruction
permitted to the labouring classes—by allowing them
to receive sound and salutary lessons on the subject of population, or those maxims of prudence and
foresight necessary to their comfort and respectability—

might give much greater room than at present for the action of the check entitled by Mr. MALTHUS, *moral restraint.* It is impossible to foretell the precise effects of such an arrangement of the social elements, or to say what would be the relative ratio in the increase of food and population, on such a supposition; but that it would be very different from that which is generally exhibited in the present or any past condition of the species, I am satisfied.

THE END.

ERRATA.

Page 12, note 1, line 2, for " labours" read *labourers.*
   20, note 2, line 10, for " the" read *be.*
   23, line 24, for " so also his corn rent" read *his corn rent by the absolute quantity of raw produce,* and dele the words " a part of " immediately following.
   47, line 9, for " to" read *with.*
   77, " 26, for " proportions" read *proportion.*
   81, " 1, insert *from* between the words prevented and falling.
  103, " 7, for " restriction" read *restrictions,* and for "no" read *on.*
  119, " 29, for "his tax" read *the tax.*
  120, note, line 6, for " here" read *there.*

APPENDIX I

Political Economy.—Rent

The Southern Review, February 1828

ART. VII.—*Lectures on the Elements of Political Economy.* By THOMAS COOPER, M. D. *President of the South-Carolina College, and Professor of Chemistry and Political Economy.* 8vo. Columbia, S. C. Sweeny. 1826.

WHILE Political Economy has been thoroughly investigated in many of its parts and divisions, its fundamental principles are still far from being satisfactorily elucidated. Whether the period has not arrived for a comprehensive examination of the phenomona, in consequence of the imperfect manner they have been observed, recorded and arranged; or, whether there is an inherent uncertainty in all such investigations, remains to be determined by results more positive, than any yet furnished by the labours of economists. We have reasons for doubt, were the elements of a comprehensive and complete system and theory at hand, whether the fulness and force of evidence, by which they most be accompanied, to command general assent, are attainable. And such must be the state of every recent science, whose leading truths do not admit of the tests of direct experiment or precise calculation. The satisfactory demonstration of fundamental principles, must, under such circumstances, await the slow accumulation of materials proper for the construction of a system generally applicable, and a theory fully explanatory.

It is but very recently that statistical inquiries have been made available in those more limited investigations which profess to explain particular phenomena. The materials of national comparison must be supplied, in at least equal copiousness, for advantage in all general reasonings which profess to develope the real foundations of wealth, and the invariable causes of its increase. We know that the riches of countries augment from circumstances widely contrasted. For example, experience assures us, that on that division of the globe on which our lot is cast, a high degree of wealth results from involuntary services, accompanied by a greater share of enjoyment to the labourer, than on many of those sections of the earth where the relation between the employer and the employed is totally different. How does this state of things agree with the explanation of economists, that the relation which anciently subsisted between the master and the slave, was an impediment to the increase of riches? How can it be shown that the payment of wages is an essential ingredient in a modern system of wealth? We might multiply illustrations of this kind, if necessary. They are calculated to rebuke the presumption that would construct systems of general application from only one point of observation.

It has been deemed not a little remarkable, in economical science, that discussions should have arisen as to the causes of certain phenomena before the real character of the phenomena themselves had been ascertained; that theory should succeed to theory, and system supplant system, in an examination into the sources of wealth, before the problem had been satisfactorily solved what weath is? It would appear as if the first proper step was to agree in the sense we should affix to certain essential terms. We believe, however, the influence of this circumstance on the progress of economical discovery, has been stated in terms much too broad. We do not know, that the determination of the fundamental question, what are the sources of wealth? has been at all assisted by those controversies (that even, at this late day, so frequently cross the path of investigation) which profess to resolve the points, what is wealth, and what productive labour? We all have a sufficiently distinct perception of the character and constituents of riches, and of the instruments by which they are increased, without the aid of any shadowy and metaphysical distinctions between wealth composed of products that perish in the instant of production, and products of a durable character—between quantities evanescent and quantities permanent and palpable. We all know what objects contribute to our comfort, accommodation and luxury, and are, at the same time, susceptible of valuation. What more is requisite to conduct us in the true path of inquiry? It is the real foundation of those products of labour which constitute the sources of our enjoyments, both mental and bodily, that we feel desirous to develope, and not whether, in a system of wealth, the artist is to be classed with the artizan, and the magistrate with the merchant, under a common denomination.

The complete accuracy of our classifications may be a subject of speculative curiosity; but the detection of some anomalies in the arrangement of the phenomena, or a few examples that may not exactly square with the rule laid down, is far from helping forward the investigation of leading principles. We consider many of the recent discussions in regard to definitions, as embracing questions of arrangement too refined to be useful, and as involving the propriety of classifications, meant merely as aids to investigation, and never urged as differences founded in the nature of things. We, of course, do not mean to deny the utility of some brief description at the outset of an inquiry of the sense we affix to certain words of leading signification and frequent employment, but there can be no difficulty in collecting the sense from the reasonings in the context, whilst in many instances, the definition is far from corresponding with the doctrine laid down. How frequently do we see definitions which are either too circumscribed or too comprehensive, as compared with the theory to which they are introductory. Whilst, therefore, pages are filled with ingenious refinements, to show the incompleteness of the definition, the theory to which it is the mere formal appendage, receives much the smallest share of attention.

It is, also, not unworthy of remark, that the order of investigation never having been properly defined the results of economical investigation have reached us in disjointed parts, and insulated by long intervals of time.   This sufficiently explains why its discoveries have multipied so slowly.   In scientific investigation, in general, the development of one principle or general fact promotes the elucidation of another.   Each point gained is a farther step in the ascending series of discoveries. There is, in such cases, a certain continuity in the succession of principles   In political economy, however, the different branches having been investigated in a detached and desultory order, there has not been that concatenation and dependence of parts which so greatly promotes investigation, and its discoveries have consequently been effected, not only more slowly, but more laboriously.

It is also to be observed, that in many instances men must be made to feel before they can be brought to investigate.   This applies, generally, in the science of politics, and with peculiar force in the science of political economy.   Truth, in these cases, follows, and rarely precedes individual and national suffering. It is after countries, classes and persons have been greatly oppressed by some external or internal cause, that the attempt is made to establish general rules of conduct, founded on the immutable distinctions of right and wrong, truth and error.   It has been in this order that the principles of economical science have been elucidated and developed.

The extreme abuses which accompanied that tampering with the currency which characterized the public authorities of the Italian States, between the end of the sixteenth and the beginning of the seventeenth centuries, gave the first impulse to political economy, and led their distinguished writers in this branch of science, at that period, to an investigation, in several admirable treatises, of the true doctrine of money.   In this manner, we may trace almost every truth of the science to its source in some public disorder or abuse of the times.   The ruin of thousands of individuals, connected with the South-Sea and Mississippi schemes, was followed by the discussion and clearer comprehension of the laws and limits of paper currency: and down to a very recent period, the principles applicable to paper issues, in connexion with payments in gold and silver, had not attained that certainty and general assent in England, which the state of the science, in the nineteenth century, might have led us to expect, until the utmost violence had been offered to the relations between debtor and creditor, and landlord and tenant, in the native country, as it has been called, of political economy.

If we pursue this train of investigation, we shall find that the comprehensive examinations, instituted within the last thirty years, into the policy of the British system of poor laws, and restrictions on the import of corn, were intimately connected with the extreme pressure of the former on the payers of the rates, and the latter, on all classes, except landlords: and, it is even not improbable that the reaction of extreme suffering, immediately succeeding inordinate excitement, has had as much to do with the recent modifications of the British commercial system as any conviction that its principles are erroneous. The history of the discoveries of political economy is, it would appear, then, in a great degree, the history of certain public disorders and abuses, and, in some instances, we may add, of intense public suffering. Whilst this explains the desultory progress, or irregular march of the science, it sufficiently accounts for the late period at which its separate truths have been digested and arranged in the form of elementary propositions.

Dr. Cooper has performed a highly acceptable service to the students of the science, by combining these propositions in a luminous and instructive order. The plan of his work embraces, however, a much wider scope than falls properly within the limits of an elementary treatise. He has blended with his exposition of established truths, a brief description of those points of the science which are still in controversy, accompanied by a judicious commentary of his own. By this plan, the student is led to a full knowledge of the present state of the science—its unquestioned truths and established doctrines, with the systems and theories yet in dispute, and the evidence and reasonings by which they are supported. The directness, simplicity and clearness of expression which characterize Dr. Cooper's manner of communicating instruction, is not more admirable than the facility with which he appears to digest and appropriate the discoveries of others—the acuteness with which he detects sophistry, and the impartiality with which he weighs the merits of opposite systems and theories. These are the real, and not less rare than real, qualifications of the teacher of science.

We differ with Dr. Cooper on two leading subjects of dispute, in the present state of the science; these are RENT and POPULATION. He adopts, on both these questions, the doctrines of the new school. As no investigation into the sources of wealth can be satisfactory while the real theory of rent and the true principle of population are unsettled, we purpose to bestow some attention on *these* two topics in the present article. A short preliminary view or outline of the points of difference which have essentially distinguished the two leading divisions of econonists, namely, those who have preferred the agricultural system, and those who have regarded the system of commerce and manufactures with most favour, may assist us in the investigation of these questions.

The characteristic difference between these two divisions, is, that one looks to LAND, and the other to LABOUR, as the *principal* source of wealth ; a small number of each class regard the one or the other as the *exclusive* origin of riches. The sect of the economists, presents an example of such as consider land, and the Ricardo school of those who regard labour as the sole source of reproduction. Dr. Smith and Mr. Malthus hold a middle place in these different divisions, although the latter inclines most to the school of Quesnay, in his views with regard to the land, and some of the doctrines of the former approach very nearly to the opinions of labour entertained by Mr. Ricardo.

The economists of the Continent of Europe, at the head of whom we would place M. Say, are not ranged under any of these classifications. Their views of the sources of wealth, are, generally considered, far more complete and comprehensive than those which characterize the British writers. From the earliest period of investigation into economical science, in England, labour has been the predominant element or principle, in the explanations offered, from time to time, as to the sources of wealth, and the means of its increase. Passages from Berkeley, from Hobbes, and even from Hume, might be cited in confirmation of this opinion. Mr. Locke and Mr. Harris, whose views on economical subjects, are deserving of the greatest attention, are, it is well known, very explicit on this point ;—they assign to labour a disproportionate share of the effect in production. The same idea, in a more qualified sense, pervades the system of Dr. Smith. It is evident he regarded the various divisions and subdivisions to which labour had been carried in Great-Britain, as among the primary sources of that general abundance which manufacturing and commercial countries so strikingly exhibit, although he considered the land as the source of higher relative profit to individuals.

The system which has been framed since his period, and which has obtained the most extensive popularity, has raised labour to a still higher importance, both as an agent of reproduction and an element of value. The Ricardo school, which has given so much weight to this agent, that it has, with metaphysical refinement, generalized it into the *sole* ingredient of price, numbers not only the eminent names of Mill and McCulloch in England, but several distinguished followers in the United States.

It would seem, however, that although Dr. Smith regarded labour as the great elementary principle of the modern wealth of nations; he did not overlook the co-operative powers of nature, in, at least, one of the leading departments of production, namely, agriculture. But conceiving that as nature did not work for man in those processes, by which rude produce is fashioned for his convenience, a nearly proportionate subdivision of labour was necessary in those employments which admitted of it, to maintain a certain level of benefit between agriculture and manufactures. The powers of land and labour were somewhat, in this manner, balanced in his system. He refused to manufactures, what he gave to agriculture, of the bounty of nature, but as he was forced to deny to agriculture, what he was compelled to allow to manufactures, of the mechanical skill and invention of producers, to save in the expenses of production, a sort of equipoise and scheme of compensations were established in his system. Dr. Smith, had, therefore, no *exclusive* bias to *land* or *labour*, in the formation of his system; but he failed to explain, in a satisfactory manner, the real sources and laws of production, from overlooking the aid which nature gives to the industry of manufacturers, in common with agriculturists. His scheme of compensations and theory of wealth was, therefore imperfect; he left a balance in favour of the land, for he deemed its cultivation a more productive employment than either commerce or manufactures. This, of course, on his theory, left a surplus for rent. That he inclined to labour, as a power of very great influence in production, notwithstanding, is evident from the place it occupies in his system, and his regarding it as the invariable measure of value.

It is easy to comprehend why the economists failed to elucidate the sources of wealth. Their theory is defective, for a reason the very opposite of that which renders the system of Mr. Ricardo incomplete. As *they* overlooked that application of material laws and use of natural agents which enable the manufacturer, by a skilful modification of raw materials, to give additional value to matter, so the framer of the new system is chargeable with the oversight of regarding these laws and agents as limited in their influence, in modifying the matter of the earth, so as progressively to increase the productiveness of the land. Accordingly, labour in his system is the substitute for the parsimony of nature in agriculture. Its essential principle is, that manufactured products fall in the progress of society, from inventions which save labour, whilst raw produce rises, during that progress, from the failing powers of the soil, which render increased physical exertion necessary to an augmentation of subsistence and raw materials. That the later economists of the Continent of Europe, allow a proportionate influence over all the departments of production, to those agents and properties which nature has gratuitously and abundantly supplied, for multiplying our enjoyments, it would be unnecessary to say to those who are acquainted with their works. No system of wealth can be complete, and no theory of production satisfactory, which does not ascribe equal effect to the powers and principles of the material world in raising, manufacturing and transporting those products to which value is annexed, in the estimation of mankind.

We have thus endeavoured, briefly to shew, in what manner the two leading divisions of economists are separated, and it is not difficult of comprehension, why the agricultural system has found the greatest favour in countries, where nature has been bountiful in fertile territory; and why, on those sections of the earth, where she has been more sparing of her favours in this form, but true to her great scheme of compensations, she has given superior facilities for manufactures and commerce; the system by which they are best promoted, should be preferred. Theories, in fact, in almost all cases, may be traced to some bias or prepossession, resulting from the position of those who devise them. The economical system owed its formation to a partial point of view of its author, who limiting his observation to agricultural phenomena, naturally looked to land as the exclusive source of wealth. The native of a country more restricted in its capabilities of riches from the soil, but exhibiting unusual results from commerce and manufactures, will incline to that system of wealth which gives them the precedence.

From this exposition, it is less remarkable than it would otherwise appear, that the rent of land should have been deduced from two opposite sources. The idea of there being a surplus or *produit net* from agriculture, it seems natural should be the origin or foundation of rent with the sect of the economists; nor is it a less consistent deduction of that school, of which Mr. Ricardo is the head, that the origin of rent should be traced to the diminished productiveness of the land. It will be seen from the preliminary remarks we have offered, that we consider both these explanations unsatisfactory.

The foundation of the supposition that land alone yields a surplus, which admits of rent being paid, is to be found, we apprehend, in the notion, that it is paid for by the tenant for the use of the natural agency which its temporary possession is supposed to convey. But this is certainly a misconception. Land is not a natural agent in the ordinary sense of that expression. We know that there can be no modification of matter, by which value is given to it, unless by the application of certain principles, and the employment of certain natural properties and powers common to all the arts. Man accomplishes nothing by unassisted labour. There is no element or principle in the earth, as such, by which it admits of being turned to a productive account without the air, the rain, and the sun, and without a skilful application of the laws of matter, and these are agents and principles independent of the land on which they act. We might, with equal propriety say, that the value paid for the use of a ship is a consideration given for the employment of the wind and water by which she is navigated, or that the price allowed for the hire of a steam engine, is the equivalent given for the use of that form of vapour by which it is put in motion. The manufacturer converts the money he borrows into the raw materials of his work and the means of subsistence of his labourers. Those materials, when worked up, and the provisions consumed during the process of manufacture, enable him to give a new form to matter, but whoever contended that he paid in the value he borrowed for the use of the natural agents, by which the change of form has been effected? He is a borrower, however, precisely in the same sense as the tenant, that is, not of the properties of the atmosphere, and the principles which co-operate with him in his labours, but of the instrument by which he produces a productive result. Land is substantially such an instrument. The fact, that it is the immediate source of those supplies which constitute the materials of our food, clothing and habitations, cannot entitle it to a peculiar character. These materials could not have been procured, except as we have already observed, by the aid of the same agents and properties that subsequently adapt them to our use and convenience.

In this point of view, agriculture is only the first stage of manufacture: the depositions in the earth, and the compost by which they are nourished, are as much among the raw materials of this art, as the matter collected from its surface, or extracted from its bosom, constitutes the raw materials of the process of manufacture. There is no portion of matter, therefore, however modified by human labour, but must owe that modification, in part, to the use of certain agents and the application of certain laws of the material world, which, of course, make no portion of its inherent properties, and exist independently of it. To this general description, land, as we have endeavoured to shew, forms no exception.

That nature produces spontaneously from the soil, does not affect this view of the subject. The quantity of subsistence and raw materials from spontaneous growth, is very inconsiderable; and natural luxuriance is sometimes so prejudicial to profitable cultivation, that labour is required to correct or to repress it. Admitting, for a moment, therefore, that there is a greater re-production in agriculture than in manufactures, so as to admit of a specific surplus in the form of rent, the cause is not to be sought in any properties of the soil itself, or its greater adaptation to the laws of the material world and the agency of nature, than is possessed by *matter in general,* which admits of appropriation and of value being given to it.

It is evident, that the natural power of production is a distinct consideration from the extent to which that power is actually developed, admitting that rent is connected with natural fertility. It is not by this criterion that we are to measure the surplus, which, on this admission, would go to rent, or even that which goes to profit, or whether there be any surplus or not from the soil after the payment of the unavoidable expenses of its cultivation. The undeveloped capacity of the land can have nothing to do with the gains of landlords, any more than the latent energy of steam has to do with the profits of navigation and manufactures. The natural powers of the soil may not be fully called forth, from the want of adequate demand, as is the case in new as well as old countries, whilst the real productive energies of many of the natural agents, in the process of various manupilations, may be, as yet, only imperfectly unfolded; as for instance, in the application of steam to branches of manufacture, to which it is entirely new, and the further extension of it to that of cotton. Admitting, however, the highest natural re-sources in the land, and, that they are fully called forth by adequate demand, this has nothing to do with a surplus for landlords. When Dr. Smith speaks of the superior productiveness of agriculture, and the economists of a *produit net,* it is on the supposition that there are certain inherent and indestructible qualities of the soil, which admit of a surplus for rent, above what can be so derived in manufactures.

It may, however, be said, that the value obtained in the most productive branch of manufacture known, is not as large as is usually obtained in agriculture, so as to yield rent in addition to profits and wages, as the worth of the goods produced is not in proportion to the increase of quantity, whilst, as regards rude produce, the value in exchange always tends to approximate to the value in use. It will not be denied, however, that if the produce of the land increased, without a correspondent exten-sion of the demand, the surplus or supposed excess of value, would disappear, as in manufactured products. If supply produces demand, as well as demand supply—this is not more applicable to agriculture than to manufactures. We know that with the augmentation of the quantity of cotton goods, the demand, with temporary interruptions, progressively increased from the fall of price, notwithstanding the great productive power of the agent applied. With every successive improvement in the application of this power, the consumption has been enlarged, and as the fall of price, for the whole period that the improvement has been in progress, has not been equal to the increase of quantity, the surplus or excess of value has been augmented that goes to profit. This is in reference, of course, to the whole value, and not to individual profit. The entire value of the products of manufacture, as well as those of agriculture, may be increasing whilst the rate of profit may be falling, and this value may be higher in the former department of production than in the latter, even with the greatest resources in land, and those resources fully called forth. The division of the produce among a smaller or greater number of capitalists, has nothing to do with the entire value of that produce. The derivation of a large general surplus above the unavoidable expenses of production, *in proportion to the quantity produced*, is not then a peculiarity that attaches to agriculture any more than to manufactures, in any stage of society that can be named, or under resources of the land, natural or acquired. Men cannot subsist without clothes or habitations, any more than without food; and the demand for these equally necessary resources to an increase of population, is as ready to appear and follow the supply as the demand for subsistence itself.

It must be admitted, however, that it is more usual for the demand to be in advance of the supply of food and raw materials than the converse, and that there is a tendency to an overbalance of profit or larger excess of value, from price and quantity combined, in cultivation, than there is from the latter alone in manufactures. But this is not more peculiar, although more usual, in one department of production than another. The large excess in both cases, from quantity and price united, or even from price alone, may admit of the application of very expensive instruments of production. Labour, instead of being displaced, may become more and more in demand, notwithstanding the progress made in inventions and processes, to save in so expensive a machine as man, and in despite of the advance of wages. The expense of a recourse to inferior soils, requiring more costly instruments of cultivation, may thus be supported. And this brings us at once to the notice of the other and opposite hypothesis—namely, that the origin and sole cause of rent is the necessarily diminished productiveness of the land in the natural progress of wealth and population.

The source of that principle is to be traced to the idea that nature, in presenting fertile territory, as one of her most valuable gifts to man, terminated her services and her bounty together. The doctrine, accordingly is, that if the species are to draw a larger fund of subsistence from the earth, in proportion to their own increase, a greater number of cultivators is absolutely indispensable, or starvation must ensue. Thus, as nature is supposed to labour *less*, man, it is alleged, is compelled to labour *more*, or just in proportion as her assistance becomes necessary to an increase of food, must be the bodily exertion to obtain it. That this is a supposition quite as gratuitous as that which assigns a greater reproduction in agriculture, than in the other arts that minister to human comfort and accommodation, we think demonstrable on rational theory, if not so susceptible of proof from a direct appeal to experience.

There is no evidence to support the opinion, that improvements in agriculture, by which exertion is saved on the land, are not progressive. That they are not so, in a manner so uniform and uninterrupted, as in manufactures, affords no proof that a physical law here prescribes a limit to those ameliorations of the soil which augment its produce, and those inventions to save expense, which, in their progress, economize land as well as labour. There is no such boundary marked out to skill and ingenuity, when the co-operation of nature is properly solicited, whether it be to aid the exertions of the cultivator, or those of the manufacturer. It is by the skilful imitation of her processes that this is effected on the soil. It is by the same *modus operandi*, by which she toils herself, that her great law of reproduction and renovation is copied, on a reduced scale, in the labours of agriculture. It is by analysis and combination, that all the wonders of art, as manifested in the increase of the physical enjoyments of the species have been wrought since the beginning of the world. Nature has scattered abroad the elements of this power of reproduction, in the greatest abundance, and she is ready to unite her agency to that of man, whenever the state of his knowledge shows that he is prepared to profit by her services. What, in this respect, has she done more for one branch of production than another—for the manufacturer, than for the agriculturist? She has spread out before both, the principles and properties of the material universe, that they may be made subservient to the uses of humanity. There is no reason whatever to conclude from theory, that nature is arrested or pauses in her labours, more in any one department of art and skill than in another, except when the instruments and modes by which her aid is solicited, are imperfect. In any seeming interruption of her operations, we must learn to see the limit which circumscribes the science and skill of producers, and not the boundary of her labours, or the failure of her bounties. We throw upon her the fault which is chargeable to the defects of our observation or the unskilfulness of our combinations. Whilst she operates her changes gradually, by equal and general laws, we complain that she proceeds too irregularly in her unceasing transformations for our increasing wants. Thus it is, that when we are either unskilful, or unobserving, or improvident, we deduce one law for one department of production, and a different law for another—one law for agriculture, and another for manufactures.

Historical evidence shows, that generally throughout the corn countries of Europe, the prices fell for fifty years together after the treaty of Utrecht; a period, it must be confessed, favourable from the absence of unusual stimulants, to the gradual extension of cultivation. This fall was most striking in France and England, accompanied by an addition in the latter country, including Ireland, of three millions to the population.* That this extension of the growth and increase of supply must be attributed entirely to improved management of the land, can admit of no doubt, and totally discredits the supposition, that at any period of wholesome and moderate stimulus to agriculture, those ameliorations that increase the produce, and such inventions as abridge and save labour on the land, are necessarily interrupted for longer intervals than affect other departments of industry. It would appear, then, that the origin of rent is connected neither with the natural powers of the soil, by which a surplus is created, nor with any physical necessity, that we should employ more labour on the land, by which, as affirmed, an addition to the prices of raw produce, and a rent on the most productive soils are the results.

What then is rent and its origin?—Rent, where land is valued as a source of profit exclusively, is the interest on a capital invested in its purchase, or laid out in its improvement, and has its source, when of this character, in the same principle that governs the proprietor of value in any other form, when he consents to forego the profit for an adequate consideration in favour of another who employs that value productively. Land, when acquired by purchase, with the same facility and on the same principles as capital in general will obey its laws. Its rent, in

* See Lowe's Present state of England, p. 208.

these circumstances, must be regulated by the general rate of interest at the time, for the tenant will never pay the landlord more than this, when, by borrowing money at this rate, he is enabled to become a proprietor himself, and derive the usual rate of profit in agriculture. The prevailing rate of interest must regulate rent where land is as easy of acquisition as capital in general, and is purchased solely with a view to profit.*

But when the monopoly of land is established, and certain incidents usually connected with its possession, in this manner, have grown out of its ownership, it makes a considerable difference in the principles by which rent is produced and regulated, as it prevails in most countries, and as it may exist in all. When the soil has been purchased as an instrument of political influence, or as a source of dignity and power, its price will not be subject to the rules which govern its market-value as a commodity, in those countries where it is sought purely for the profit that can be made from it. Something must be paid for the additional value acquired by land in consequence of these circumstances. This addition to the price will not be given, of course, by those who purchase land exclusively with a view to profit. The interchange of capital between agriculture and other employments, so far as regards the acquisition of the soil, with a view to profit, is consequently impeded to this extent. Capitalists are necessarily compelled to become tenants in place of proprietors, and the effect is, that instead of the level of profit being effected by this interchange, it is produced by the rise and fall of rent. Rent then, or its payment, when land is not sought solely on commercial principles, is essential to the level of profit, and will be regulated by profits in those businesses or departments of production which afford the greatest advantages to producers.

Accordingly, when the territory of a country has been monopolized, although only in part, if it is purchased principally as a means of political influence, or for the dignity and power usually connected with its possession, and not with a view solely to profit, every rise in commercial and manufactured products, by which higher returns are derived than in agriculture, will be attended by a fall of rent, equally as when a rise of agricultural produce, by which a difference is created the other way, must be accompanied by the elevation of rent. We see then, that it is not the rise of the products of the land absolutely, any more than the fall of manufactured and commercial products absolutely,

* The rate of interest referred to here, it will, of course, be understood, is what is paid for the use of money, with the view to a profitable result, and not what the borrower allows when he wishes to discharge debts, or to spend unproductively.

that admits of a surplus for rent, but such a difference in the returns from the soil, compared with those from commerce and manufactures, as renders rent essential, when land is purchased (in the circumstances and for the considerations abovementioned) to the equilibrium of profit. As the fall of rent on the worst lands, when they are forced for additional produce, is absolutely necessary to obtain the usual profits in agriculture, so when the supplies are derived from the better soils alone, if they should afford higher returns than commerce and manufactures, rents must rise on them to effect a similar level between profits in cultivation, and profits in those employments.

But such an excess or surplus from the land, above the average rate of profit, in those employments which afford the greatest advantages to producers, as admits of rent, and its separation generally, or the formation of a class divided from that living on profits and wages, are things entirely distinct. The proprietor of land, where it is wholly or partially monopolized, may choose to have the profit as well as the rent. That he does not so choose, is evidence that the amount of rent is sufficiently large to enable him to forego the profit. The perpetual splitting of landed possessions, by which the aggregate value of rent to each proprietor is too small to enable him to live luxuriously, as a landlord, would, perhaps, prevent the separation of rent generally, where the soil is acquired on purely commercial principles, and freely alienated; but this does not preclude particular owners from deriving a rent regulated by the general rate of interest, if they choose to live as landlords on a limited income. Rent, then, admits of being paid, and may be derived under any arrangements, with regard to the soil; but such rent as arises from a surplus above the general level of profit, is prevented from appearing, unless there is such a division of the territory as connects political influence or other real or fancied advantages peculiarly with its ownership, and this rent will not be generally separated without such an amount of income from large landed possessions, as will enable the proprietors, notwithstanding having relinquished the profits, to live on rents, in that style of expense in which landlords, under such circumstances, are naturally inclined to indulge. The greatest pressure of the population against the limits of the food, or the highest degree of relative scarcity, may not, therefore, afford a fund of sufficient magnitude for landlords generally, although it may admit of a surplus above the general level of profit, for rent, to particular proprietors.

It is obvious, also, that whether the rent that arises in fully peopled states, originates in the manner we have described, or results from the unavoidable scarcity of fertile territory, still the rent which we consider more natural, because regulated proportionably to what can be made from any other investment of capital, may be produced under any disproportion between the population and the produce, or any degree of external demand. As long as good land shall be abundant in the United States, compared with capital, and the science and skill of more matured countries continue to be applied to a virgin soil, by which a large amount of produce is derived with a small expenditure, the disposition, as well to hire as to rent land, to any but a very limited extent, will not, perhaps, appear: but whilst the arrangements with regard to the land, continue favourable to its alienation and its value is regulated solely on commercial principles, this state of things will indefinitely delay the appearance of that rent which is produced from a surplus or excess, as we have described it; and this, although the whole of the territory should be fully occupied and peopled. The high relative returns, from particular tracts, whether originating in increased productiveness or the gradations of land, would pass under the appellation of profits, and the excess or surplus produced by the greater acquired fertility of one tract compared with another, or arising from these gradations,* and which is supposed, most peculiarly, to constitute rent, would never be visible. The difference would be precisely of that character which enables some particular cultivators to obtain higher annual returns than others from superior management of the land, even when none but the richest soils have been broken up. If the gradations of the soil, where a high stimulus forces the additional quantity of produce required from inferior tracts, is to entitle the difference, or the value of the difference, to the appellation and character of rent, why should not every saving of expense or increase of skill, by which a larger return is obtained by some cultivators to what is derived by others, even in the early stage of agriculture, merit the same character and title? The payment of rent is not then a necessary condition of the supply of raw produce in any state of society, and its appearance and separation, generally, do not exemplify a natural progress.

---

* We have termed the difference from the gradations or different qualities of the soil, a surplus or excess; but it must be understood in a different sense to that in which it is employed by the writers of the Ricardo school. It is not to effect a level of profit in agriculture, by the rise of rent on the better lands, that this difference is caused, but by the fall of rent on the poor soils, to enable them to be cultivated, with the existing and average rate of profit. There cannot, it is true, be two rates of profits in cultivation, as alleged by the advocates of this doctrine. There may, however, be two or more rates of rent.

Whenever the separation, generally, of rent has taken place, its amount is settled, of course, on a mixed principle—the actual power of the land, whatever that is, and the existing price of its products.   When Mr. Ricardo denies that increased fertility will augment rent, he overlooks the first of these considerations.   He attends solely to the rise of rent, which has its source in relative scarcity.   It is disregarded, however, in his view of rent, that such rise is not incompatible with an augmentation of the corn rent.   If, indeed, the increased quantity from additional fertility were thrown on the market all at once, the conflicting influences of increased demand and increased supply would be balanced, for they would necessarily counteract each other : the price would, of course, fall as the supply had augmented—the tendency to a depression of the corn rent would exactly equal the opposite tendency to an elevation of the money rent, and it would remain at its former amount.   But this is never the case with any commodity.   The additional quantity produced is thrown upon the market in portions successively, and never altogether: consequently, the price is sustained.

It makes no essential difference as to a rise of rents, when they have been generally established, whether the land from which the additional supplies are derived, is of an uniform or of a different quality.   The last capital applied to the soils already in cultivation, or to new and less productive tracts, with a diminished return as to quantity, can never produce a rise of rent, unless the price has been forced up previously, so as to yield higher profits in agriculture than in other employments.   If the value of the produce should merely place the cultivator on a level with other capitalists, there would be no surplus for rent; but if the price should exceed this level, and, at the same time, the soils in cultivation yield a quantity of produce which would augment this difference, then the surplus for rent would be determined by this excess, in addition to the other.

The definition of rent by Mr. McCulloch, (which is in substance that of Mr. Ricardo) "that it is nothing but the excess or value of the excess of the produce obtained from the best, above that obtained from the very worst soils in cultivation,"* is defective in not noticing the excess or surplus caused by the higher price, (all other things being equal) of agricultural compared with commercial or manufactured produce, as well as that originating in the increased productiveness of the land, and the saving in the costs of cultivation, by each of which circum-

---

* See article, "Political Economy," in the Supplement to the Edinburg edition of the Encyclopedia Britannica.

stances, a difference in the returns may be produced. But, be this as it may, how, we should like to be informed, can a resort to a worse or more unproductive quality *increase* this difference, and increase it, moreover, in a *two-fold degree?* If the tenant on the better soils improve them, whilst the produce increases in price, so as to yield higher returns in cultivation, than in commercial and manufacturing employments, there must be an accession of rent on those soils, from price and quantity combined; but, if the difference is not increased in this manner, the landlord's gain can only be in proportion to the relative scarcity. Why, if a given portion of land, No. 1, yields 100 quarters of corn, and an equal quantity of land, No. 2, but 90 quarters, the owner of No. 1 should obtain the excess or difference, equal to 10 quarters, as corn rent, from the price being forced up, we can very readily conceive; but why the corn rent of No. 1 should increase, whilst its powers of producing continue the same, we are totally at a loss to comprehend.

This scale of rent, whether in reference to the gradations of the soil, or to the difference in the corn returns, from the application of equal capitals on the old land, is an attempt to apply a sort of mathematical sequence or progression to a subject that does not admit of it. It is not by such a rule that we can measure the gains of landlords, so far as they depend on quantity. It is not by commencing on the second quality of soils, or with the difference as to quantity produced by the application of equal capitals on the lands already in cultivation, and increasing in both corn and money rent, in the descending progression, as this difference augments, that the law of rent, founded on relative fertility, is to be inferred; but it is by beginning at the highest degree of productiveness, and falling in the rent for the inferior soils, at every step in the descent, and rising in the rent on the better tracts, if they yield higher returns than the general and average rate of profit, that that law is to be truly deduced. As then, profits in commerce and manufactures will regulate profits in agriculture, where lands are generally occupied and under lease, so will rents on the superior soils, govern rents on the worst lands in cultivation, when they are forced for additional produce. It is to enable the cultivator of No. 2 to obtain the same rate of profit with the cultivator of No. 1, that the rent on No. 2 falls, in proportion to its more limited powers, and from no other cause. No. 2 must, however, pay a rent at least equal to what this quality of land would yield to its owner in a natural state, or it would not be allowed to be cultivated. The same circumstance that enables the most productive tracts to yield a high money rent, enables the most barren soils cultivated, to pay a corn rent.   It is the rise of price that elevates the former, but without the payment of the latter, cultivation could not be extended.   If, therefore, it be admitted that money rent, or rent which is founded on value and demand, cannot be a component part of price, this does not apply to corn rent, or rent in proportion to fertility, natural or acquired.

It is invariably the case, we believe, that when considerable wealth has been attained by States from commerce and manufactures, that profits in them will govern profits in cultivation. As the price of those commodities raised at the least expense, will regulate, in ordinary circumstances, the price of the others, in the same department of production, so will profits follow the same general law, as regards different employments.   Those branches of business that afford the greatest advantages to producers, can be carried on with lower profits than those in which equal facilities are not to be had.   Under the existing arrangements with regard to the land, in most parts of the world, capital has been prevented from accumulating on it, whilst the population has been unnaturally stimulated—a system which has resulted in a corresponding addition to rent.   If this explanation be correct, profits in commerce and manufactures, in countries so circumstanced, must govern profits in cultivation, just as on those parts of the globe where more natural arrangements prevail, and whose inhabitants enjoy superior facilities of production from the soil, the rate of profit, generally, will be regulated by what can be made by the capitalist from the land.

Now, admitting that an unusual stimulus to cultivation from demand, may force the additional produce required from inferior soils, or those already in cultivation, but partially exhausted, it does not follow that such a state of the demand presents the natural, or even the usual circumstances.   They are, on the contrary, such as attend an extraordinary excitement.   Still the increased expenditure on the inferior or less productive tracts, is compensated in the great excess of price above what is ordinarily derived.   And, practically, the high price *precedes*, and never can *follow* extension of cultivation.   It is never the *effect*, but invariably the *cause* of additional expenditure.   Although it were true, therefore, that the return in *quantity*, from the inferior or less productive soils, should be smaller than from the superior lands, or from those already in cultivation, with the same or even additional expense, still the return in *money* may allow of a considerable rise of profits and wages as well as rents.

If we are correct in these deductions, it will not be difficult to decide whether facility of production on the land is so widely different from facility in manufactures, as is affirmed, not only by the new school of economists, but by Mr. Malthus and Mr. West, who presented to the world at the same time, that doctrine of rent, from which all the leading conclusions of the school alluded to, have been derived. If it be true that the commodities raised from the soil, are not capable of regular increase from improved modes of cultivation, in the same degree nearly as articles produced by machinery, then has agriculture one law to regulate its returns, and manufactures another. But we have endeavoured to prove that there is no just ground for the conclusion, that improvements in cultivation are necessarily partial and not progressive like manufactures, and that a physical law bounds human skill and invention more in that art which provides us food, than in the others that minister to our necessary wants. We have said that clothes and habitations are elements just as necessary to a proper standard of comfort as subsistence itself. Mr. Lowe estimates that the corn wages of the English labourer are 56 per cent. of his whole consumption, when not over liberally paid.* If we make a small addition for the raw materials necessary for clothing and lodging, we shall find that the demand for the produce of the soil is but little in advance of that for commercial and manufactured products, taken together. But as the condition of the labourer improves, his scale of comforts and conveniences is enlarged, and his relative expenditure on mere necessaries, diminishes.

Facility of production on the land, like facility of production in manufactures, is dependent, therefore, on those arrangements which best stimulate, in all departments of industry, the invention and efforts of producers, and on these alone. The price, generally, of the products of the soil, like the price of articles produced by machinery, will be governed, in the absence of all unnatural excitements, by the expense of raising that portion which is produced at the least cost. This is restoring the principle of Dr. Smith, from which Mr. Malthus was the first to depart, as relates to production on the land, and thus became himself, the cause of those heresies in the school of Ricardo, as to the influence of costs on prices, against which he has so much protested. He has, in consequence, in his "Principles of Political Economy," embarrassed himself with two conflicting principles, which he vainly attempts to reconcile, to-wit, the operation of supply and demand on prices, and, consequently, on

* Present State of England, p. 229.

profits, and the modified influence of an alleged necessarily increased expenditure in cultivation, in reducing profits.

The idea that nature made a present in the different grada-tions of the soil, of a number of machines of unequal powers, and that, by a sort of physical necessity, resort must be had, in the progress of population, to those which require a greater quan-tity of labour to work them, is very plausible and striking; but nothing is more common and more dangerous in these specula-tions, than to mistake metaphor for truth. It is not susceptible of evidence, admitting there are many qualities of land, that man must necessarily go from the best to the worst of these, to obtain increased supplies from the soil. Nature has made a present to us of agents of unequal powers, as well as soils of unequal qualities. Steam is more powerful in propelling ma-chinery of the same character, than wind or water. If they were capable of appropriation, their value would be determined by what they could produce, as is the case with land. The soil has no intrinsic worth. It derives its whole value, as the immediate source of necessary supplies, from the returns ob-tained by the influence of labour, and the agency of nature united. Admitting then, the justness of the comparison, and that the best machines are first worked in agriculture, whilst the worst are put earliest in operation in manufactures, the value of land may be increased, if only of moderate powers, and kept up, if naturally of the richest description, by that union of science and skill, to which it is impossible to prescribe a limit, or allege with truth, that their influence is controlled by a phy-sical principle or law of nature.

On the whole, the attempt to show, on the part of Mr. Mal-thus, that land is not subject to the laws of monopoly as rent is generally established in old countries, because its produce sells at its necessary price, or that price which is necessary to yield the actual supply required, must be deemed unsatisfactory. It would be the same thing, so far as the consumer is concerned, if such a demand were created as would raise the value of raw produce enough to admit of rent, whether that value fell to landlords or to those who both owned and worked the soil, with this difference, however, that in the latter case, a part of the excess arising from the high money price, would be returned to the land, in the form of reinvested capital, whilst, in the for-mer, nearly the whole is spent unproductively. Capital is ac-cumulated on the soil more abundantly and rapidly when large money returns fall into the hands of cultivators who are owners, than when they are divided with landlords. It would, of course, be the same, should both spend alike, but the circumstance of ownership makes all the difference possible in the results.* The saving from profit to add to capital, is a principle that is never weakened when the security of property is complete, and when the increased value given to capital, in whatever form that value may exist, continues with the improver instead of passing into the hands of others. Now, the effect of the whole of the rents being spent unproductively, and scarcely any part of them returned to the soil, in the shape of reinvested capital, is to cause a greater relative scarcity of the products of the land than would prevail under other arrangements. If the saving of income from rent to add to capital took place in agriculture, as the saving from profit from land, where there is no rent established, there could be no greater monopoly connected with rent than there is with the high money prices of commodities in general ; but as the effect of the high rents which the scarcity originates, becomes a cause in turn to aggravate that scarcity, there must, to this extent, be a greater transfer from the consumer to the landlord than in other instances of high money prices.

In opposition to this view, it may be said, that the landlords expenditure encourages the industry of the manufacturing and commercial classes, and, that the welfare of the society is as much promoted by this species of demand and consumption, as if their rents took any other form of expenditure. But the effect is, that by diverting capital from the land, a greater relative encouragement is given to commerce and manufactures than to agriculture. It may be inferred, as a positive consequence, that the establishment of rents, as they exist generally in countries where the land is held under strict or even partial monopoly, postpones to a late period, if it does not preclude, those improvements on the soil which require capital equally with science and skill. Landlords, in general, are always more disposed to take the chance of an increase of their rents, from the high price of the products of the land, than from returning to the soil, or leaving in the hands of their tenants, a portion of their rents, to add to the quantity of produce. When they, besides, constitute a class possessed of political influence, the elevation of the price of raw produce and subsistence costs nothing but the exercise of their power, but to receive an accession of income from increase of fertility, if effected by their own means, they must forego present enjoyment, with the view to a distant return. Such motives

---

* The custom of allowing long leases is a practical recognition of the truth of this principle. The nearer the tenure approaches to permanent possession, the greater the improvement of the land.

do not generally govern when the same results may be effected by an exercise of power.

If these views are correct, they assist to determine whether, and to what extent, profits depend on the fertility of the land last taken into cultivation, or whether they are solely governed by the demand as compared with the supply of capital. We have endeavoured to show that improvements on the land may be progressive and not partial, and that consequently the value of the returns may be augmented either by diminishing the expenses of cultivation or by increasing the quantity produced. And in those cases in which the supply of raw produce and subsistence could not be augmented as rapidly as population increased, without additional expenditure on the soil, the question of falling profits would be practically answered, if the reward of labour kept pace during such increased expense, with the gains of capitalists and the rents of landlords. The universal prosperity of labourers, as well as the high profits of capital in Great-Britain, between 1793 and 1813, when more inferior soil had been broken up, than in any equal period of her history, decides this question. If it could be made to appear, that at every recurrence of more than usual comparative scarcity, the increase of profit could not proceed, proportionally, with the additional expense of forcing inferior land, the inference would be just, that profits must fall if wages rose, with every step made in this progress; but it is overlooked in this theory, that the gains of the capitalist admit of being *more* than proportionally extended, from the stimulus originating in a foreign demand for commercial and manufactured products, terminating in a correspondent demand for those of agriculture. It is not recollected that such an excitement produces money returns that provide a fund more than sufficient, not only for the payment of the additional *quantity*, but the additional *price* of labour, to which the capitalist is subjected in such circumstances. If these returns were no more than sufficient to meet the expense of the cultivation of the poor soils, produced by employing a greater *number* of labourers, the higher *rate* of wages he would be compelled to pay, if the demand for labour should exceed the supply, would leave him less for profit. As it is demand, therefore, that raises wages, it is demand that raises profits, and we may add, that raises rents, notwithstanding the necessity of employing more labour in cultivation, and paying for that labour at a higher price.

Mr. Malthus has much insisted* on the necessity of a fall of profits as well as wages, to the extension of cultivation over in-

Principles of Political Economy, ch. iii. p. 120.

different soils, but we believe it never happens that such extension takes place in this manner, but is invariably caused by the
high money prices of raw produce. If profits should fall it would
lessen the inducement to an increase of expense, when there
would be no fund to meet it. The fall of profits and additional
expenditure are absolutely incompatible effects. But to make
such fall indispensable to the cultivation of bad land, and to make
it also the consequence of that cultivation, is still more inconsistent. It is the same thing as saying, that the return *in money*, from
the difficulty of finding employment for capital, must be first
reduced to admit of additional supplies from the soil, and then,
that the return *in produce* being less, compared with the same
expenditure, than before, will be accompanied by a still further
reduction in the rate of profit. This inconsistency results from
abandoning the principle of demand and supply, as regards the
products of the soil, or which is the same thing, supposing the
increased expense of raising the last portion of subsistence and
raw materials, is the *cause* instead of the *consequence* of the
price being elevated.

With regard to the fall of money wages or the price of labour,
on which so much stress is laid, as also necessary to the cultivation of indifferent land, the heaviest portion of the expense in
reclaiming such soils from their natural poverty, is in *manure*,
and not in *labour*, except in some peculiar situations. Nearly
the whole of the inferior lands of the county of Norfolk, (Eng.)
have been brought into profitable cultivation from the application of composts, to obtain which, the greater part of the outlay
has been in stock, and in what are technically termed, artificial
manures; instances of levelling and draining, in which labour
is the principal ingredient of cost, constitute exceptions rather
than the contrary. There is, then, never any transfer in consequence of the fall of profits and money wages to rents, under
any circumstances; and, we may add, that there is never any
transfer, as insisted on by the new school, of profits to wages,
as the difficulty of procuring the subsistence of the labourer
increases, unless the working portion of the population can
submit to no further reduction in the quantity or quality of
their food, and no increase of physical exertion.

The capitalist has every interest in that excess of population,
which, while it tasks the labourer to the utmost of his bodily
energies from the pressure of want, keeps down his money
wages to their lowest possible limit. The landlord has an equal
interest in the depression of his corn wages. The toils and
privations of the working classes may not always measure the
amount of profits and the value of rents, for wages may advance

proportionally with both; but, in the ordinary state of things, the sacrifices of the labourer will very nearly determine the gains of landlord and capitalist, excepting where, under a system of poor laws the former is compelled to refund a portion of his high rents in the form of rates. It would appear then, that the stages between a moderate and a low standard of comfort for the labourer are so far separated, that the point at which the fall of profits commences, from the pressure of the population against the limits of food, is scarcely if at all to be prescribed. It is impossible to say where it can be placed. The situation of the people of Ireland, with great natural resources in land, is conclusive evidence of this. But admitting the influence of this circumstance on the population, it is in no instance a resort to inferior soils that affects profits by influencing wages. The cultivation of indifferent land is never forced, as we have endeavoured to show, except under a very high stimulus, and in that state of things it is great excess of value or most extraordinary money prices that rewards labourer, landlord, and capitalist liberally.

We are not disposed to deny the influence of fertility on profits. They must be limited by the capabilities of the soil, supposing them fully called forth by adequate demand. But, as Mr. Malthus has, himself, well observed, *limitation* is a different thing from *regulation*. They cannot exceed the natural or acquired powers of the soil, nor be depressed below them, should the proper stimulants be present. The land cannot support a greater number on the profits of stock, than, after allowing for the labour devoted to its cultivation, it can be made to yield in subsistence and raw materials; but this does not invalidate the principle, that profits as well as wages depend on the great law of demand and supply; on the contrary, it is in strict subordination to it. It is the demand of the manufacturing and commercial classes, for the produce of the soil, that measures the value of the general returns obtained in agriculture, as it is the proportion of capital to population that governs the rate of wages and profits respectively. The principle that regulates the division of the produce of society between the labourer and capitalist, lies so open to observation, that it cannot be misunderstood. It is competition that must determine the share that falls to each class under every condition of things, whether rent be paid or not.

The principle of the new school, therefore, by which that law of profits, which is founded on competition, is superseded, is neither true in fact, nor rational in theory. What is gained by the labourer, is not *necessarily* lost to the capitalist, and vice

versa. If it were true that population must be always excessive, compared with the demand for the produce of its labour,
and the means of setting it to work, still, until it be shown that
the labourers wages in money must rise as his wages in corn
diminish, the rate of division will not be as stated. There is a
different scale of comfort for the working population in the same
country, at periods not very far separated, and it cannot be conceded that habit is so connected with a certain and invariable
standard of necessaries for the labourer, that the rate at which
he is recompensed in money, must be necessarily raised as the
rate of his reward in commodities in general is lowered. The
division then of the whole produce between labourer and capitalist will, when the population increases faster than the produce, or the converse, be adjusted by the law of competition.
The labourer must receive fewer commodities when they exist
in relative scarcity, and a smaller sum in wages, if there are a
greater number seeking employment than there is demand for
the products of capital and industry. This is agreeable to universal experience. But in a just theory, it is more natural to
suppose that the demand should not be so far separated from the
supply of provisions, as well as the commodities produced by
labour and capital generally, than, that wages should always be
encroaching on profits, and, that an unavoidable action and
re-action each on the other, should present a necessary progress.
It is more rational to infer, that if some disturbing influence
were not, in the division of the whole produce or its value, constantly varying the proper proportions—that as a greater share
fell to the lot of the labourer, a larger quantity would be assigned
to the capitalist. Under no circumstances, however, would we
be entitled to reject the influence of the law of demand and supply. The supply might admit of being a little in advance of the
demand for commodities, and the labour by which they are produced. The price or money value of both might fall slowly
and progressively together.

It is a mistake to suppose that supply will not produce demand as well as demand supply. The *expectation* of an extension of demand, from increase of quantity and fall of price, is
sufficient to stimulate producers, equally with a pre-existing
demand. The love of indolence, by which the demand may be
suspended or lessened, or the markets not fully supplied, is not
a stronger principle, as assumed in too many of the reasonings
of economists, than the wish, in the majority of mankind, where
property is well secured, to better their condition and to accumulate. Activity is, on the contrary, the overbalancing motive.

The illustrations of the superior force of the opposite principle, have been necessarily drawn, in the greater number of instances, from those parts of the earth where, although possessed of great natural resources, the inhabitants have been sunk in slothful habits, from the absence of the stimulants that best call forth those resources, and the powers of human labour and invention. Those systems of political economy, therefore, in which a greater influence is ascribed to indolence, than to that activity, mental and physical, which is the main-spring of all improvement, because connected with increase of enjoyment, the desire of possessing and transmitting property and a dominion over others, must be false. The occasional recurrence of gluts, is a symptom of the faulty distribution of capital and of a disturbance in the regular exchanges of its products, and not a proof that man must cease to produce from the want of consumption in the ordinary way.

But those writers who are not advocates of the passion for expense, appear to lay too much stress on the necessity of accumulation. Whilst one class of economists seem apprehensive, therefore, that men will spend too freely, another appear to dread that they will accumulate too fast. Both apprehensions we think equally unreasonable. These desires are in equilibrium in the conduct of the majority of men, when left to their natural impulses, and the enjoyment of the fruits of their labours. There is an equal absurdity in the doctrine that teaches the necessity of unproductive consumption, to a balance between produce and expenditure, as in that which is the foundation of sumptuary enactments.

The length to which we have extended these remarks, precludes us from explaining the points of difference between us and Dr. Cooper, on the subject of *population*. We hope, however, at no very distant period, to redeem the promise with which we set out, in noticing the very useful contribution he has made to science, by his "Elements of Political Economy."

APPENDIX II

The Tariff: Its True Character and Effects Practically Illustrated

[1830]

THE TARIFF:

ITS TRUE CHARACTER AND EFFECTS

PRACTICALLY ILLUSTRATED.

————————

CHARLESTON:
PRINTED BY A· E. MILLER,
No. 4 Broad-street.

1830.

ERRATA.

In page 5, line 11—for "56," read 46 millions of dollars.
   " 8, last line—for "$2.50" read $1 per head.
   " 9, line 4—omit the word "same."
   " 9, line 6th from the bottom—for two dollars *twenty-five*, read two dollars *fifty* cents.
   " 36, line 8th from the bottom—for "7½ per cent." read 9¾ per cent.
   " 37, line 6th from the bottom—for "$596," read $607 50.
   " 37, line 5th from the bottom—for "9½," read 9¾.
   " 37, line 3d from the bottom—for "$1946," read $1957 50.
   " 38, line 11—for "9¼ bales," read 9¾ bales.

ADVERTISEMENT.

The following Essays appeared originally in the " Southern Patriot." They give an experimental account of the
effects of the Tariff on Agriculture and Commerce. Our
Author has been induced by the solicitations of his friends
to add somewhat to his first plan, and prepare them for publication in the following form.—The facts on which our
Author's reasoning is founded, have been collected with much
care; and his opinions are submitted with his reasons in the
way of liberal discussion. There is no subject on which it
is more important, at this time, to be well informed. Those
who are desirous of information on the actual effects of the
Tariff will find in the following sheets much that is useful
And even those who differ from our Author, will, it is presum-
ed, be pleased to see the discussion of the subject promoted
by an investigation, the only object of which is Truth, and
which is carried on in a style altogether free from bitterness
and personality.

THE TARIFF.

NO. 1.

THE whole subject of the Tariff has been thoroughly sifted, as far as *principles* are concerned. Yet the people appear to be unsatisfied. Amidst conflicting statements from quarters entitled to equal confidence, they call for *facts.* They ask for *evidence.* They wish to know the *extent* of the injury they receive from the interference of the Federal Government with the pursuits of industry. They wish to ascertain *how much* is taken out of their pockets to be paid as a bounty to a very small and favoured class of the people of the United States engaged in manufacturing. They are anxious to see what they lose by this bounty, both in its direct and indirect operation. In what degree the demand and price of the staples for export may be affected, if affected at all, by the amount paid the Government and the manufacturers together, to protect the latter.

It is impossible to answer these questions entirely, satisfactorily. The subject does not admit of exact elucidation. Many of the circumstances most important in their bearing on the various parts of so complicated a matter, are, as it were, locked up from the view of the most scrutinizing inquirer. The means of ascertaining them are very imperfect. And these circumstances, when obtained, are so involved in their relation to each other, as cause or effect, that no positive conclusion can be drawn from them, even when authentically ascertained. When they are disentangled from their state of complication, they leave on the mind only vague results, in very many cases, from the utter impossibility of assigning to each fact its due portion of influence, in producing a general effect. As the demand, however, is for facts, we will endeavour to furnish such as industry and care can supply.

The first point of inquiry is—What amount is there paid into the Treasury of the Union by means of the duties for protection?

The following table of the duties, with a list of prices, has been prepared with much care by a respectable and intelligent merchant of this place. It exhibits a comparative view of the Tariffs of 1816, 1824 and 1828. The articles selected are those which are most heavily dutied, and comprise, generally, about one-third in value of our annual imports retained for consumption. The first column of the table shows the present cost in dollars and cents of the articles enumerated without duty, and with expenses, estimated at 20 per cent. for the cotton and woollen goods, and 30 per cent. for the iron, which are about the present expenses. The second column of the table shows what would have been the present importing prices, including charges and duty, on each article, if we possessed the Tariff of 1816. The third column shows in like manner what would have been the present importing prices, including duty and charges, if we had continued with the Tariff of 1824. The last column exhibits what is paid under the Tariff of 1828. Exchange is assumed at 10 per cent. and commissions at 5 per cent. and we have dropped the fractions or parts of a cent when they exceeded, and have taken them up when they fell short of half a cent. The average of the duties under the Tariff of 1816, for the articles enumerated, will be seen on calculation to amount to 25 per cent. The average of the duties under that of 1824 will be found to be 28 per cent. And the average under that of 1828, 47 per cent. The duties for protection on the articles selected were raised, therefore, between 1816 and 1824 only 3 per cent. but they were advanced in 1828 from the Tariff of 1816, 22 per cent. and from that of 1824, 19 per cent. This is only one part of the tax for protection. The bounty paid the manufacturers in the purchases from them or their agents, by the people of the United States, constitutes another portion of the burthen. And here the difficulties of our subject commence. The extent of the supply and consumption of woollens and cottons of American manufacture is involved in the utmost obscurity. We know the sum we pay Government, and can thence ascertain this portion of the protection. But it is difficult, if not impossible, with accuracy to arrive at the amount introduced through illicit trade, as well as the portion of the supply brought into the market by the American manufacturer. We will endeavour, however, to furnish such data as we can obtain on these heads.

Comparative view of Merchandize without Tariff, and under the Tariffs of 1816, 1824 and 1828.

Article	Price	Width / Unit	Cost, adding expenses 20 per ct.	Tariff 1816	Tariff 1824	Tariff 1828
Coarse Baizes costing	8d per yard,	36 inches wide,	$00 18	00 22	00 23	00 40
Good do. "	12d "	"	27	33	34	53
Coarse Flannels "	30s per piece of 46 yards,	42	7 99	9 83	10 19	15 48
Coarse Flannels "	40s " 46 "	26	10 65	13 12	13 61	18 43
" Blue Yorkshire Plains	10d per yard,	27	22	27	27	33
Good do. do.	13d "	27	29	35	35	39
Fine do. do.	18d "	27	40	49	52	63
Coarse Welsh Plains	13d "	31½	29	35	35	41
Good do.	15d "	31¼	33	41	41	46
Fine do.	18d "	33	40	49	51	60
Blankets	70s per piece,	52	18 66	21 27	22 95	24 66
Flushings	22d per yard,	36	49	60	62	63
Carpeting	20d "	54	44	55	64	84
Broad Cloth	6s "	54	1 59	1 95	2 02	2 30
"	8s "	56	2 13	2 62	2 72	4 02
"	10s "	62	2 66	3 27	3 40	4 57
"	16s "	62	4 26	5 23	5 44	6 35
"	18s "	62	4 80	5 90	6 13	6 92
"	21s "	62	5 59	6 87	7 14	9 26
Cotton Cloth	3d "	27	7	11	12	14
"	6d "	36	13	20	21	22
"	8d "	36	18	24	25	27
"	12d "	41	27	34	35	37
Bar Iron, costing £6 15s	$1 50 per ton,		1 95	3 45	3 45	3 80
Sheet Iron, " £11	2 44 per cwt.		3 18	5 98	6 54	7 10
Wrought Nails, 18s 8d	3 70 per cwt.		4 81	7 81	9 81	9 81
Axes, costing £1 4s	per 100 lbs.		6 92	8 12	8 38	9 20
Hoes, costing 14s 6d	5 33 per doz.		4 18	4 90	5 13	5 75
Spades, " £1 10s 6d	6 80 "		8 84	10 34	11 10	11 85

In the above comparative statement it is unimportant what standard is taken, whether the prices of 1816 or 1830. The goods would be relatively higher or lower in proportion to the duties they would be subject to. For instance, a piece of red flannel in 1816, 22 inches wide, costing 42s with the expenses and duties of 1816, would be $13 76. In 1830, the same quality of flannel would cost about 21s, with the present duties and expenses, $11 91; therefore, it is clear, that if the Tariff of 1816 prevailed, the consumer would get the article costing 21s 10d, $5 03 less per piece, being a difference of 10¾ cents per yard.

Also, a piece of white Welch plains in 1816, 31½ inches wide costing 2s 6d per yard, with the expenses and duties of 1816, would be 82 cents per yard. In 1830, the same quality of plains would cost 18d, with the present duties and expenses 59½ cents per yard, shewing a difference the consumer has to pay of 21½ cents per yard on the article. The average fall in price of British woollens since 1816, is estimated at fully 40 per cent.—of cotton goods since 1816—60 per cent. Since 1824, the fall in the former has been 20, and in the latter about 30 per cent.

NO. 2.

The first inquiry that naturally suggests itself, is, what do the People of the United States pay, out of their income, for the Protection of American Manufactures? The first branch of this inquiry again is—how much is paid out of this income *through the Custom House,* and how much in *the purchases made from the American Manufacturers or their Agents?* The *whole* price of protection—the *whole* amount of the tax, can be ascertained in no other way than by prosecuting these branches of the inquiry separately. On the first of these heads, a pretty near approach may be made to the truth; on the second, the elements of any calculation are much more difficult to be obtained, and the results must consequently be more uncertain.

It is seen from the Table of comparative prices we have exhibited, that the average difference of duties, under the Tariffs of 1816 and 1828, on imported cotton and woollen fabrics and iron manufactures, of most general consumption, is 22 per cent. We assume, of course, in all our views and calculations, the Tariff of 1816, as purely and entirely a Revenue Tariff. Twenty-two per cent. is, therefore, the amount of protection, on a fair average, for imported cotton and woollen fabrics, and manufactures of iron of most general demand and use. If we assume a general average for all imported articles, which come under the denomination of protected, at 25 per cent, we are certain that we are within safe limits. The present average of duties on the whole of the imports, is about 45 per cent. As 20 per cent. was about the general average of the duties in 1816, the difference, or 25 per cent, is what is now paid *for protection through the Treasury.*

Assuming this basis, then, and deducting the articles of which there are no similar articles, either grown or manufactured in the United States, we shall arrive at a tolerably correct estimate of the amount paid for protection *through the Government.* It is of course obvious that silks, linens, lace, wines, teas, coffee, cocoa, fruits, spices, and some few other imported productions, should be deducted from the list of protected commodities. These constitute the bulk of unprotected articles. They formed in 1829, according to the Secretary of the Treasury's Report, a value of nearly twenty millions of dollars, almost one half of our dutiable imports retained for consumption, these imports constituting a value in that year of a little more than 46 millions of dollars.

The dutiable imports retained for consumption were on an average for a series of years, from 1821 to 1829, inclusive, about 36 millions of dollars.* Assuming the proportion of articles imported, not falling within the class of those protected, to have been the same as above stated, within an equal series of years, it follows that protection is paid, through the duties, on about 26 millions of dollars.† This at 25 per cent. would of course constitute a sum of between 6 and 7 millions of dollars, on that branch or division of the tax for protection which is collected by the Government, and goes into the National Treasury. This, taking the present population at 13 millions, constitutes an assessment for protection of 50 cents per head, for the population of the whole Union, *supposing that the whole consume imported commodities.*

We shall present, hereafter, such data as will enable us to estimate, with as much accuracy as perhaps can be attained on such a subject, the amount of the tax for protection paid by the people of the United States, *through purchases of the Manufacturers or their Agents*, and then we shall be able to form a probable estimate of the *aggregate* of that protection.

———

NO. 3.

In the observations previously submitted, we endeavoured to show that the people of the United States paid 50 cents per head for protection to American manufactures, *through the Government*, on the supposition *that the whole population consume imported commodities, (on which more than a revenue duty is paid) and domestic manufactures which receive protection.* The principles on which that estimate was made cannot be disputed. It will not be denied that from the entire value of our importations the amount re-exported should be deducted, to ascertain the real amount of foreign goods on which the people pay duties for protection. This we have done. It will not be questioned that what comes in *free of duty* should also be deducted. This we

---

* Watterson & Van Zandt's Statistical Views,
† It will be recollected, that the average annual imports *free of duty* amount to about 10 millions of dollars.

have also done. Nor will it be doubted that all imported articles, of which there are no similar articles either grown or manufactured in the United States, should likewise be deducted. This we have done, and the result is an average annual import of about 26 millions of dollars, on which protecting duties are paid. We have endeavoured to establish that 25 per cent. is the average difference between the Revenue Tariff of 1816 and the Tariff of 1828, which, on 26 millions of protected imports, gives 50 cents per head, estimating the population of the Union at 13 millions.

This is all sufficiently clear. The proportion paid for protection *through purchases of the Manufacturers or their Agents*, presents, however, the great difficulty. We have here nothing but conjectural data, on which to proceed. If we assume a certain sum per head for the income of the people of the United States, and assign a fair proportion of this income for the purchase of American manufactures, we know not that we can estimate this part of the tax for protection from better elements. The income per head of the population of the United States, is of course all matter of mere conjecture.

Mr McDuffie in his late Anti Tariff speech in Congress, assumes 325 millions of dollars as the entire annual income of the people of the Union. We think with him that it is rather under-rating than over-rating it, at this sum. Mr. Everett in his speech in reply, computes the National income at 1000 millions of dollars. This is we think much too high an estimate. A medium between these sums we conceive to be nearer the truth. If then we assign 40 dollars as the income of every man, woman and child in the Union, it would carry the whole annual revenue of the people of the United States to 500 millions of dollars. Let us, therefore, assume 40 dollars per head. The proportion paid out of this for protection is next to be conjectured. The great bulk of protected articles purchased of the American Manufacturer consists, we know, of Cotton and Woollen Goods. They constitute we are sure four-fifths of the expenditure of our people, both on articles imported which pay a protecting rate of duty and fabrics manufactured in the United States, which come into competition with them. We must here, then, endeavour to introduce another element into the calculation. We must conjecture the value laid out by each person in the purchase of these fabrics. The proportion of cotton to woollen, we may suppose, as three is to five, for all parts of the country. The proportion of woollens consumed at the North, from the greater severity of the climate, is much larger than at the South, and the proportion of cottons, of course, largest at the South: but as the Southern population stands, in relation to the whole population, as four is to thirteen, we have assumed the relative consumption of cotton to woollen in the ratio of three to five, as nearly correct.

It is computed in the Boston Report, that the consumption of woollens in the United States is six dollars per head. We think this estimate rather high. We will assume it, then, to be five dollars for woollen, and three dollars for cotton goods, which will give an aggregate expenditure on these fabrics of eight dollars for each person in the United States. As they absorb four-fifths, by our estimate, of the sum annually laid out in the purchase of articles as well of those imported, paying more than a revenue duty, as those protected which come into competition with them, it follows on this calculation that ten dollars per head for each individual in the Union, must be about the sum expended in purchases from the European importer and American manufacturer of protected commodities.

On these principles, it is possible to make some approach to accuracy. We have shown that 25 per cent. is the average excess of price, in consequence of protection, for imported articles, comparing the Tariff of 1828 with the Tariff of 1816. That is, for every two dollars expended by each person in the United States on foreign productions, which interfere in the American market with similar articles, there is paid as tax to the Government 50 cents. Now, we cannot err materially if we assume the same proportion of 25 per cent. for excess of price paid the American Manufacturer above what a similar foreign article could be purchased for, with merely a revenue duty, and the expenses attending importation added to the cost. The difference can be be but small that will determine a preference either way, in favour of the American or the foreign article.

Proceeding on these views and calculations, we would compute the *entire* tax paid for protection at $2 50, being 25 per cent on ten dollars, for each person in the United States, $2 to the Manufacturer, and 50 cents to the Government, and as the proportion consumed of woollen and cotton goods to the whole consumption of protected articles, foreign and domestic, is four-fifths, the sum paid, on this calculation, for protection *in purchases of cotton and woollen goods of the Domestic Manufacturer or his Agent*, should be estimated at $1 60 for each individual. But here there is another circumstance that interferes with our calculations. The above estimates are founded of course on the assumption that the *whole* of the cotton and woollen fabrics consumed in the United States are the product of the looms of the American and Foreign Manufacturer.

This would exclude that large body of Domestic Manufactures of cotton and wool in the United States, called Household. In computing the bounty received by the American Manufacturer from the American consumer, an allowance must be made for this circumstance.

NO. 4.

There are no means of ascertaining the proportion of Household manufactures of wool and cotton in the United States. We know not where to find the data for computing that proportion with any thing approaching to certainty. It is stated in the Boston Report, founded on official statements, that three fourths of the woollens consumed in the United States from 1790 to 1794, were supplied in the Household way, and one fourth imported. We may conclude the Household manufactures of cotton to have been in about the same proportion. But it may be supposed that for both descriptions of manufacture, assuming one fourth part only to be imported, would be too small a proportion at the present period, whatever it might have been at a very early era of our national history. Let us suppose that between *one-half* and *two-thirds* of the cottons and woollens consumed in the United States are manufactured in a household way, and between *one-half* and *one-third* imported. Our present numbers are about thirteen millions.

Let us then assume that between five and six millions of our people consume articles receiving protection through bounty and duty together. On this supposition, the whole annual expenditure on these articles would amount, at $10 per head, to fifty-five millions of dollars. Twenty-five per cent., it will be recollected, is the protecting rate of duty for woollen and cotton fabrics. It will be also borne in mind that a value of $26,000,000, comprising articles which come into competition with our own protected fabrics, is imported, on which a duty to this extent, over and above a revenue duty is imposed. It follows on this supposition that the bounty paid the American Manufacturer, amounts to $7,250,000, being one-fourth or 25 per cent on twenty-nine millions, the difference between twenty-six millions paid to the Treasury and fifty-five millions, the entire sum contributed for protection.

Let us compute it, however, at the sum paid through the Custom-House, being $6,500,000. This would give one dollar twenty-five cents as bounty for each person who consumes manufactures of domestic origin in the United States, supposing the number to be as above assumed between five and six millions. On the same principle, the sum paid the government as protecting duty, estimated on between five and six millions of persons, making an aggregate of $6,500,000, would amount for each person to the same sum of one dollar and twenty-five cents. The whole sum for protection on this supposition would reach the aggregate amount of $13,000,000 of which the government would receive one-half, and the Manufacturers the remainder. We see then that computing the burthen on *the whole* population, it would amount to $2.50 per head. Estimating it on the number we have assumed, between five and six millions of the population, which are supposed to consume domestic manufactures receiving protection, and foreign articles paying higher than a revenue duty, it would amount to the same sum per head of $2 50.

<hr>

No. 5.

We assumed in our last that the purchases made of protected commodities from the European importer and the American manufacturer together, constituted about one-fourth, or ten dollars in forty of each individual's income in the United States. We have also assumed that between five and six millions of our population are consumers of those commodities. It will be recollected, assuming these proportions to be correct, we estimated the bounty paid the American Manufacturer by the American consumer, *in purchases from him or his agent*, at about one dollar twenty-five cents annually for each person. We computed the amount, on the same principle, which is paid the *government*, through the importer, also at about one dollar twenty-five cents for each individual per annum, forming an aggregate amount for protection of about two dollars and fifty cents per head, on between five and six millions of the whole population.

We have assumed the above proportions which are even thought by some to be high, for the purpose of showing on these data that the sum paid by South-Carolina for protection, is not so large as has been estimated. If the whole Union pays for protection in bounty and duty together, about thirteen millions of dollars, the proportion of South-Carolina, her numbers being one-twenty-fifth part of the whole, cannot exceed five hundred thousand dollars. It will be recollected it has been computed, and strenuously maintained, that she pays four millions of dollars to the revenue of the Union, and on this extravagant estimate her proportion of the tax for protection cannot be less than two and a half millions of dollars.

But let it not be concluded that we do not think the price paid for protection, even if reduced to its narrowest limits, as not constituting an annual burthen of a very large amount on the people of the Union. Let us suppose the bounty paid the manufacturer only equal to the amount we have estimated, and we see it will constitute a tax of two dollars and twenty-five cents per annum for each person in the United States. The entire amount for protection, on the supposition that 5,500,000 persons pay it, constituting an aggregate of thirteen millions of dollars, of which the manufacturers would receive one half; the other half going into the National Treasury.

Many practical men with whom we have consulted, are of opinion that the proportion we have assigned as *bounty* to the American manufacturer is high. In this opinion we cannot concur. If we assume the number of the population clothed in household manufactures at between seven and eight millions, it is as liberal an allowance as can be made, and if we assume the sum of $10 per head as the proportion of each person's income expended on protected articles, purchased either of the importer or manufacturer, it is as moderate an estimate as can be admitted. The entire amount computed for protection agrees with various modes of calculating this amount, which will be detailed hereafter. Thirteen millions of dollars per annum, is, as we have already conceded, a heavy tax on consumption, but it operates in proportion to income. If it bears oppressively on the industry and enterprize of South-Carolina, or the Southern States generally, it also operates on the revenue and resources of those other parts of the Union which are either directly or indirectly interested in foreign commerce, in *at least an equal degree.* We shall next offer some statements in illustration of the admitted influence of the protecting duties as they affect the income of the whole country, derived from and dependant on our foreign commerce.

NO. 6.

The object of these essays being to ascertain the effect on the powers of production of the Union by the whole sum contributed for protection, we have separated that portion paid the Government, in purchases from the importer, from that paid the manufacturer, in purchases from him or his agents. We have made the former portion of the tax for protection one dollar twenty-five cents for each person in the United States. For that other portion of the tax which is given as a direct bounty to the manufacturer, who have estimated at about the same sum of one dollar twenty-five cents for each individual, taking as the basis of the calculation the most moderate sum which we could suppose to be expended on protected articles purchased of the domestic manufacturer, and of the importer of foreign articles.

It is necessary to agree on some principle of calculation by which to ascertain what is paid out of the pockets of the people, to force domestic manufactures, that we may know with tolerable accuracy to what extent protecting duties operate as a tax on American capital and industry. Let us then see if we can adopt some mode of proof to establish the probable accuracy of our estimates. It will be recollected we had estimated the whole of the tax at about thirteen millions of dollars, on a calculation of ten dollars for each person's expenditure on protected articles, between six and seven millions of which go into the Treasury, and the remainder, into the pockets of the Manufacturers.

Let us, however, adopt some mode of proof. Let us compare the domestic exports for an average of five years between 1820 to 1824, both inclusive, and the domestic exports for an average of the last five years, that we may ascertain if they have kept pace with the increase of population. If not the extent of the deficiency will afford a good test of the extent of protection for domestic manufactures. We have chosen the domestic exports in preference to the imports, from not having any data by which we can allow for the quantity of illicit imports. The domestic exports on an average of five years from 1820 to 1824, both inclusive, amounted in value to - - - $48,606,905
From 1825 to 1829, - - - - - - - 57,058,401

Difference, - - - - - - - - - - 8,451,496
We thus perceive that the domestic exports have increased in value, in five of the last ten years, within a fraction of 17 per cent. The population of this country doubles in about twenty-five years. The increase of numbers in ten years is, therefore, 40 per cent. We have, then, augmented our numbers 40 per cent., while we have increased our domestic exports only 17 per cent. on a calculation of their comparative value for the last ten years. This embraces the period within which our first Tariff of protection was passed. If our domestic exports had augmented in proportion to our numbers, they would now have amounted to about sixty-eight millions of dollars. If they had increased by the addition of thirteen millions, which we have supposed to be paid for protection, they would now amount to about seventy millions.

But the domestic exports have in former periods of our commercial history increased at a rate somewhat beyond that of the population. It is a striking fact showing the folly of restrictive measures that the domestic exports divided by the population, do not yield more per head for the average of the last ten years than they did in 1790. The entire exports in that year were $19,000,000. The population, within a small amount, four millions, which gives for each person $4 84.* The Treasury returns of that period did not distinguish the domestic from the foreign exports, or the amount which is re-exported of foreign produce from the amount exported of domestic produce, but we may suppose sixteen millions to have been the amount of the domestic exports of that year. This would give about four dollars per head for the domestic exports of the year after the adop-

* To avoid repeated references, we state once for all that our statements are made up from Seybert's Statistics, Waterson and Van Zandt's Statistical Views and the Treasury Reports.

tion of the Federal Constitution. The average annual value of the domestic exports for the last ten years is $52,832,653, which divided by our present numbers gives a fraction over four dollars per head. In 1800, the population being between five and six millions, the domestic exports reached per head $8 92. This was a period, however, of uncommonly prosperous commerce to to the United States. But in 1810, just after the restrictions were removed of our Embargo and Non-Intercourse Acts, they yielded $6 25 per head ; our population being then a little more than 7 millions. The conclusions properly inferrable from these facts are of the highest importance.

From 1790 to 1800, the domestic exports had more than doubled, while the population had augmented a little more than one-third If the domestic exports had increased between 1820 and 1830, in the ratio they did between 1790 and 1800, they would now amount to near one hundred millions of dollars, instead of being at their present amount, between fifty and sixty millions. We have estimated that as the tax for protection takes out of the pockets of the people about thirteen millions per annum, were we free from that tax, or had we continued the Tariff 1816, the present value of the domestic exports would amount to about sixty-eight millions,without allowing any thing for accumulation. If we take a mean sum between what they yielded per head in 1790 and 1795, they would amount at the present period to about seventy millions. We, therefore, in adopting various modes of proof, see, that the present National loss from the system of protecting duties, is somewhere about thirteen millions per annum. The effect on our powers of production from this heavy assessment on American income, will next be considered.

NO. 7.

We have shown that the domestic exports do not now yield, for the whole population of the Union, more than they did in 1790, the year after the adoption of the Federal Constitution. We have shown that they yielded more than twice as much in the most prosperous period of our commerce, namely in 1800, than they now yield per head. If we take a medium between these periods, they yielded at least one-half more than they now yield per head. They amounted in 1810 to $6 25 for each person. They now amount to little more than $4 for each person. If they now produced $6 25 for each individual, they would amount, estimating the population at thirteen millions, to an aggregate value of nearly eighty-two millions. If they had augmented only in proportion to our numbers, they would now be about seventy millions, which would be a little less than $5 for each person. According to this estimate, the difference between the present aggregate amount of the domestic exports, and the amount at which they would have been, without the payment of duties, according to the increase of population, is, somewhere about thirteen millions.

But it will be said that the revenue duties, quite independent of the tax for protection, have diminished the domestic exports in some degree. This is true. But it will also be recollected that these exports, calculated on a principle of increase in proportion to the augmentation of our population, embrace a period of the last ten years only, in which period the protecting policy has been adopted. Assuming then, that the increase ought to have been at least as great as our numbers, the diminution of our domestic exports cannot be placed at less than thirteen millions annually, from restrictions on our commerce, to foster manufactures. This is the price paid for protection to this small branch of the national industry, calculated on the principle of increase of population. Let either principle then be assumed, that of an increase of our numbers, or a comparison of our present exports divided by the population with former periods of our history, and all candid men cannot but admit, the assessment on the capital of the country, for the benefit of a very small moiety of its population, is very heavy. Mr. Everett, in his speech on this subject, at the last session of Congress admits it to be eight millions per annum, but he limits his calculation to the amount paid through the duties to the government, overlooking the amount received in direct bounty by the manufacturer, in the enhanced price of his fabrics, from all those who purchase of him.

Let it not be supposed from these remarks that we consider this comparative diminution in the domestic exports, as bearing on this section of the Union, in any thing like the proportion to the other parts of the country, of *three* to *one*. We consider it a general tax on our foreign commerce, or on the income derived from that commerce, and as bearing on the different parts of the Union in proportion to the capital and numbers employed in carrying it on. It is the greatest of all fallacies to estimate the relative loss, comparing one part of the Union with another, simply by a comparison of their domestic exports as they appear on the returns from the Treasury department. These returns present a very imperfect notion—even of the revenue which is *directly* derived from the foreign commercial intercourse of the Union by its different sections. As to that portion of their income *indirectly* drawn from the foreign export and import trade, they afford no idea at all.

Thus if the income *directly* derived from our commercial intercourse with foreign countries, were to be estimated from the Treasury returns of *the domestic exports alone*, that income would stand nearly as thirty-two to twenty-two in favour of the Southern and South-Western States. The value of the exports in Cotton, Rice and Tobacco, are on an average about thirty-two millions of dollars annually, and the exports of domestic produce from the other parts of the Union about twenty-two millions. But on this principle of computing the income of the different parts of the country drawn from its foreign commerce, all the mercantile capital which is employed in purchasing, insuring, and transporting the domestic produce of the United States is excluded. We believe it will be admitted that nineteen-twentieths of that capital is owned North of the Potomac. It was estimated in the Boston Report, which is an authority on matters of this kind of the highest character, as the gentlemen engaged in preparing that important work had been eminent merchants, that the income, including freight, interest on mercantile capital, and premium of insurance arising from the shipment of such portion of our cotton crop as was in 1826 exported to Europe, amounted in that year to $5,000,000. This, of course, does not include that portion of freight, interest on capital, &c. for the domestic exports to foreign countries of the rest of the Union. Nor does it embrace that part of the freight, &c. derived from the carrying trade or the re-export of foreign commodities.

If, however, the export of a value of between twenty-nine and thirty millions of dollars in Cotton alone yielded to the mercantile and shipping interests in 1826, an income of five millions of dollars, then as the domestic produce of the rest of the Union could not be computed at less than twenty-two millions of dollars, the revenue to those lasses engaged in its purchase and transport could not be estimated at less than four millions more. This would amount to an aggregate income from these sources of nine millions of dollars; and as the proportion of the export of foreign articles is to the entire exports of the Union about one-third, this would form an addition of three millions more. But the increase since 1826 of the tonnage of the country employed in its foreign commerce, is about ten per cent. This would carry the National income from the sources above indicated to at twelve millions of dollars. If this sum is added to the domestic exports of those States which are not classed among the great staple States, it would amount to an income of thirty-four or thirty-five millions of dollars, *exclusively* and *directly* derived from and dependent on foreign commerce. This is about the annual value of the domestic exports of the South and South-Western sections of the United States. It is thus clearly seen that the revenue of those parts of the Union, immediately interested in foreign trade, is *at least equal* to the income from the same source of the large exporting States. In this estimate we have not included the *indirect* revenue of the Northern and Western States derived from a coastwise commerce with the great staple States. This commerce enlarges considerably the limits of the foreign trade of the Southern and South-Western sections of the Union, and by necessary consequence, gives greater expansion to their natural resources. We shall proceed in our next to present some illustrations of the nature and extent of that commerce.

NO. 8.

It is obvious that on the preservation of the European markets for the Southern staples, depends the Southern market for Northern and Western commodities. With the loss of the one must perish the other. If Southern industry is deprived or curtailed of its fair remuneration, by the policy of prohibition, Northern and Western labour must suffer in a nearly equal proportion. If the South lose a commerce worth thirty millions of dollars, as carried on in their products, the West and North must be cut off from a share of the profits of that commerce, in the ratio of at least ten millions out of the thirty. If the South has been already deprived, through the operation of high duties, of a market for fifty thousand bales of Cotton, or a value equal to one million and a half of dollars, or in any other proportion, the North and West must have suffered, by re-action on their own powers of production, in nearly an equal ratio. As the tax on imports leaves a diminished value in the pockets of the Southern payers of the impost, so must a less value fall, in the nature of things, to Northern and Western producers of commodities for Southern consumption. If Southern consumers of Northern and Western articles of commerce lessen their consumption of those articles, to the whole extent of the tax, or any proportion of it, the loss falls, as to diminished demand, in an equal proportion on those different classes of producers, who are customers of each other, and who concur in the general result.

We do not overstate the proportion of our exports from the South, which indirectly furnish the equivalents for Western and Northern produce, at one-third of the whole. We think ten millions of dollars expended on commodities produced in those divisions of the Union, for the markets of the South, a moderate estimate.* Now, as it must require a population of three millions, exclusive of the Southern and South-Western States, to produce a value of between twenty-two and twenty-three millions for foreign exportation in the other quarters of the Union, a va-

* The Boston Report computed the export to the Southern States of Northern produce and manufactures alone at this amount. If Western produce is added, we feel assured that the import into the Southern States from the North and West, would at the present period amount to fifteen millions of dollars.

lue of ten millions exported from those quarters to the South and South-West cannot be produced by less than one million of persons. And if we add the number engaged in navigation and ship-building, connected entirely with the foreign commerce of the country, we shall not make the amount of industry in the North, East and West interested in the preservation of that commerce, and suffering from all losses inflicted on it, much less than from five to six millions of persons.

On this view of the subject, ten millions in value produced in the Southern States, has the co-operation of the labour of at least one million of the population of the Western and Northern States. Our own resources of population, on the presumption that we imported nothing from the North and West, would enable us then to produce an annual value of twenty-two millions, as thirty-two is the aggregate annual value of Southern produce exported. If we are able to import commodities of Northern and Western production to the value of ten millions, at a less cost than we can produce them ourselves, or import them from Europe, we liberate our capital for a more productive use to the extent of ten millions. As to articles of raw produce imported from the North and West, and as to all articles introduced from those quarters, requiring small capital and little machinery for their manufacture, importation beyond the Atlantic is out of the question. No one believes that we can import carriages and cabinet furniture, shoes and saddlery, or corn, horses and mules, as low as they can be furnished by those parts of the country engaged in raising or producing them. Whatever might have been the degree of protection to the manufactures of the United States requiring a small outlay of capital, and executed almost solely by manual dexterity and skill, in the infancy of those manufactures, the time has arrived at which protection of any kind whatever, given to them, can be but nominal. Excluding iron, and the cotton and woollen manufactures, the great mass of articles made by hand in the United States, and with the aid of little capital, cannot be imported with the charges of transportation from Europe, added to their value, so low as they can be supplied in the United States.

NO. 9.

Our object in attempting to analyze the complicated character of that commerce which is carried on between certain parts of the Union and foreign countries, through the intervention of other parts, is to show how intimately all sections of the United States should be united in the preservation of that commerce. We are for giving to each division of this great Republic, such an allotment in that commerce as it is entitled to from its resources of soil and extent of population. We have said, and still contend, that income constitutes the best measure of the productive power of the different parts of an agricultural country, however divided by parallels of latitude, or discriminated by a difference in their productions. It is the only measure we have of the ability to consume as well as the power to produce, varying somewhat, as one portion of a country may be more luxurious, or its soil more productive than another. The limits, however, either as to capacity for production or amount of consumption, cannot much exceed the aggregate of the population. When it is stated, therefore, that one-third of the people of the Union produce a value for export to foreign countries of two-thirds of the whole, while the other two-thirds of the population create a value of the same kind, of only one-third of the whole, the mere enunciation of the proposition startles from the disproportion between the value produced on each side, and the numbers by which on each side it is said to be effected.

This led us to examine the subject somewhat in detail, and disentangle, if possible, the elements of a commerce which appeared to be so complicated. We came to the conclusion, of necessity, that the income of a country, or any division of it dependent on commerce, was to be measured by its entire trade, taking in its circuitous as well as direct exchanges. That as production and consumption are as much correlative terms as demand and supply, the power of a country, or any division of it, to consume foreign productions, is to be estimated by the whole amount of its productive labour, employed either directly or collaterally in foreign trade.

Applying these obvious principles, it is evident that the coastwise exports of the States of this Union, by which they obtain foreign produce by an intermediate exchange, are to be added to their other exports, in ascertaining their ability to purchase and consume foreign commodities. Deny these principles, and the exports and imports of a country can never be balanced. Refuse to admit them, and should North-Carolina (whose exports abroad for her numbers are the smallest in amount of any State in the Union) export the whole of her corn, lumber and naval stores to her sister States, producing cotton, rice and tobacco, and exchange these staples for foreign goods, her exports will appear *as nothing*, while her imports will stand, in proportion to her numbers, between *three and four millions of dollars.*

Now, we do not mean to deny that a tax, whether in the form of a duty or an excise, by leaving less to be expended on imported commodities, by a necessary consequence, diminishes demand, to the amount of the tax, for domestic produce, which would be exchanged for such imported commodities. But in assigning the proportions of this diminished demand to different parts of a country having mutual exchanges, the ratio of income must be assumed as the true rule of apportionment, as we determine proportionate consumption by the same rule, making some allowance, as we before said, for the greater productiveness of the territory of some portions of such country, to what there may exist in other portions. According to this rule, if North-Carolina has one million of dollars less to expend on foreign commodities, by means of duties on imports, on the supposition that she paid for her imports by exchanging her corn, &c. for the cotton of South-Carolina, that appears to be a diminution of demand falling *exclusively* on South-Carolina, but it is in reality a diminution of demand for the commodities of North-Carolina, to the amount of one million, for it is by the produce of her labour that the purchase of foreign commodities is ultimately made, the produce of South-Carolina, to the amount of one million, being merely in this case the *medium of payment.* Extend this rule, and if the Southern and Southwestern States constitute one-third of the people of the whole Union, the diminution of demand for their produce, like the diminution of their power to consume foreign articles by an impost, is in the proportion of one-third of the whole. Now whether this diminution of demand for domestic produce is experienced by that produce falling in price, or a smaller quantity being purchased, the division of the evil or disadvantage, in the one or the other mode, must take place on the same principle. It must be felt in the proportion of one-third of the whole, nearly, or according to income, in the Southern and Southwestern States, and in the proportion of two-thirds of the whole in the rest of the States.

NO. 10.

The view which we have taken of the co-operation of Northern and Western labour, in augmenting the amount of Southern exports, is absolutely essential to a correct understanding of the final operation of high duties on foreign imports. The circuitous or indirect exchanges between the North, the South, the West, and Europe, disguise the real character of the transactions in which the parties are thus engaged. It is by no other process of trade that the North and the West could pay for a part of their importation of foreign commodities. It is true, that Southern exports is the medium of this complex operation. It is accurate in saying, that but for our Cotton and Rice, the North and the West would have to look to other sources for the means by which the people of those sections are now able to exchange the fruits of their labour for the fruits of European labour. It is a fact of which there admits neither doubt nor dissent, that by breaking up or abridging the European market for Southern staples, the Southern market for Northern and Western commodities would be lost or curtailed, to an extent corresponding with the value we import of those commodities.

But is not this the strongest of all proofs, that the North and the West will, in such event, suffer in powers of production precisely in proportion that their Produce and Manufactures constitute an offset for the value of the Cotton and Rice which may be said to be shipped to Europe on Northern and Western account? How could South-Carolina export to Europe a value of ten millions of dollars, unless she were able to liberate her capital from every other mode of production, and limit it solely to the growing of two staples? How could this be effected, unless by the indirect concurrence of Northern and Western labour?— The articles which we import from the other divisions of the Union, must be considered as the equivalents, therefore, for a portion of our European exports.

We could not make our capital work doubly for us. We could not render it fully effective in raising Cotton and Rice, and equally effective in producing provisions or articles manufactured by the aid of little capital, and principally by manual labour, which are not protected, and which we purchase from other sections of the Union. The impossibility of this is obvious on a moment's reflection. To take a comprehensive view of the whole scheme of American industry—of the degree in which the labour of different parts of the Confederacy concurs in the great business of production—is the only mode of arriving at correct results on this subject. According to these views, then, the loss of income to the Northern, Eastern and Western States should be computed:

1st. As regards these States, on the capital employed in raising that portion of their domestic exports which finds its way to foreign countries:

2d. As regards the Northern and Eastern States, on the capital invested in the purchase and carriage to foreign countries, of nearly the whole of the National exports; and

3d. As regards the Northern, Eastern and Western sections of the Union, on the capital employed in the exchange of their Produce and Manufactures for that portion of the annual crop of Cotton, Rice and Tobacco, which has become the *medium of payment* for their imports from abroad.

The two first of these portions of Northern and Eastern capital, depend, as we have seen, *directly* on our foreign trade, and the last portion *incidentally*, or, *through the Southern demand*, on that trade. We have estimated the gross annual revenue to the growers of that portion of Northern, Eastern and Western produce which is exported to foreign countries, computing its average annual value at the ports of shipment, at $23,000,000. From freights and interest on mercantile capital drawn from the shipment and transport of nearly the whole of the National exports to foreign countries, at $12,000,000, and from the coastwise exchanges which indirectly constitute an essential part of our foreign trade at $10,000,000, forming an aggregate of Northern, Eastern and Western income, dependent either in a direct or remote manner on our foreign commercial intercourse, of $45,000,000. This revenue we have assumed, for the moment, to be divided between five and six millions of persons. The gross annual income of the Southern and South-Western States, computing it on the value of their domestic exports at the ports of shipment, which form at least four-fifths of their whole annual revenue, amount, as we have seen, on an average of years, to about thirty-two millions of dollars,* which we may also suppose, for the moment, to be divided among a population of four millions. It is then seen that the annual revenue of the Southern and Southwestern divisions of the Confederacy, dependent on foreign commerce stands to its other divisions, as thirty-two to forty-five, and the population among whom it is divided as four is to five and a half. On these principles, therefore, the comparative loss of income to the different parts of the Union from the system of protecting duties must be computed. This will be the subject of our next number.

NO. 11.

On the principles laid down in our last, the annual income of the Northern, Eastern and Western States derived from and dependent, either immediately or remotely, on foreign commerce, omitting the various internal transactions connected with

---

* This estimate is founded on the amount of the export of Cotton, Rice and Tobacco, and if we add the other portions of their domestic exports to foreign countries, consisting of Lumber, Corn, Flour, &c. it cannot exceed $35,000,000 annually, or three millions more than we have stated. Deducting, therefore, on this account, three millions from the domestic exports of the Northern and Eastern States, and adding them to the Southern and South-Western, their income from foreign commerce would stand as thirty-five millions for the latter to thirty-two millions for the former. But it will also be recollected, that we have computed the freights at a low amount, and have adopted the principle of the Boston Report, in estimating their entire value on the transport of Cotton alone, when it is well known that the articles shipped to foreign countries of Northern and Eastern production are in the aggregate of much greater bulk, and yield, consequently, a greater amount of freight. For these considerations, the income of the Northern and Eastern parts of the Union *immediately* connected with its foreign trade is *at least* as large as that, derived from the same source, of the Southern and South-Western States.

it, cannot be computed at less than between forty and fifty millions of dollars, and the annual revenue of the Southern and Southwestern States, estimating it on the value of their domestic exports at the ports of shipment, is allowed to be rather more than thirty-two millions of dollars, which if it be admitted should be divided among four millions of Southern population, the remainder of the national income, between forty and fifty millions, derived from raising and transporting the other staples of our foreign commerce, must be shared between at least five and six millions of Northern and Western population. We say that these proportions should be observed in apportioning the aggregate of that revenue, whatever may be the aggregate numbers engaged. We ourselves think that not above three millions of the Southern population are employed in raising produce for exportation, and in the ratio we have laid down, not more than between four and five millions of the population of the rest of the Union engaged in the pursuits connected with the raising and transporting of those Northern and Western products, which are the equivalents for the foreign importations of those sections.

The present loss from protecting duties, which we have estimated at about thirteen millions of dollars, must be apportioned, therefore, in conformity with these principles. The great staple States lose, according to the proportion of their numbers and capital engaged in foreign commerce, an annual income of between five and six millions of dollars, and the rest of the Union, on the same principles, between seven and eight millions. We have shown, computing the amount of revenue of the Northern and Eastern States from the capital they employ in navigation and in the foreign trade of the country, that the aggregate of that revenue cannot be stated at less than thirty-five millions of dollars, omitting all inland transactions connected with it, and entirely excluding that portion of their income which is drawn from their coastwise commerce with the great staple States. It exceeds by three millions of dollars the average annual revenue from foreign trade, of the Southern and South Western States. That the income derived from the exchanges between the States, and which furnishes the means of payment for the foreign imports of a part of them, should be added, we have already shown.

The next inquiry, is—What amount of the national income derived from foreign commerce, both immediately and remotely, if not drawn from the pockets of the people by duties of protection, would be expended on foreign productions? for it is in this proportion that the demand for the whole of our staples of export to foreign countries, for mercantile capital to effect the returns in foreign merchandize, and the tonnage for transportation both ways has been lessened. This is a point somewhat difficult to determine. An approximation may be made to it, however, sufficiently near for the purposes of truth. We may suppose the expenditure on foreign productions of that part of our population, whose revenue is derived from foreign commerce, to be *one-fourth* of their whole income. We are confident that this is not too low a proportion. If we suppose that between seven and eight millions of the people of the United States are engaged directly and indirectly in foreign commerce, including the various internal exchanges and transactions connected with it, this number divided by forty, the sum in dollars which we have assumed to be the income of each person in the Union, would give three hundred millions of dollars, as the aggregate income of the Union from foreign trade, including all the extensive inland transactions connected with it. The imports from foreign countries retained for home consumption amount on an average of years to between fifty and sixty millions of dollars, the value being computed at the ports of shipment, to which of course the charges for freight, &c. are to be added, as well as the quantity of illicit imports. This would carry the amount at least as high as between seventy and eighty millions of dollars, which on the sum we have computed to be the aggregate income from foreign commerce, would amount to 25 per cent. or *one-fourth* of that income. On this calculation the *whole* Union loses in its export trade and the branches of business dependent on it, about three millions of dollars, being nearly *one-fourth* of thirteen millions, the entire sum paid for protection: the Southern and South Western States, between one million and one million and a half of dollars, and the Cotton-growing States, about one million. The effect of this loss on the productive powers of the Cotton-growing section of the Union will be next considered.

NO. 12.

We have estimated the present annual loss to the income of the people of the United States from protecting duties at about thirteen millions of dollars, calculating that loss on the principle of an increase of numbers, or supposing each individual in the Union to produce as much per head for exportation now as was produced between 1790 and 1800, not the most prosperous period of our foreign commerce. On this calculation, computing the proportion of foreign productions consumed by those engaged in that commerce, and the pursuits connected with it, at *one-fourth* of their whole income, we have made the present loss to the export trade of the country in its domestic produce, to be about three millions of dollars per annum.

Supposing these data to be correct, the Southern and South-western States lose in their foreign commerce by a protecting Tariff, about one million two hundred and fifty thousand, the Cotton growing States, about one million, and the State of South-Carolina, about two hundred and fifty thousand dollars. But if the Southern and South-Western States lose, as they are estimated to do, between five and six millions of dollars per annum, of their *entire* revenue from foreign commerce, by protecting duties, and about *one-fourth* of this sum, or between one million and one million and a half of that revenue, connected with the export of their staples, the Northern, Eastern and Western sections of the Union are deprived by these same duties, of between six and seven millions of dollars, also of their *entire* revenue from foreign commerce, and of the same proportion of *one-fourth* of this revenue, connected, in like manner, with the export of their peculiar staples, and with those branches of business dependent on the transport and shipment of almost the whole domestic exports of the country. If then the Cotton-growing States lose about one million of dollars, to produce this amount, computing the price of Cotton at ten cents, and the weight, per bale, at three hundred pounds, would require between thirty and forty thousand bags. We would then say that the export of Cotton to foreign countries, would have been about thirty-five thousand bales, in addition to the present export of this staple, had the Tariff of 1816 been the maximum of the duties. The difference between this sum and nearly a million and half, the entire loss to the export trade of the Southern and South-Western States, would be made up in the export of other staples peculiar to the cotton growing region of the United States.

Our readers will perceive that all this is based on calculations of which it is impossible to obtain the elements with any thing approaching to certainty. We do not think we have over estimated the present loss to the annual income of the Union from protecting duties, at thirteen millions of dollars, when taking the sum of our population and dividing the value of the exports by it, we compute what the exports *should be* by what they *were* between 1790 and 1800, not, as we before said, the most active period of our foreign commerce. Nor do we think that we are very wide of the truth in assigning the proportion of *one-fourth* of the whole income of those engaged in the foreign commerce of the country, as the amount of their consumption of foreign commodities, and as the measure consequently of the loss to that commerce from protecting duties.

It is quite immaterial to this question whether there is *any* loss or not to the export trade of the Union, or the interests connected with it, by taking out of the pockets of the people a sum which would have constituted an addition to their income of thirteen millions of dollars. Whether we assign one-fourth, one-third, one-eighth, or no amount at all for expenditure on foreign commodities makes no difference. It would be the same thing in effect, if an increased expenditure had been confined to domestic articles, or had been altogether limited to what is called unproductive. In either case there is a deduction from the enjoyments or the comforts of the people.

But let the amount of the loss to the country be estimated on any principle that may be assumed—let it be calculated that eight millions per annum constitute the tax towards the support of Manufactures, paid through the Custom-House, as computed by Mr. Everett, adding only fifty per cent. for what is contributed as immediate bounty to the Manufacturers, in purchases from them—let the amount of Cotton for which we have supposed an additional demand would have been created without protecting duties, be reduced from thirty-five to twenty-five or twenty thousand bales, and in the same proportion for the products of Northern and Western labour, and still we say the sum of the protection amounts to a larger assessment on the capital of the community, than ever was imposed in any country, in the infancy, as it were, of manufacturing power.

Let the amount then, of the assessment, be somewhat larger, or somewhat smaller, than we have assigned it to be, what would have been the effect on the price of that staple, which is the medium of payment of nearly two-thirds of the imports of the Union, and through that staple, collaterally, on Northern and Western produce, if the tax for protection had never existed? The loss of foreign trade to the amount of three millions, or even two millions, or even one and a half millions of dollars, must lessen relatively either the price or the quantity (in either case the *value in amount*) of the National exports. Which does it lessen? Or to put the question in its true shape, which would have been the consequence? Would the *price* of American produce for exportation have been *higher*? Or would the *quantity* have been *greater* without protecting duties? We say unhesitatingly that the effect on the price, whether the reduction of demand be great or small, can be but temporary. Let us trace the circumstances that would attend a supposed restoration of the demand. Let us suppose the Tariffs of 1824 and 1828 repealed. The first effect of this would be an increased demand for foreign goods in proportion to the sum applicable to their purchase from the saving of income, in consequence of abrogating our Protecting duties. Until there is an equivalent amount of American produce created, to pay for the additional imports, the foreign exchange would advance, and with it whatever could be employed, as the means of payment, for these imports. Our principal staples of export would of course correspondingly rise with the premium on bills. Unless the powers of production were limited the additional quantity of produce required, as the equivalent for the additional imports, would soon follow. It has been found by experience that an advance of two cents per pound in Cotton stimulates the production, and the supply so rapidly increases that the price falls to the former level in two years, unless a fresh stimulus is given to the production. It follows necessarily that an increased price can be but temporary, and that if our protecting duties were removed or had never been imposed the price would not be higher. The protecting duty by lessening the demand is felt, therefore, by the producer, in taking off less of his produce than would have been purchased without that duty. But it will be said that the actual phenomena contradict this explanation—that the price of Cotton has fallen two-thirds since 1816, and one-third since 1824, and that these facts furnish the evidence that the protecting duties have affected the price of our principal staple. This branch of the subject requires to be fully opened up, which we shall attempt in future numbers.

NO. 13.

We have attempted to prove that protecting duties have not permanently reduced, nor can they permanently reduce, the *price* of our principal staple of export, but that they have lessened the *quantity* comparatively to what would have been exported by their operation. We have established from the well-known laws of trade, that any effect on the price could be but temporary, while the import of foreign goods exceeded the export of American produce, and an additional value was required in one form or other as a remittance, to restore the balance between the value exported and the value imported. We have shown that this temporary difference of price would be an accompanying effect of an advance in bills, from an increased competition among the importers, to pay the excess of import above export; but that the additional produce, the real equivalent for additional imports, being soon supplied, the effect on the price is necessarily quite temporary. It would be the same consequence, however, to the producer, were the *quantity* or the *price* relatively reduced, if to him the *whole value in amount* is equally lessened.

But it has been insisted that this explanation is not in agreement with the fact of the fall of cotton, since in 1816, to the present period, of 66 per cent. and its fall from 1824, to the present period, of 31 per cent. It will be admitted that the fall between 1816 and 1824 has nothing to do with a protecting Tariff, and that the cause of the fall of 31 per cent. since the the Tariff of 1824, is the only true point of investigation. Yet, as the fall between 1816 and 1824 throws much light on the subject, and explains in part the causes of the subsequent fall, we will take up the subject of the comparative supply, consumption and price, from 1816. We shall confine ourselves to the import, consumption, &c. of Great-Britain, as being the great market for cotton, and influencing all others.*

It is necessary to divide the period since 1816, into three portions, to understand this matter thoroughly. It is from that period that all the considerable fluctuations in the supply and price of cotton take their date. Going as far back as the year 1802, and until 1815, there was a remarkable uniformity in the supply of cotton. In no one year within this period did the supply vary more than 80,000 bales, from any other year with which it might be compared, if we except the three years of interruption to regular commerce, 1808, 1809 and 1810, yet the average supply of these three years was nearly the same as in the preceding period. In the aggregate of almost the whole fourteen years, there was not a variation of more than 25,000 bales in the supply. It was in 1815 that the excess of supply became apparent. In 1815, the quantity imported into Great-Britain exceeded that of any previous year from 1802, upwards of 80,000 bales, if we exclude the above-mentioned three years which interrupted regular commerce.

In 1815, a new era commenced in the cotton trade. From 1816 to 1822 is the first of the three periods to which we wish to direct the attention of the reader. In that period, the first great fall of cotton took place. In that period, the average annual import was about 500,000 bales, which was between 2 and 300,000 bales above the average annual import in the whole period between 1802 and 1815. During this same period, while the supply was so rapidly increasing, for three years, 1818, 1819 and 1820, the consumption received a very trifling augmentation, checked by the high prices of 1817 and 1818, and the resumption of cash payments in 1822. This excess of supply, meeting w th the other circumstance of the return to specie payments, brought the average price of Uplands down from 20d in 1816, to 8¼d in 1822, or a fall of 62 per cent. It was in 1822 the full effect was produced on prices from the resumption of cash payments in England. Much the greater part of the decline during this period was owing to this measure. From the debates in the British Parliament in 1822, and the concurring testimony of all practical men, cotton, in common with all British commodities, was proved to have fallen 45 per cent. The fall in cotton, then, between 1816 and 1822, was principally owing to the return to cash payments in England, and in a secondary degree to the excess of the supply over the consumption. The

---

* The statements we may make on this branch of our subject, are founded on commercial letters from houses of the first respectability in England.

consideration of the other two and most important periods we must reserve for our next number.

====

NO. 14.

We have attempted to establish that all the great fluctuations of supply in the cotton market take their date from about the year 1815. That before that period, there was a remarkable uniformity in the supply. That there was not a variation of the whole import into Great-Britain from 1802 to 1815 of more than 80,000 bales, between any two years of this time, while the average variation was not more than 20,000 bales during this whole period, excluding the years 1808, 1809 and 1810, years of uncommon derangement to all commercial relations. It is well known that the average variation in the supply since that period, both from the United States and the East-Indies, has far exceeded this. We have shown that the average annual import for seven years from 1816 to 1822, was within a fraction of fifty per cent. larger than the average annual import for ten years from 1802 to 1815, excluding the years 1808, 1809 and 1810, and the same fact shows that the aggregate import for the same period of *seven* years, between 1816 and 1822, was as large by a fraction as the aggregate import for *thirteen* years, between 1802 and 1815. We have attempted to prove that the fall in Cotton in the first period, between 1816 and 1822, which we have selected to illustrate our views, was *mainly* attributable to the resumption of cash payments by the Bank of England in the latter of these years, and the fall only *incidentally* owing to the excess of the supply over the consumption; 45 per cent. of the fall being assignable to the alteration of the currency, and about 15 per cent. to the excess of the supply.

We come now to the second period, between 1822 and 1824, inclusive, when prices were remarkably steady, being at an average of 8⅜d during this period for Uplands. In this period there was also a considerable increase in the supply, but the rate of the consumption far exceeded it, and prices must have risen, but from the accumulation of stock, owing to the supply having so far outrun the consumption in the previous six years. The annual average export from Great-Britain between 1822 and 1824, inclusive, had been the same as for some time before. The advance of price could have been prevented, therefore, by nothing else than the large accumulations of the previous years.

We come now to the third and most important period between 1826 and 1829, inclusive. We, of course, omit the speculative year, 1825, in all our views of this subject. The price was, on an average of these four years, about 6½d, being a fall of 30 per cent. from the period between 1822 and 1824. It will be recollected that it was from 1824 that the new supply from Egypt began to make its appearance, so as to be felt on the market. In 1825, the import from that country into Great-Britain was upwards of 100,000 bales, and the average annual import between 1825 and 1829 was between 50 and 60,000 bales. The increase from the East-Indies within the same period was tolerably large, the supply received from Brazil had not much varied, but the receipts from the United States were very heavy. Let us exhibit these accessions severally, that we may judge what must have been the effect on the market.

From the United State, the average annual receipts from 1826 to 1829, inclusive, exceeded the average annual receipts between 1821 and 1824, inclusive, by - - - 146,302 bales

From the East-Indies the average annual increase within the same period was - - 41,295

From Egypt (a new supply) annual average 31,924

219,521

We thus see that there had been more received in Great-Britain between 1826 and 1829, by nearly one-third, than during the same number of years previous to the year 1825, the year of great speculation, the average annual receipts from all quarters, from 1821 to 1824, being 558,502, and between 1826 and 1829, 754,318 bales. The consumption had also increased between these two periods in a greatly accelerated ratio, owing to low prices commencing with 1826, but nothing, of course, in this proportion. The average annual consumption in the first period was 552,225, and in the second period 665,777, an increase of about 20 per cent., while, as it is seen, the supply had augmented 40 per cent. We thus have the complete key to the fall of prices between 1826 and 1829 ; and the wonder is that they did not decline to a lower point. They were assisted, however, in their reduction, by the calling-in of the one pound notes of the Bank of England, or rather the apprehension in the public mind of the effects of that measure. The general conclusions we draw from this examination are :—

1st That between the years 1816 and 1822 prices fell about 60 per cent. *primarily* from the resumption of cash payments by the Bank of England, and, in a *secondary degree*, from the excess of the supply over the consumption.

2d. That between the years 1826 and 1829, prices again declined about 30 per cent. from those prevailing in the period between 1821 and 1824, *mainly* from the excess of the supply over the consumption, and *incidentally*, but in a small degree, from another alteration in the value of the English currency.

3d. That in periods of three years the supply and the consumption powerfully act and re-act on each other, and cause considerable variations of price, but in periods of ten years the irregularities are rectified, and the supply and consumption very nearly equalized. The final conclusion from the whole of this review, is, that the fall in the prices of Cotton indicated in the periods selected by us for comparison, is entirely disconnected with the supposed operation of the Protecting duties. Some other views growing out of this comparison will be presented in our next number.

NO. 15.

We think we have demonstrated that the fall in cotton since 1824 has no relation whatever to the establishment of duties of protection. That the difference of about 31 per cent. between the price now and the price then, is attributable to the excess of the supply; that whilst the consumption since 1827 has been increasing at the rate of 20 per cent. the supply has been augmenting at the rate of 40 per cent. In this ratio the price ought to have fallen 50 per cent.

We have remarked that the supply and consumption most powerfully act and re-act on each other in short periods, from two to four years, producing great irregularities of price, but that in periods of about ten years, the supply and consumption are equalized. Several most useful conclusions admit of being drawn from these facts. There is a limit to be found somewhere between the high prices which stimulate production and retard consumption, and the low prices which stimulate consumption and retard production. To discover this limit is of the highest importance. We have asserted that in periods of two, three and four years, the alternations are produced, and prices may be said to ascend and descend in a sort of geometrical, though not absolutely regular scale. Let us see if we can mark some of them. We find from 1818 to 1821, inclusive, the rate of consumption retarded by the high prices of these four years, assisted by the return to cash payments by the Bank of England, for whatever checks the power of purchase generally, by lessening the quantity of circulating medium, retards consumption as well as high prices. Again, the rate of consumption was increased in 1822, stimulated by the low prices commencing with 1819; it did not much increase in 1823, but a considerable augmentation took place in 1824 and 1825, until the high prices of the latter of these years again checked it, and the consumption fell to nearly as low a point as it had been in 1821. In 1827 it again received a considerable impulse from the low prices, commencing with 1826, and having got, in 1830, to the estimated large amount of 15,000 bales per week, or 780,000 for the year, it is almost certain will not augment, in the same ratio, in the next four, as in the last four years, if prices should increase to much beyond those of the present year. In the last ten years, the consumption has increased 75 per cent. being in 1820 within a small amount of 9,000 bales per week. This is a much greater increase in the consumption than that of the most rapid addition to numbers known, the population of the United States augmenting at the rate of 40 per cent. in ten years. It would, therefore, appear, that from two to four years all the considerable changes take place in the prices and rate of consumption, and we have every reason to believe, that a re-action having taken place, the production may be stimulated for the next three or four years, from some addition to prices.

We have entered into this detail to show what reasonable hopes of encouragement are held out to the American cultivator, provided the extension of the cultivation is gradual. The consumption will and must go on increasing, for there are every year more people to clothe as well as feed, and the use of cotton clothing is every day more and more superseding that of linen, as well as lessening that of woollen and silk fabrics, by a mixture of cotton with them. But it would be unreasonable to look for such a stimulus to the consumption as took place between 1826 and 1830, as this was owing mainly to the extreme low prices between these years.

Before concluding this branch of the subject, we wish to correct a prevalent delusion as relates to the competition of the American buyer in our market, in enhancing the price of the raw material. On general principles it would seem impossible that the purchasers for one-sixth of the entire crop—admitting 150,000 bales as the amount of this year's consumption of the American manufacturers, to be the extreme extent of that consumption—it is impossible we say on general principles that so small a portion of the demand confined to the finer qualities, could materially influence the price of the whole. We find on comparing the prices and supply of American, Brazil and East-India cottons in the Liverpool market, in an average of years, between 1816 and 1820, and 1825 and 1829, that although the supply from the United States had increased 120 per cent. that from Brazil had diminished 2 per cent. and that from the East-Indies had augmented 55 per cent. yet they had all fallen equally in price 60 per cent. thus conclusively proving that the greater portion of the supply being from the United States, governed all the rest, although the proportions of the supply from each quarter had so much varied. What applies to the sellers applies to the buyers.

But, to rest this matter on practical knowledge, it is well known that the competion is, in reality, between the French and the Northern buyer, for they appear in the American market together, and purchase the same quality of cotton from similar inferiority in French and Northern machinery, as compared with British. It is only in the commencement of the season, when the supplies in market are small, that the above two classes of buyers appear as purchasers together, and raise the price of the finer qualities a fraction, and by consequence, those below them a little also. But their wants are soon supplied; the English buyers then come in, and the price falls fully in the proportion it had previously advanced, and, perhaps, on the whole, somewhat lower than it had risen from the early appearance of the buyers on Northern account in the market. Every business-man, conversant with our cotton market, will vouch for the accuracy of this representation.

NO. 16.

If the course of reasoning which has been adopted in the previous portion of these essays is accurate, we shall assume as having been established, that the annual income of the Northern and Eastern States derived in a *direct* manner from foreign commerce, is *at least* equal to the annual income of the Southern and Southwestern States dependent on that commerce. But if the coastwise and inland exchanges of the Northern, Eastern and Western States, with the Southern section of the Union (by which the imports into those States are in part paid for) are admitted to furnish a portion of their annual revenue from foreign commerce, then their income will stand as nearly *two-thirds*, and that of the Southern States as nearly *one-third* of the whole annual National gain from this source.

This conclusion runs counter to the doctrines advanced by the greater number of our Southern statesmen, both in speeches and in public papers. They contend that it would be in effect the same, whether the duties were levied on the exports or imports, and as a consequence of this doctrine, that as the Southern States furnish two-thirds of the exports to foreign countries, they contribute in this proportion (between sixteen and seventeen millions of dollars) to the Federal Treasury. It might be supposed by many that this tenet had been sufficiently refuted in the remarks already offered, at least as far as *the proportions* paid by the different sections of the Union, respectively, form a part of this question. But as the doctrine has been authoritatively put forth in the Exposition submitted by a Committee of the Legislature, and ordered by that body to be printed—as this paper has become most extensively circulated, and the portion of its contents containing this doctrine, has met with advocates all over the State, a detailed explanation of the fallacy on which it is founded, seems to be necessary.

That fallacy consists in the misapplication of a well known principle, " that exports and imports must be equal, in a series of years." From this admitted truth it has been concluded, that duties whether laid on exports or imports would be the same in effect. We would say that the value of the imports must be *at least* equal to the value of the exports, in a series of years, by the addition of freight, insurance and interest on the capital employed, both ways, or inwards and outwards, in effecting the exchange of domestic for foreign produce. Were this not the case the different portions of capital engaged in the whole operation would not be replaced. But what in this respect is true of *the whole*, is not true of *a part*—what is true of the *entire* population, is not true of a *moiety* of it. If the imports were distributed in the same manner, or among the same number of persons by whom the exports, which are their equivalents, are raised, it would be correct to say that a tax on exports would be in effect a tax on imports. But if we suppose these exports to be produced by one-fourth or one-third of the population, we must admit the imports to be consumed by a much larger proportion of the whole—by all who can furnish in their labour or revenue the means of payment for foreign productions—by all who are employed in foreign navigation, and the arts connected with it—by all who live on the income of the capital engaged in the innumerable channels of circulation for imported merchandize—by all who are concerned as labourers in the inland transportation and the retail trade dependent on its effectual distribution to its respective consumers.

Imported productions derive a vast augmentation of value, after they have reached the ports of importation, and before they come to their final destination, the hands of the consumers, in consequence of these circumstances. It is out of this increased value, and from this diffusive circulation of imported commodities, that the importer is able to replace his capital, and derive the ordinary rate of profit. He purchases of the producers the whole annual value of their labours, and he draws back from them, *as consumers*, about *one-fourth*, we may suppose, of this value, exclusive of charges and duty; but he looks to the other classes, who have equivalents to offer in money, or labour, to replace the other *three-fourths* of his capital employed in effecting the exchange of domestic for foreign produce.

To illustrate this principle, let us assume, for the sake of the argument, the number employed in raising agricultural staples for foreign markets to be four millions, situated exclusively in one section of the Union, and those engaged in the export and import trade of the country, situated in a different section, to purchase these staples for thirty-five millions of dollars. They would be augmented in value, estimated in the returns, by the freights and charges, we will suppose, eight millions more, making forty-three millions. The growers or producers of these staples would take off, we will imagine, between eight and nine millions, being about one-fourth of the money value for which they sold the produce of their labour. The importers, therefore, must find a market among the rest of the American consumers for between thirty-four and thirty-five millions, forming the other portion of their money capital, with such an addition to the value as will replace to them the duty paid the Government.

Now, it is quite immaterial in what quarter of the Union the producers are situated, whether all at the North, or all at the South, or unequally, as is the fact, in both divisions. As regards the number engaged in raising the staples for exportation, the value of the exports must exceed the value of the imports (reversing the principle, in its application to *the whole*) by a sum which will be *at least* sufficient to meet their unproductive expenses, and keep their capital entire. As regards the population *in general*, viewed as *one whole* or *entire nation*, the value of the imports must exceed the value of the exports, by a sum which will *at least* be sufficient to cover the expense of freight and the other charges attending importation. Suppose South-Carolina to export $10,000,000; did she import to the whole of this amount, the sum which her citizens have to pay for taxes, (State and City) for maintaining the various unproductive classes engaged in divinity, law, medicine and instruction, for the services of those who contribute to the amusement of her citizens, and the labours of household servants, would necessarily, on this supposition, have to be deducted from her capital.

The money amount for which South-Carolina sells her cotton and rice, constitutes the only fund out of which she can discharge these various payments. If we suppose that these expenses amount to $2,000,000, or only $1,000,000 annually, her exports must exceed her imports by the sum of these expenses, whatever they are. But, besides this, to continue her capital entire, supposing she accumulates nothing from a surplus, there must be a further excess of the money value of her exports over her imports, for this purpose. This peculiarity arises from the circumstance that South-Carolina lives almost entirely by raising staples for foreign exportation. But the same principle will apply to any portion of the American population engaged in producing articles for foreign markets, in whatever quarter of the Union they may be situated.

It requires no explanation in detail to show in what manner the imports of the entire country, viewed as *one whole*, must exceed its exports. The whole mystery, if any, of the matter consists, as we have shown, in the way the imports are distributed, and in the successive augmentations of value which they undergo, before they finally reach the consumers. If we suppose, therefore, that one-fourth or four millions of the population engaged in raising staples for foreign markets, consume twenty millions of the imports, and these imports amount at the ports of importation to a money value of sixty millions, the other forty millions must be distributed to the remaining eight millions of the people. It is, then, obvious in what manner a principle which is true of *the whole*, is false when applied to *a part* of the country, and is with regard to such part exactly the converse.

NO. 17.

We have endeavoured to show the fallacy of the doctrine that exports are equal to imports, as regards *parts* of a country as well as the *whole*. If this were even admitted, an export would not be in its consequences the same as an import duty. If an export duty were to take effect on that portion of the exports, or their value, which is parted with by the producer, as the equivalent he furnishes for the foreign commodities he consumes, the substitution of the one for the other impost could make no difference in the result. But the argument against which we contend proceeds on the assumption, that the duty is levied on the *whole money value* of the exports to foreign countries. It takes for granted that the producer of the staples for distant markets, consumes the *entire amount* for which his staples sell, *in foreign productions.* This we have shown to be impossible. On such an admission, there would be no fund (supposing there were no coastwise imports of raw produce and manufactures of Northern and Western origin) from which to discharge the various items of unproductive expenditure, as we have endeavoured to prove. But as regards the Southern States, and particularly the State of South-Carolina, the coastwise imports of Northern and Western produce, consisting of provisions and manufactures which have ceased to enjoy protection, amount to a large sum.

Let us admit that the State of South-Carolina sells the annual produce of her labour for ten millions of dollars. Let us suppose that she reserves two millions for the services of the Divine, the Physician, the Lawyer, the Schoolmaster, the menial servant, and for the State and City tax-gatherer; she will, on this supposition, expend seven millions annually on other objects, admitting that one million is necessary to replace the annual waste of her capital, and form a small surplus for accumulation. Of this seven millions, on the calculation we have all along proceeded, she would expend two millions five hundred thousand dollars (being one-fourth of her gross annual income produced from the sale of her staples) for commodities of foreign origin of *every kind*, exclusive of duty and expenses attending importation.

The amount of the duty at the average rate of 45 per cent. would not exceed $1,000,000, as about one-fifth of the foreign imports are not duitable. The expenses attending importation are on the average about 20 per cent.. This amounts on a value of $2,500,000 to $500,000, forming an aggregate of annual expenditure on foreign articles paying duty of about $4,000,000, On these suppositions the coastwise imports of South-Carolina, consisting of raw produce and manufactures *not protected* of the other States, must amount at least to $3,000,000. On this amount there is of course no duty paid, and adding three millions more for unproductive expenses and to replace the waste of capital, $2,500,000 (being *one-fourth* of the money value of the exports of South-Carolina) constitute the amount which is subject to the impost of the Federal Government.

On the same principles, instead of the Southern and Southwestern States paying upwards of sixteen millions of dollars annually into the Treasury of the Union, they pay about four millions. Instead of South-Carolina paying four millions annually, she pays one million. Instead of her paying upwards of two millions for protection annually, she pays between five and six hundred thousand dollars, in bounty and duty together, estimated on her population, as compared with the rest of the Union, and computed on her exports, valued at $10,000,000, about $525,000.

But it has been contended that as the various classes engaged in the mechanic arts, and all others of whom the Planter purchases his supplies, consume foreign articles paying duty, all taxes on *their* consumption must fall on the produce of the soil, as the only fund, where there are no manufactures and no capital scarcely invested in commerce, from which these taxes can be ultimately paid. Admitting this, the Planter's expenditure is not greater from this circumstance. The money value of this produce when sold is divided among the different classes who contribute to the wants or enjoyments of the producer in various ways, and the proportion of their *separate* consumption of foreign articles being on supposition the same as that of the producer, the *aggregate* of the tax on the annual produce of the State must also be the same. If the produce itself were divided before being exchanged for money, the same proportionate distribution would necessarily follow, as regards the various classes of society. Each one who has services to exchange for that produce, must receive a portion of it, according to the value of the equivalent in labour he has to offer, and he parts with a portion of it again to provide for his consumption of foreign goods, in nearly the same ratio on an average as the immediate producer.

Let us, however, as regards the planter, take the case of barter, put in the speeches and essays on this subject, and suppose the grower to be the exporting and importing merchant. The return will then be, to adopt the illustration of Mr. M'Duffie, one hundred pieces of cloth for one hundred bales of cotton. The duty is paid on the entire quantity. What proportion of that would the planter retain for his consumption?—for on this, as we see, the whole question hinges. He must part with that portion which he is not able to consume himself, to supply his other wants—to meet his other objects of expenditure. If he continue the operation of barter, and exchange his duty-paid cloth for butter and bacon, and sugar and coffee, he charges the duty by giving a smaller quantity of cloth than is usual for the same quantity of those articles; or, which is the same thing, he obtains a greater quantity of those articles for the same quantity of cloth. He must be remunerated for the tax he pays the Government. He acts as the merchant, and cloth imported by him cannot be brought into the market on lower terms.

Now, let us suppose he sells, instead of bartering, the residue of his duty-paid cloth, can this make any difference? Must he not obtain the duty from the consumer, on three-fourths of the value he sells, supposing he retains one-fourth for his own consumption? And on the supposition that each purchaser consumes the same proportion of foreign cloth, are there not three-fourths of their income, whether consisting of dollars or of commodities—whether of cloth or cotton, untaxed? In whichever mode the subject, therefore, is considered, it cannot but be apparent that the duty, if even levied on the exports, falls on that portion only which is exchanged for articles of consumption of foreign origin.

Instead, then, of its being 45 per cent. on thirty-two or thirty-five millions of Southern exports, as the case may be, it is 45 per cent. on only *one-fourth* of thirty or thirty-five millions. Instead of the whole impost being 40 per cent. it does not exceed 10 per cent. on the gross income of the planter, and instead of the tax for protection, independent of the duty for revenue, being 20 per cent or any higher proportion of that income, it is only $5\frac{1}{4}$ per cent. if estimated on the value of the exports, and only $4\frac{1}{4}$ per cent. if computed according to comparative population. As this matter will, however, be better understood by an illustration in figures, applied to the income of an *individual*, the following statement, which is thought to be as accurate as can be framed on such a subject, is subjoined. It will be perceived that $7\frac{1}{2}$ per cent. for the *whole* duty is the result of the calculation. The proportion paid the Government for protecting duty, compared with the whole impost, is, it will be recollected, as $6\frac{1}{2}$ is to $22\frac{1}{2}$ millions of dollars, or between one-third and one-fourth of the entire duty. Consequently, on this estimate, the tax for protection paid in *duty* alone by the planter, is a little less than $2\frac{3}{4}$ per cent. on his gross income, and an equal amount being supposed to be paid in *bounty* to the manufacturer, makes the aggregate, on the same estimate, rather a fraction less than 4¾ per cent. on that income for protection. It will also be seen that the planter's consumption of dutiable commodities, by the same estimate, is even *less* than *one-fourth* of his gross annual revenue.

We will suppose an Upland cotton planter the owner of 150 negroes which will turn out 75 workers, producing, on an average, 3 bales of cotton to the hand and raising their own provisions; the bales to average 300 lbs.—price, in the Charleston market, 10 cents per lb. Deduct $2 per bale for freight, factorage, &c. will leave $28 per bale:—

150 negroes, at $300 round,	-	-	-	-	$45,000
Plantation,	-	-	-	-	15,000
Out-fit of plantation,	-	-	-	-	4,000
					64,000
225 bales of cotton at $28 per bale,	-	-	-	6,300

This is exactly 7½ per cent. on the planter's capital, after deducting $1500 for plantation expenses, which must be acknowledged to be a liberal per centage on an agricultural investment.

We will now endeavour to show what the planter actually pays in duties:—

150 negroes, 5 yards each of English plains, at 40 cents per yard,	- - - - - -	300
Osnaburgs for 150 negroes, at 60 cents each,	-	90
Plantation tools, &c.	- - - -	100
1050 yards cotton bagging, at 20 cents per yard,		210
		700
Woollen and cotton cloth for family,	- -	250
Other dutiable articles, in addition to those enumerated, estimated at	- - - - - -	400
		$1350

The above is the cost of the articles *without duty;* the Government, we will suppose, charges 45 per cent. duty on the $1350, amounting to $596. On the planter's gross income this gives a fraction over 9¼ bales out of every hundred, instead of 40 as estimated by Mr. M'Duffie. The cost of the articles, with duty added, amounts to $1946, which is allowing nearly one-third of the planter's gross income to be expended in articles, raised in price 45 per cent. in consequence of duties.

NO. 18.

It is evident from the statement we annexed to the last number, that the utmost amount of duty paid by the Planter of South-Carolina to the Federal Government, is 10 per cent. on his gross income, or ten bales of Cotton out of every hundred he raises within the year. It has also been made evident that the extreme sum he pays for protection, both in duty and bounty, is $5\frac{1}{4}$ per cent. on his gross annual revenue, or $5\frac{1}{4}$ bales of Cotton out of every hundred he raises within the year. If estimated again in a different mode, making the most liberal allowance, we have shown that the entire duty does not amount to but little more than nine and a half bales, and the protection, in bounty and duty together, to not quite five out of every hundred bales.

The estimates we have made proceed all along on the assumption, that expenditure, both productive and unproductive, is equal or nearly equal for all parts of the country. This has, however, been denied. It has been contended that the *aggregate* of expense in agriculture, regarding the *number* of hands employed, and not merely *individual* consumption, is larger at the South than at the North, and that as the classes not engaged in this section of the Union, in the culture of the soil, live more luxuriously than similar classes at the North, the burthens of the protecting policy must consequently fall heavier where the consumption is greatest. We feel assured that the aggregate of consumption in the Southern States generally, is not greater, if it is not even less, than for other sections of the Union. We admit that it is impossible to form a correct notion of the sum total of the expenditure in production of two different parts of a country, employing slave and free labour respectively, simply from a comparison of their *numbers*. The greater *effectiveness* of free labour would render such a comparison entirely fallacious. We are satisfied that it requires twice, if not thrice, the number of labourers in bond to what it requires in voluntary services, to produce an equal value, or to speak with more precision, an equal *net income* from the soil or in any other pursuit whatever.

It is no use here to dwell on the causes and consequences of this difference. The fact is so. We are *compelled* to employ a species of labour, which from principles of universal operation is far less effective than any other equal amount of voluntary service whatever. This forces us to reduce our expenditure *in some quarter*, to enable us to derive the ordinary profit in agriculture. The whole mystery of the matter, if any, is unravelled by the simple fact, *that the standard of comfort for our labouring population is necessarily reduced far below that of other parts of the Union, not being compelled to employ a similar class of rural labourers*. Without a reduction of our productive expenses, corresponding to the greater number of Agricultural labourers we are compelled to employ, it would be impossible to cultivate the Southern region scarcely at all, and certainly not within fifty miles of the sea-board. It would be impracticable to raise a value for foreign markets, unless with this reduction of expense, that would yield a net income of 3 or even 2 per cent. per annum.

It is scarcely possible to ascertain with any certainty the difference of *aggregate* expense in maintaining those in bond and those free, when comparing those parts of the country which employ them respectively. The average annual hire of a rural labourer at the South is about $50. The same expense to a Northern Farmer is about $150, estimating three hundred working days at fifty cents per day. This is a difference of *one* to *three*. In other words a grower of wheat at the North is not compelled, from the greater effectiveness of free labour, to employ more than *one* hand, where *three* would be necessary, all other things being equal, to produce the same net income, to the Planter of Cotton at the South. If we allow, therefore, the annual hire to be as *three* to *one*, or as $150 is to $50, then this would measure the difference in the *number* of labours required at the South in the cultivation of the soil to what is required at the North. If this is admitted, it follows that the *aggregate* of the expenses of production, as far as labour is concerned, must be equal between the two divisions of the Union.

But there is a higher average rate of Agricultural profit at the South than at the North, or, in other words, a larger net income from the employment of an equal capital in raising cotton to what there is derived from the growing of wheat in these two divisions of the country respectively. Now as regards certain sections of the Southern country, this arises from superior natural fertility. As relates to the Southwestern States, for instance, it is the effect of the bounty of nature. But as relates to the other divisions of the Southern section, it is the result of a smaller expenditure in production. There can be no other conceivable cause for the difference. There are but two modes by which a difference of Agricultural profit is produced. First: greater natural or acquired fertility; and, second: less expense in production. As regards the Southern States, generally, the higher profit they enjoy, or larger net returns they derive from Agricultural investment, is not produced, we know from improvement of the soil, or skill in the arts of husbandry, or in the application of labour. It can originate in nothing but the same cause that compels us to reduce the standard of comfort for our slaves from their comparative ineffectiveness, that we may receive a fair remuneration or living profit on our capital. Whatever, therefore, may be the difference between the rate of agricultural profit between the North and the most northern portion of the Southern States measures the difference of their expenses in production.

The general rate of interest, allowing for temporary fluctuations in the money market, is a fair measure of the difference of profit, in comparing countries, or sections of the same country of which Agriculture forms the main pursuit. On any other supposition the level of profit could not be maintained. It is by the equality of the return, having regard to the *aggregate* of the annual outlay, that capital is kept in equilibrium not only between different employments in the same country, but between different countries and different divisions of the same country, regard being had to the greater or less risk and the greater or fewer enjoyments, real or imaginary, connected with particular climates. We have seen how rapidly our Virginia friends turned their tobacco into cotton fields, as soon as the inducement was sufficient, and we beheld how equally rapid has been the emigration of capital from one portion of the Southern country to another, more naturally fertile, from the same inducement. Were this not a general law governing all parts of the Union—were there higher profits in one section as compared with another than in proportion to the risk and other peculiarities attending climate, taking into view the relative expenses of production and the relative money value in foreign markets of the produce raised, nothing could prevent the flow of capital from the North to the South until the equilibrium was restored.

It is obvious from these considerations, that the *aggregate* of our expenditure, with regard at least to that portion of our population employed in rural labours, is less than in other sections of the Union, by the difference in the general rate of agricultural profit between the larger portion of the Southern country and those other sections. If the difference in the general rate of interest should be thought to measure this difference of profit, then, whatever that may be, would also measure the difference between Southern expenses in production and similar expenses in other parts of the Union. The burthen of protection does not fall, therefore, with greater but rather with less severity on the Southern States, than on other portions of the Confederacy engaged in the labours of Agriculture, as far at least as relates to the expenses of production. It will be recollected that better than one-half of the Southern population consists of slaves.

As relates to the other classes at the South, if they are admitted to be more luxurious than similar classes in the other divisions of the Union, this difference cannot exceed that which we have endeavoured to show subsists between their expenses in production. But it must also be admitted that the greater severity of a Northern climate requires a larger consumption of woollens, an article more heavily protected than other descriptions of imported merchandize, and that the balance is in this way more than restored.

NO. 19.

Having contended that the protecting duties operate on all parts of the Union in proportion to their relative income from foreign commerce, and in this aspect a National evil, we are not insensible to the benefit yielded by those duties to the States which exclusively enjoy the income and expenditure they produce. We have endeavoured to show that the entire tax paid for protection is equal to an assessment of thirteen millions, or about 4¼ per cent. per annum on the income of that portion of the people of the United States engaged in foreign trade, estimating that income at three hundred millions of dollars. On this estimate it amounts to about one dollar on each man, woman and child in the United States, and one dollar and fifty cents on that portion of the people, supposed to be connected, directly or indirectly, with the foreign commercial intercourse of the Union. Now, the Manufacturers cannot constitute at present more than one-twenty-fifth part of the whole population. They were computed by the Census of 1820 at 349,247. If they now amount to 500,000, it would give them an increase of about 40 per cent. in the last ten years; and if we suppose that there are an *equal number* engaged in agricultural pursuits, who depend on the consumption of the Manufacturers to absorb the surplus they create, it would be a liberal estimate.

On this calculation there would be one million of persons, directly and indirectly interested in the expenditure of thirteen millions of dollars, raised from the rest of the population interested in the foreign commerce of the country; or, in other words, between at least eight and nine millions of persons are taxed for the benefit of one million; or to state the fact in another form, each man, woman and child in the United States, whose income is in any manner dependent on that commerce, exclusive of those benefited by domestic manufactures, may be considered as assessed in the sum of one dollar and fifty cents annually, to put in the pockets of each person so benefited $13 annually.

This tax, it must, however, be kept in recollection, although an exclusive advantage to *particular States*, and in this aspect a *sectional advantage*, yet is the price paid for monopoly by a large majority of the people of those States, in common with the people of the rest of the Union. It should be considered as a sum raised from the income of at least between eight and nine millions of persons, for the benefit of one million, between five and six millions of which happen to occupy the same section as the one million. This *accidental* circumstance should not be deemed sufficient to detach them from the other portions of the people of the United States, who have a community of interest with them. They are common sharers of a common burthen, not for any National good, but simply and solely to enrich the few at the expense of the many.

We have now gone through that branch of our subject, in all its different divisions but one, which embraces the *present* or *existing* evils of protecting duties. That other division is the relation of our *income* to our *ordinary expenditure*, and to our *money engagements*. These are most important topics, in explanation of our present embarrassments. All who possess powers of observation could not have failed to remark that the general scale of our expenses continues to be adjusted to a standard of income with which it bears no just ratio. Can it be with truth affirmed, that we have reduced our ordinary expenditure, generally, in proportion to the reduction of our income, since money has become twice as valuable as it was ten years since? Can it be contended that we have lessened our usual expenses in the ratio that our revenue has been curtailed, in the period of the last five years, during which our principal staple has fallen in price 30 per cent.? Let all who are insisting that the disproportion between our revenue and our expenses is exclusively attributable to the Tariff, look into their household establishments with a courageous mind, and a scrutinizing eye—let them sum up the items, small as they may seem, of their expenditure, and compare the aggregate with the aggregate of their expenditure only five years since—as relates to their income now and their income then. Let them cast a glance of only one moment on but one item of that expenditure, *the number of their household servants*, who are rapidly eating out their substance, and then honestly pronounce whether this single branch of their unproductive expenses does not go far beyond the standard of their income, and exceed, far exceed, any thing but what would be justified by hereditary opulence? Let us be candid—let us be self-accusatory, if justice demands it—let us concede all to truth that is due to truth, when we declare, in the face of the world, the Tariff to be an odious monopoly!

We come now to the subject of our *money contracts*, and we ask, if much, very much of our present embarrassment is not imputable to the disproportion between our engagements and the money value we can command to discharge them, owing to the fall in the price of our staples from over production? We ask whether lands and slaves contracted for when produce was 30 per cent. higher than at present would not impoverish any but the most skilful manager and the most provident spender? This fall has taken place in five years, and looking at the usual period in which a borrowed capital is doubled, we inquire, in the spirit of truth, what must become of all that property now under mortgage in the face of a reduction of 30 per cent. in the value of the income with which the debt it secures is to be discharged, unless liberal indulgence is given, and the most prudent management and economical expenditure follow. Let these questions be answered in all candour and sincerity, and the causes of a great portion of the existing embarrassment in the State of South-Carolina are at once explained.

On this branch of our subject we have a few words to add as to the effects of Absenteeism. That this practice is sufficient of itself, if extensively pursued, to impoverish the wealthiest country, the instance of Ireland is a most striking and calamitous proof. It divorces those from each other which should be intimately united by the interchanges of internal commerce. It separates the possessors of income from those, who, by their labour, contribute to that income. Unless there is a reflux of the revenue, in expenditure, of which labour forms an integral part, an essential element, the sources of individual wealth must be soon exhausted, and rapid and general impoverishment follow. The Irish landlord will find ere long the limit of his revenue from his rents, if the other classes besides those connected with the soil receive none of the benefit of his expenditure.*

Can the planter of South-Carolina expect different results on the general prosperity, from the same custom? Can he expect to behold the aspect of smiling industry around him, while he spends his revenue far from his vicinage? Can he expect his neighbourhood to put on any other than the face of poverty, while his income is lavishly bestowed on that labour which fertilizes a distant territory, and builds up towns and villages abroad? It is impossible to say to what degree of general impoverishment this practice may not lead, in the Southern section of the Union, united especially, as it is, with that spirit of gain, which, restless after rapid accumulation of wealth, is impatient of slow returns wrought from reluctant nature. It is sufficiently destructive to our present interests, and the most injurious of impediments to progressive future improvement, that a more inviting country than we possess, stretching to the South and West, with almost boundless limits, and irresistibly tempting,

* The British Government have now in serious contemplation, judging from the debates in Parliament, to introduce the *principle* of the Poor Laws into Ireland, as a check to the practice of Absenteeism. Not such a compulsory poor's rate as exists in England, but the substance of Elizabeth's celebrated statute, free from the perversion or misapplication of its salutary principle, in actual practice in England, by which any deficiency, as to wages, is made up out of the allotted poor's rate. This extension of the principle of that system to Ireland is deemed essential to the salvation of the sister Kingdoms, for the separation of the Irish landlords from the rural peasantry of Ireland, by the annual emigration of the former to England and the Continent, to spend their incomes, throws, at certain periods of every year, numbers of the latter on the shores of England and Scotland, who work for such reduced wages, that it threatens to bring the whole labouring population of the three Kingdoms to one common level of misery and destitution

from the richness of its virgin soil, to the spirit of change and adventure, should drive a part of the Southern population to constant emigration, and to give up their inheritance to waste and sterility from ruinous exhaustion. But this injury receives a most fearful aggravation from the practice of Absenteeism. The first is an all pervading cause of the increasing poverty of the Northern section of the Southern States: and they are together concurring and almost constantly operating causes of that distress which is spreading with rapidity over almost the whole lower region of South-Carolina.

Nor in illustrating the causes of a distress which is *all-pervading*, and not merely *local*, should the circumstance be overlooked, of the change, within the last fifteen years, of the commercial relations of the whole civilized world. We are a part of the great community of nations, and the transitions from war to peace must affect the whole and every part. As we have shared in the profits which accompanied general hostilities, so must we participate in the reverses that attend a general pacification. Capital, manual exertion, inventive power, and practical skill, have been diverted in an unexampled degree from those employments which ministered to the wants and demands of war, and are hourly enlarging the circle and multiplying the labours of peace. In all departments of business—in all modes of commercial activity—in all the varieties of agricultural enterprize—in each sphere, great and small, of adventurous industry, a spirit of the most boundless competition and untiring energy has entered. It would be singular if under such circumstances the Southern States, and South-Carolina in particular, should escape the effects of a change so general in its operation.

NO. 20.

Having, we trust, established that the Protecting System injures the prosperity and, lessens the resources of the Southern States, in no higher proportion than their relative income, we come now to a consideration of the *probable consequences* of that system, if persisted in and run out to its final results, on their capital and industry. While we contend that its *present* operation is not *unequal*, and that the Southern States suffer from it no *partial* injustice, we must concede that its *prospective* effects threaten irreparable injury to their revenue. It is *here* that the Protecting System will bear with unequal pressure on the resources of the South. It is to the *future* we must look for that suffering, distress and inequality, which, it is falsely affirmed, the Southern States now sustain from that system.

This, as we have always contended, is the strong point of our case, and which too many of our public men have comparatively neglected, to dwell like unskilful advocates (we speak with no feeling of disrespect) on untenable positions, which, in proportion as they were susceptible of overthrow, by the most ordinary practical men, did the great cause of Free Trade the worst of injuries. If it did not lose, for that cause, some supporters, it threw on our particular case discredit, from *exaggeration*. That we suffer a loss of income of 40 per cent. or that our great staple of export, is reduced in value *in this proportion*, by the operation of protecting duties, is an allegation which, if true, would prove the system that supports them, not only the most exorbitant scheme of assessment that ever the ingenuity of man devised. but would, before this, have impoverished the country, compelled to bear it, more rapidly than any plan of taxation of which history gives an account. *One tenth* of the gross annual produce of the land in England, for the support of the Church, is thought to constitute an immense burthen on the Landlord. What effect would *four times* the amount of this assessment produce in a similar pursuit? Could the most unbounded fertility of soil, or the most skilful application of labour, sustain it four years together? We answer, impossible that it could!

Now, let us look for one moment to the *future*. Let us see what this system *threatens*. Let us cast but a glance towards the imports from Great-Britain, for a few years past, to judge of the *probable consequences* of this system, if not abandoned. Great-Britain purchases four-fifths of our whole supply of Cotton. She takes between twenty-six and twenty-seven millions of dollars of the whole value of this article. Our imports from that country, and its dependencies in Europe, have fallen off in *absolute* amount, on an average of the four years from 1826 to 1829, inclusive, as compared with the average of four years from 1822 to 1825, inclusive, $2,263,302, and diminished *relatively to the increase of our population* within that time, nearly $5,000,000 annually. The population of the Union having increased within the last ten years, about 40 per cent., our imports from Great-Britain should have amounted by this time to about thirty-six millions of dollars, instead of being, as at present, between twenty-nine and thirty millions. Mr. Baring lately stated in his place in the British Parliament, to show the superior importance of the British trade to Mexico, as compared with that to the United States, that they stood as fifty to thirty millions of dollars, in favour of the former. This is a plain proof of the great relative diminution of our commerce with Great-Britain.

When, however, these facts are taken in connection with the natural capabilities of those British Colonies which have, and may again furnish almost unlimited supplies of the raw material of the British Cotton manufacture, the apprehensions from this source are any thing but groundless. Under a moderate stimulus to production, the quantity of cotton which has been poured into Great-Britain from the East-Indies, is almost inconceivable. In the year 1816, the supply from that quarter was not larger than about 30,000 bales, for British consumption, although it had occasionally before reached a much higher amount. But in 1817, only one year after, it increased to about 120,000 bales, and in the succeeding year, it rose to nearly 250,000, at that time constituting one-half of the whole British consumption, and now forming one-third of that consumption, thus increasing *eight-fold* in *two years.* Can any fact be more striking and conclusive to establish the capacity of the British dominions in the East, to furnish, under a moderate stimulus to cultivation, a full supply equal to all the British wants, in four or five years?

When it is recollected also, that the British Government are now on the eve of determining whether they shall or shall not renew the charter of the East-India Company, these fears are much strengthened. We do not expect that that charter will be wholly abolished, but it will and must be essentially modified. What will be the effect of transferring British capital and skill to the East, under such a modification of this charter as will permit British subjects to hold and cultivate land in that quarter, so as fully to develope its productive powers, we need not state to the intelligent reader. No British subject can now cultivate land in the East but under restrictions imposed by the East-India Company, which check the investment of capital.* When the

---

* No British subject can even resort to that portion of the East under the dominion of the Company, without a license from it. This license is frequently an object of patronage, and when obtained, is clogged with various fees and forms. No British subject can go beyond ten miles of one of the seats of Government, which are the Presidencies of Calcutta, Madras and Bombay, without a special license from the Company. All British subjects are prohibited from engaging in the great *inland trade* in the principal staples, nor are they permitted to hold or farm lands without the limits of the above towns, and the remedy for the abuse of this privilege, is summary deportation —that is, if found without those limits they may be seized, imprisoned and sent within the bounds allotted them, by the meanest of the Company's servants. When allowed to cultivate land within the prescribed limits, the Company takes, as tax, nine-tenths of the rent of all lands, estimating such rent, generally, at *one-half* of the gross produce of the soil,

From an examination before the East-India Committee, recently appointed to inquire into the affairs of the Company, it appears from the evidence of Mr. Rickards, formerly an eminent India merchant, that the Company not only take one-half the cotton crop in kind, but the ryots or cultivators are compelled to surrender the other half to the Company's agents at a certain price, agreed on by a committee, consisting of the judge, the collector and the commercial resident of the district. This price was stated, by Mr. Ricards, to be far below what could have been obtained from private merchants. The consequence is a great obstruction to the cotton trade of India.

This detail is entered into to show what is likely to be the consequences, as to an increase of the quantity and melioration of the quality of cotton, as has been the case with Indigo, if only a portion of these restrictions on the enterprize and skill of British subjects in India should be removed, on the renewal of the charter of the Company.

motive is given by our prohibitory policy for the removal of those restrictions—when the inducement is still more strengthened by the enlargement of an increasing market for British manufactures in the East—when it is recollected that 130,000,000 of people in that quarter acknowledge either the sway or influence of the Britsh sceptre—when it is seen that the standard of comfort for the population of the East is far below that of our slaves, in so far that a discriminating duty of 7 shillings per cwt. in favour of West-India over East-India Sugar is necessary to counteract the superior cheapness of East-India as compared with West-India labour—when the force of all these circumstances is candidly admitted, we know not how it can be contended that our capital is not threatened with irreparable loss.

It must also be admitted that if it be the interest of Great-Britain to procure her supply of Cotton from her Colonies in the East, she will pursue the dictates of that policy which induced her to encourage the cultivation of Indigo in that quarter of her empire, whether or not we persist in following out our scheme of restrictions.

NO. 21.

We have affirmed that a persistance in restrictive measures, threatens an irreperable loss to the Southern States. To what can we resort as a substitute for a staple of export that will not diminish our revenue and our wealth materially? To what shall we apply our capital in Slaves where we may not meet disastrous competition? To sustain the value of that capital depends on the possession of foreign markets for a product in which there is some limit to competition from peculiarity of climate. Pass that limit, and our property in slaves and lands may be reduced one third if not one half in value. A value of 600 millions of dollars, to estimate merely that of our slaves, is not to be put in jeopardy to sustain 200 millions, which constitute the utmost amount invested in protected manufactures, without the grossest violation of rules of ordinary equity, as well as the principles and spirit of our National compact.

We hold it to be indisputable that we can have recourse to no species of profitable cultivation or form of successful industry wherein our climate does not give us a decided advantage, and consequently exclude competition within certain limits. We may reduce our scale of living, so as to enable us to cultivate an agricultural product common to the South as well as to the North, but where should we find the markets for Wheat or any other such product? Nor can we change our culture for any other form of investment, without such a loss of capital as would threaten general ruin. The slowness of the return, or the limitation of the market for any of the articles which have been mentioned as substitutes for our peculiar staples, must render all attempts at a change of this nature hopeless, unless with such a revolution of our habits as would make existence scarcely tolerable.

The same remark is applicable to Manufacturing in the Southern States. It is mere mockery in reply to our objection against restrictions on our foreign commerce, that they threaten ruin to our interests, to tell us there is no *monopoly*, for we are free to enter, in common with other parts of the country, into this pursuit.. Independently of the fact, of itself, that from the greater effectivenes of free, as compared with slave labour, which forbids any species of industry of which climate does not confer an advantage, how can it be seriously contended, that there is no privilege conferred where the possession of extensive coal districts, (which must become the principal seats of Manufactures) the density of population, and abundance of capital, give natural and factitious aids, which it would be vain for a division of the country, destitutue of these aids, to contend against. Now the change or removal of capital from one employment to another, in a section of country where circumstances render it a comparatively safe operation, presents some compensation, or at least the promise of it, for the present or future loss of those who suffer in such section from monopoly. We have seen with what apparent facility large capitals have been transferred in the Northern and Eastern States, from commerce and navigation to manufactures. Although, therefore, the present loss or disadvantage from restrictions on our foreign commerce, bears on all parts of the country in something approaching to equality, it follows, that from natural or acquired advantages for manufacturing of the more densely peopled portions of this Union, the prospective injury to this division of the Confederacy, threatens a most grievous inequality.

From the whole of this examination we think we are warranted in affirming, that we have demonstrated, as far, at least, as such a subject is susceptible of the mode of proof we have adopted, the truth of the following principal positions :

1st. That the tax for protection on the people of the United States amounts at the present period to about 13 millions of dollars per annum, about one half of which is paid in duty and the other half in bounty.

2d. That the loss to the Union from the protecting policy, being in proportion to its income from foreign trade, that proportion is about *one-fourth* of the whole annual revenue of those engaged in that trade.

3d. That this loss should be apportioned nearly according to relative numbers between the different parts of the Confederacy, and that the Southern States sustain their share of the general loss at least in no greater than this ratio.

4th. That, granting this, whatever taxes for protection diminish the money value in foreign markets of Southern in common with Northern produce, by an unavoidable reaction, fall equally on the owners of American shipping, and mercantile capital engaged in carrying on the foreign export and import trade of the country, as well as on the growers of Northern and Western produce transported inland and coastwise to the Southern portions of the Union.

5th. That the restrictive system has not reduced the price of our principal staples, particularly cotton, although it must, of consequence, have lessened the demand for those staples, in proportion to the sum applicable to the purchase of foreign commodities.

6th. That on these principles the loss to South-Carolina, from that system, is about $500,000 annually, in bounty and duty together, or about 5 per cent. per annum on her annual revenue.

7th. That much of the present distress and pecuniary embarrassment in this section of the Union is attributable, first, to absenteeism; second, to emigration to more fertile territory; third, to a con-tinuance in a style of living and scale of general expense beyond a proper standard of expenditure, in reference to that reduction of income which has been common to all countries.

8th. That the prospective injury from restrictions on our foreign commerce threatens the most pernicious inequality, and if fully carried out to the point of prohibition, will probably be attended with the depopulation and abandonment of the whole lower region of the Southern States. Some general reflections will close this series of essays.

—

NO. 22.

We wish to renew the effort we made some years since, for the purpose of procuring the co-operation of the people of the Manufacturing States in the abolition of the miscalled "American System." We are anxious to prove that they participate with us in bearing a very heavy tax on their powers to produce, as well as their ability to consume. We think it is by such views that the blows already received by that system may be followed up by others, which, in the end, will prostrate it. But, to produce this salutary effect, we must not overstate our case. It is a very strong one, without exaggeration. We have endeavoured to show that if the scheme of protection is carried out to its intended results, the loss and the suffering of the Southern States will be out of all proportion to what would be inflicted on the other portions of the Confederacy. We would be obliged to turn our capital into new and untried channels. We will have unsettled our whole scheme of industry. We will have overthrown the very foundations of our prosperity. When we are rendered unable to exchange our staples for their European equivalents, the very spring and fountain head of our resources will have been sealed—the grand reservoir of our comforts will have been closed. We will have suffered out of all comparison to that part of our Northern and Western brethren who are sharers with us in the *present* inflictions of monopoly. Such is the inevitable tendency of the system. It will curtail the wealth of the North, but it may leave us scarcely a fragment of our riches.

We have been steady opponents of that system in all its stages. We have been the decided, the uncompromising enemy of monopoly, we may say it, without the imputation of presumption, ever since we have been connected with a public press, which has been for upwards of fifteen years. When we differ from our leading public men, we must be allowed credit, therefore, for our sincerity. We have given the subject, in all its aspects, much close and anxious reflection. The conclusions at which we have arrived do not render the great Southern cause the weaker, if those conclusions have a basis of truth. We repeat that it is by disenchanting the majority of the Northern and Western public of the delusion which the sinister arts of monopoly have worked on their minds, that the system must finally receive its stroke of death. It is by showing how their interests are bound up with the interests of the South, that a scheme of unequal protection will ever meet its real fate. Let us then unite in this task all who have any powers by which public opinion may be shaped to those issues that will vindicate the spirit of our republican system, with which monopoly is at war.

But let us not be misunderstood. We are for getting rid of this system by no means that will place the Union of these States at hazard. We should consider it a less evil to have this system, with all its *attendant losses* and *prospective risks* to a *separation of the States.* We should prefer making a large sacrifice even to the odious spirit of monopoly, sooner than break up and scatter, never to be re-united, the elements of this glorious scheme of Republican Federative Government.

We affirm that no Statesman is justified in placing at hazard the peace and prosperity of those who are under his guardianship, in contemplation of the occurrence of a probable evil. We insist that the ill-tendency merely, of public measures, furnishes no justifiable ground of resistance, if that resistance is to be any thing but what is usual and regular. There are risks, it must be admitted, in proceeding to treat the legislation of Congress in a different manner to what is deemed by the rest of the Union to be constitutional. We are utterly in the dark, as to what those risks are. They may result in opposition---they may result in peaceable separation. There may be neither bloodshed, nor any of the attendant horrors of civil war.

But, let an issue the least injurious to our interests be imagined, and the hazard to our welfare in the one case, from the modes of resistance which have been proposed in South-Carolina, must far outweigh the risk in the other case, from the consequences of the Protective policy, at least in its present aspect. It is the duty of Southern Statesmen to weigh one probable risk of this kind against another. We can imagine a case in which it would be wise as well as honorable and patriotic, to encounter every hazard in the maintenance of our privileges, and in defence of our peculiar institutions. But we do say, that the present crisis has not furnished such a case, and we lose neither honour nor patriotism in weighing one evil in perspective against another, in determining our choice.

Now let a result, as we have just said, the least injurious to our welfare be conceived---let it be supposed that we will be at liberty to adopt our own remedy, and continue free, without molestation or hindrance from the rest of the States, to trade with all the world, according to our own sense of our own interests; we ask, if any man will venture positively to affirm, that if in that event the value of our property would not be materially impaired—that an emigration of capital would not take place to an injurious extent ? We ask, will any accurate observer of human nature hazard the assertion that that value is not dependent on *Union*— on a perception or feeling of security, derived from that source ? Persons who argue on a contrary presumption, know not how small a weight will turn the balance in favour of emigration, and the disruption of all local attachments, when the sense of security is in the least degree tampered with. This is delicate ground on wh ch for the Statesman to tread, and he cannot acquit himself properly in his great trust and function, if he does not shape his measures accordingly.

But it is said if we do not *now* resist we shall be deprived of the power *hereafter* to do so with any effect, from the diminution of our resources. Here we think there is a great mistake. Those who reason on this principle look forward to the possibility of a contest for the preservation of our property, and the power connected with it. We do not like to weigh such possibilities, but the topic has been frequently introduced in essays and speeches, and in a manner forced on us. Now, we think it a radical error to suppose that our *real power* would be either increased or diminished from the increase or diminution of our *wealth*. Wealth is not power in the same sense in the New World as in the Old. Great Britain fought the great battles of National Independence with Buonaparte, by hiring the disposable numbers of the Nations of the Continent. Her wealth is an important element of power, in maintaining the balance of Europe, for she has only to subsidize the Continental cabinets, by taking their mercenaries into pay, to preserve the equipoise. But where are our trained bands---the Swiss who fight for pay---in the United States? Where could any portion of the Union hire them, if disposed to fight either their foreign or their domestic battles by their employment? Would any of the States of this Union invite the legions of the old world across the Atlantic, either as Allies or as Mercenaries, to fight in the names of liberty and law? We say impossible. Let, therefore, any part of the Union be more or less wealthy, absolutely, or comparatively, makes no difference in a question of strength. Mere wealth then is no element of political power in the new world, where men are not driven into armies from want, unless the free States which occupy its territory should permit the corrupt politics of Europe to blend with their civil controversies, and its mercenary forces, to determine their contests as to the true limits of Constitutional power and obligation.

APPENDIX III

Systems of Banking and Currency

The Southern Review, April 1870

Art. V.—1. *An Inquiry into the Currency Principle.* By
   Thomas Tooke. London: 1844.

2. *A History of Prices, and of the State of the Circulation.*
   By Thomas Tooke. London: 1856.

3. *An Essay on the Production of Wealth.* By R. Torrens.
   London: 1821.

4. *Ways and Means of Payment, a Full Analysis of the
   Credit System with its Modes of Adjustment.* By S.
   Colwell. Philadelphia: 1860.

There are two evils in a system of mixed currency against
which society has to provide safeguards: 1. An irredeemable
paper currency employed as a fiscal resource to defray the
public expenditure. 2. An undue extension of private credit,
through the agency of banks, in mercantile loans and discounts.

The subject will be most conveniently discussed under two
general heads: 1. The regulation of Currency. 2. The regulation of Credit. Before we enter on the discussion, it is our
purpose to take a rapid survey of the English system of banking and currency from the earliest period to the present time.
The record of British failures in this department of legislation,
affords several instructive lessons.

In rapidly sketching the history of English banking, we do
not think it essential to ascend higher than the incorporation
of the Bank of England; for, although a few of the Scotch
banks were of an earlier date, owing to a peculiarity of organization they do not afford so much instruction as the English
system of banking, as they were not subjected to so many fluctuations and vicissitudes.

There are four epochs in the history of English banking. 1. From the establishment of the Bank of England in
1707, when corporate banking and the issue of paper money in
the form of bank notes were first introduced in England. 2.
From the suspension of specie payments by that institution in
1707, until their resumption in 1822. 3. From the resumption
of specie payments until the enactment of Sir Robert Peel's

bill in 1844. 4. From the passing of that act to the present
time. In the first of these epochs, the impolicy of legislative
interference in the institution and management of banks, and
the danger of any connection between a National bank and
the Government, are signally exhibited.

The history of banking in England commences with monopoly and ends in restriction. It is almost needless to state, as it
must be known to all who have any acquaintance with the
subject, that the Bank of England had the exclusive privilege
of banking within sixty-five miles of London, and that no partnership could be formed with more than six persons to carry on
the business of banking. Among the earliest fruits of this restriction, was the failure of a large number of private banks in
1793. In that year the number of these institutions 'was
supposed to be three hundred and eighty-five.'[1] From 1810
to 1816 inclusive, no fewer than one hundred and forty-seven
commissions of bankruptcy had been issued against country
banks, and in thirty years nearly three hundred,—an average
of failures in proportion to the total number of these establishments exceeding that of any other regular business.[2] It is
needless to add, that if more than six partners had been allowed
to form such associations, persons of large capitals would have
united, and the risks of failure would have been greatly diminished.

There was great enlargement of public and private enterprises within the twenty-five years previous to 1795. 'Taking
into consideration,' says Mr. McLeod, 'the two periods, that from
1770 to 1795 was fully as wonderful an effort in canal-making as
the period from 1830 to 1855 was in railway-making. Concurrently with this prodigious extension of the facilities of transport, an equal extension of the powers of production took
place. . . . . It was just at this period that the original sin
of the monopoly of the Bank of England began to tell with full
force upon the country. Now were the seeds of future ruin,
misery, and desolation, sown broadcast throughout the land.
The prodigious development of all these industrial works de-

---

[1] McCulloch's Commercial Dictionary.

[2] Essay on Banking in England and Holland. By T. Joplin.

manded a great extension of the currency to carry them on. What was required was to have banks of undoubted wealth and solidity to issue such a currency. Bank of England notes had no circulation beyond London. Its monopoly prevented any other great banks being formed, either in London or in the country, and it would not extend its branches into the country. Scotland, at this time, possessed three great and powerful joint stock banks, and it was just at this period that they began successfully to extend their branches into the country. England required to have a currency, and as it could not have a good one, it had a bad. Multitudes of miserable shop-keepers in the country, grocers, tailors, drapers, started up like mushrooms and turned bankers, and issued their notes—inundating the country with their miserable rags—men as different from the bankers of London, as the chief of a savage tribe is from the sovereign of Great Britain. In 1775 an act was passed to prohibit bankers from issuing notes of less than 20 shillings, and two years afterwards, of less than £5. It is no doubt true,' continues Mr. McLeod, 'that many of the most respectable bankers of the present day also took their rise at that time, but they were, comparatively speaking, few. The great majority were such as we have described above.'[3]

It was not till 1826 that there was any relaxation of this monopoly. In 1783 there was much alarm, but fortunately no crisis. The Bank of England 'refused to make any further advances to the government on the loan of that year, but they did not make any demand for payment of the other advances to government, which were between nine and ten millions. At length in the autumn when the favorable signs began to appear, they advanced freely to government on the loan, although at that time, the cash in the bank was actually lower than at the time they felt the greatest apprehensions.'[4]

'The period,' says Mr. McLeod, 'that succeeded the American war was one of great apparent prosperity throughout Europe.

[3] Theory and Practice of Banking. This work is an admirable repository of facts, and to it we are indebted for some of the details contained in this historical abstract. Mr. McLeod's work is not a mere statistical record, but combines political information with its statements which throw light on its general conclusions.

[4] Ibid.

People firmly believed that all wars had come to an end, and the reign of perpetual peace had begun. Mr. Tooke[5] states from his own personal recollection that there had been an enormous and undue extension of commercial speculation, not only in the internal trade and banking in this country, but also throughout Europe and the United States, for some years previous to 1792. The amount of bank notes in circulation, which was under six millions in 1784, had increased to nearly eleven millions and a half in 1792. At length in the autumn of 1792 commercial failures began both here and abroad, as well as in America. The average of bankruptcies during the first ten months had been fifty, in November they suddenly rose to one hundred and five. This unusual number created much uneasiness.'[6] The crisis was of the most severe character. Of the number of country banks, computed at the time at nearly four hundred, upwards of one hundred stopped payment. The banks of the West of England alone stood their ground. The pressure extended to the London bankers. The demand on the Bank of England for support and assistance was refused. They contracted their discounts. The government urged the Bank to come forward to support credit, but it declined. All the authorities, among them Sir Francis Baring, blamed the Bank. The most alarming accounts were received from Holland. Universal bankruptcy was threatened. A committee of the House of Commons being appointed, recommended an issue of Exchequer bills to the amount of £5,000,000. A large sum, $70,000, was sent to Holland and to Manchester. The sum applied for was £3,855,624. The transaction left a clear profit to the government of £4,348,000. We have been thus minute in recording this transaction as being the first in which direct aid to the sufferers was extended by the government, and as throwing light on a phenomenon unusual in the history of English banking. McPherson, in his *History of Commerce*, says, ' that the very intimation of the intention of the legislature to support the merchants, operated like a charm all over the country,

---

[5] Thomas Tooke, formerly a merchant of London, whose *History of Prices*, is a standard production throwing much light on the phenomena of prices, and many other topics connected with Banking and Currency.

[6] Evidence of Tooke—Committee on Bank of England Charter—1832.

and in a great degree superseded the necessity of relief by an almost instantaneous restoration of confidence.' Our readers may recollect a similar result during the crisis of 1857, in England, on its being announced that it was the intention of the government to permit the Bank to exceed the limit prescribed by the Act of 1844.

The testimony of Sir Francis Baring and Mr. Tooke is favorable to the financial condition of the country in 1794. The reaction from the crisis of 1792–93 had restored the country to apparent prosperity. The bankruptcies had greatly diminished. Gold was flowing into England in the last six months of 1793, and the two following years exhibited a tranquil money market. The interest of money fell to four per cent., and there was a difficulty in finding profitable investment for capital. This lesson had been taught by the crisis of 1792–93, that during a monetary pressure, while an unfavorable balance of trade is causing the exportation of gold, and a panic the hoarding of it, the true policy of banks is temporary expansion, to fill the void thence occasioned, and not contraction, which widens the vacuum. It was at this period that Mr. Pitt acquired his great power over the Bank of England—an acquisition exhibiting the danger of the connection between Bank and Government. Mr. Pitt wanted supplies with more rapidity than they could be furnished by taxation. He was subsidizing such of the European powers as would accept his subsidies for the formation of those coalitions against Bonaparte that were destined to crumble before the arms of the Corsican. The Bank of England was a ready resource. The subsidies paid to foreign powers in three years and a half, from 1793 to 1797, amounted to nine millions and a half, and this was not the total of the specie sent abroad, on other accounts. In the Appendix to the Lords' Committee of Secresy, the aggregate given is the large sum of £22,161,060. It would thus appear that in little more than three years, there were upwards of thirty millions of specie remitted to the continent on account of government. What portion of this was drawn from the Bank there are no means of ascertaining, but such was the magnitude of the advances as to give rise to repeated remonstrances from the Board of Directors, repeated promises from Mr. Pitt that these advances, without the previous sanction of Parliament, should be discontinued, and repeated violations of those promises.

'Several of the Directors,' says Mr. McLeod, 'being examined before the Committees of Parliament, unanimously attributed the necessity of stopping payment to the enormous amount of their advances to government, and they gave it as their opinion that if the government had repaid these advances, as they ought to have done, this great catastrophe would have been avoided.'

The first epoch, therefore, in the history of the Bank of England, which culminated in the suspension of specie payments by that institution in 1797, was marked by the crisis of 1793, the first of those periodical revolutions by which the fiscal history of England has been characterized, and by a derangement of private credit, which led to unprecedented bankruptcies, aggravated by the restriction that forbade the formation of partnerships in banking consisting of more than six partners.[7]

The period between suspension and resumption was one of controversy and discussion. It was profuse in the literature peculiar to the subject. Pamphlets, tracts, volumes, appeared in rapid succession. The press literally groaned under the burden. Bullionists and anti-Bullionists were the designations by which the parties were distinguished, according as they contended for depreciation of gold on the one hand, or enhancement of its price on the other. Some of the most remarkable examples of inconsistency were exhibited, on this occasion, in the British Parliament. Sir Robert Peel was an advocate of the views of the anti-Bullionists, a position from which he receded in 1819, when he became a convert to the doctrines of the Bullion Report. The Bullion Committee was appointed

---

[7] In condemning joint stock banking the distinction is overlooked between the conduct that leads to insolvency, and that want of prudent management which is the source of discredit. In 1793, 1816, and 1825, the numerous failures of English as well as Irish country banks, was owing to inadequate capital as well as to inexperience. Large numbers engaged in banking not only with insufficient means, but without a proper sense of moral responsibility. Surely there is a wide difference between individuals who engage in business of this character, and those who, carried away by the contagion of speculation, add to the quantity of the currency.

in 1810, and was instructed to inquire into the causes of the high price of bullion.   Their report was the first scientific exposition of the subject of the currency made by a Parliamentary Committee.   On that committee were some of the ablest members of the House of Commons—Horner, Huskisson, Burdett, Thornton, &c.   Their report excited a protracted debate, which terminated in its rejection by the Ministerial Party.   The singular doctrine was advocated by Mr. Vansittart, the Chancellor of the Exchequer, that a guinea valued in law at twenty-one shillings was, in reality, worth thirty shillings, because such was its value in paper money; and Lord Stanhope brought in a bill to punish parties who bought and sold guineas at more than their standard value, contending that a pound sterling was an ideal measure of value—an abstraction.   The gist of the controversy was, whether the currency being not exchangeable for gold, was depreciated, or whether gold had appreciated. The dispute has not been settled to this day.

In alluding to the literature of the day, connected with this subject, it is impossible to overlook the agency of Mr. David Ricardo in calling public attention to this matter.   The price of bullion, in 1809, having taken an unexpected rise, it led to the publication by him of a pamphlet with the title, *The high price of Bullion—a proof of the Depreciation of Bank Notes.* The fact of an advance in the price of bullion, was connected with a phenomenon that threw much light on the subject of paper currency.   As long as the Bank of England kept its issues within due limits—a period of twelve years, from 1797 to 1809—there was no difference between the mint or standard value of gold and its market price.   The measure of the issue was the mercantile and public, not the government, wants. But as soon as the Bank increased its advances for the public service, the effect was immediate.   Bullion rose in price.   The further rise of it that followed the extension of the war to the Spanish Peninsula, and the absolute necessity of the remittance of gold to supply the British military chest, left no doubt that the rise was, in some measure, the consequence of those advances, which, if they were partly in notes and partly in specie, would account at once for the depreciation of the paper currency, and the simultaneous rise in the price of gold. This practical result led to an extremely important theoretical deduction. It showed that if the issues of banks were kept within due limits, it would supersede the necessity of specie payments, a doctrine that had been forcibly presented in the *Edinburg Review* for February, 1826.

It was not until the modification of the usury law that the Bank brought into operation the most convenient mode of contracting the currency, namely, through the rate of discount. The limitation of five per cent. had precluded it from advancing the rate beyond that limit. After the removal of the restriction, the Bank increased its rate to ten per cent., and, we believe, at one period, to twelve per cent. The old mode of contracting the currency was by the sale of Exchequer bills, but this was attended with the disadvantage of reducing their market price. It may be said, therefore, that the modification of the usury law was productive of a total change in the policy of the Bank of England. The action of the Bank previous to the removal of the restriction, was precisely similar to that of the country banks when they desired to contract the currency. They rejected the bills or notes offered for discount, or they sold Exchequer bills. The only criterion by which they were guided was the abstraction of gold from their vaults. The testimony of Mr. Harman and Mr. Dorrien, governors of the Bank, in their examination before the secret committee of 1819, is conclusive on this point. Mr. Harman was asked, 'What regulates, in your opinion, the amount of circulating medium which is necessary for the purposes of the country; is it the amount of revenue and expenditure, and the general amount of foreign trade in the country; or on what other circumstances does the amount of the circulating medium depend? —I should think decidedly what has been suggested, the amount required for the revenue and the general expenditure, and what is wanted for inland and foreign trade.' This was, no doubt, the true index of the amount of circulating medium necessary for the purposes of the country, but it was no answer to the following question put by one of the committee: 'What is the indication of there being circulation enough in the coun-

try, neither too much nor too little, and what is the regulator
that determines that sufficiency?—If it is meant to allude to
discounts, I should have only the old answer to give: *undoubt-
edly good paper* being sent into the Bank for discount, of
which we must judge the best we can, *that is the criterion.*'
Here is a plain avowal, that the solvency of the applicants for
discounts is the only criterion of the issues—in other words,
the general wants of the mercantile public were the only regulator of the Bank's issues. Mr. Dorrien's testimony is to the
same effect.

That there was a striking change of opinion in the management of the Bank, marking a new epoch in the history of
English banking, appears from the answer of Mr. Ward, a
director, in 1832, who said in his evidence, 'In the year 1819,
when the committee sat, there were some resolutions forwarded
to the committee from the Bank, stating some of the principles
they had regarded; and it will be recollected that they dis-
tinctly denied the principle, that the exchanges were to be regarded in regulating the issues. Subsequently to that period,
opinions changed, and, of course, in the working of the machinery, they found the merits of the case such as they really
were; and a growing disposition manifested itself to heed, in a
greater degree than they hitherto had done, the principles of
exchange and bullion; but in 1827, I moved that that resolution
should be rescinded, and from that moment I have considered
it the practice of the Bank, and it was the practice, in a great
degree, even previously to that. . . . . It was first considered
a theoretical notion, but subsequently it was found, little by
little, that the practice did agree with the theory.'

It will be recollected that the principle here alluded to, was
that which formed one of the fundamental doctrines of the
Bullion report of 1810, to wit, that the issues of the Bank of
England ought to be regulated by the state of the foreign exchange and the price of bullion—that Samuel Jones Lloyd pro-
nounced it a new and auspicious era in English banking. It
will not excite surprise, therefore, that it has, to this day,
formed the rule of the Bank of England in regulating its issues.
But it should excite surprise when we state that adherence to

this rule has been the source of almost all those fluctuations in the value of money and in prices, which has characterized the history of English banking and currency, since its adoption about the year 1830.

None of the controversies connected with the currency gave rise to more bitter disputes than that about the influence, supposed or real, of Sir Robert Peel's act, in 1819, for the resumption of specie-payments. It has always appeared to us to be more verbal than real. Unless it could be proved that the fall of prices was general, the case was not made out that it was abundance of commodities, and not contraction of the currency, that led to the fall of prices. There was no proof of this. Mr. Tooke contended for the doctrine of abundance—for a change in the relation of demand to supply. Now, what do we mean to express when we say that a greater or smaller quantity of money has been exchanged for a given quantity of commodities; or, in other words, that their prices have risen or fallen? What do we mean to express by a fall of prices, unless when produced by excess of supply? Do we not mean a diminution of demand—an increase of purchasing power? and what is this but the application of a reduced quantity of money to the purchase of commodities, and consequently, *a change in the relation of demand to supply.* The idea is inconceivable of a simultaneous fall of general prices, unless by an increased value of money. If this reasoning is correct it becomes a question merely of terminology.

The years 1820–23, were years of reaction, of suffering, of sacrifices. But in 1824, the skies became again clear. It was a year of great comparative prosperity, such is the elasticity of British resources. The King congratulated the English people on their social recovery. The Minister echoed the congratulation. Before the close of the year the horizon became again clouded. Enterprise had been too highly stimulated. Speculators abounded. Credit had been stretched to its utmost tension. The reserve of cash in the Bank of England was lower than ever known before. The accidental discovery in the bank vaults of some one-pound notes which had been discarded from use, saved the Bank from another suspension.   After a short struggle and many sacrifices, the Bank and its customers proceeded again on the even tenor of their way, until speculation was revived in a new direction, and railways became the sphere of adventure.   Fabulous sums were embarked in their construction.

The year 1844 witnessed an important change in the principles by which the currency was to be regulated, and the machinery through which the Bank was to aid in the result.   After tinkering the currency for fifty years—after relaxing the monopoly of the Bank, and coaxing it to establish branches in the provinces, it was discovered that self-interest was still too powerful for the devices of the late minister, Lord Liverpool; so Sir Robert Peel conceived that although the Bank was born and nursed in restriction, there was not restriction enough, or that it was not the right kind of restriction—that there was no self-regulating check.   He imagined that by rendering debt—a portion of the public debt—the regulator he had solved the problem.   The debt due by the government to the Bank was about £14,000,000, for which the Bank held the obligations of the government.   The story is not yet all told.   An occasion soon presented itself to test the new principle of regulation.   As we have intimated the people of England in 1847 were possessed with a frenzy with regard to railways.   They subscribed all their spare capital and all they could borrow to build extended lines.   They sank millions in the soil.   They converted nearly all the circulating into fixed capital.   The returns were too slow to meet the pressure for payment of the obligations incurred.   Thousands were ruined.   The Bank of England made prodigious efforts, but without the aid of government almost universal bankruptcy would have followed.   The government extended such aid as it could afford.   The act which was to be a self-regulator—the sheet-anchor of the Bank and the currency—was authorized to be suspended.

The fourth epoch begins with the suspension of the act in 1847, and ends with the second suspension in 1857.   This latter was not preceded or accompanied by failure of the harvest and heavy purchases of grain, nor by the negotiation of large loans on the London market, nor by disturbing political influences. The crisis was produced from overtrading, said to have been connected with speculation in the United States. The aid of the government was invoked. Sir Robert Peel's act was suspended. The commercial cycle re-appeared. The year 1866 witnessed another of those ever-recurring revulsions which has signalized English commercial history. It assumed the phase of excessive joint-stock speculation. The power was given to the Bank of England to suspend the act a third time; but it was not used. And here is the proper place to offer our theory of this remarkable failure.

In the first place the act of 1844 is founded on assumption. It assumes a larger agency of paper currency in the abuse of credit than can be proved. It does not assign the due measure of influence to those other forms of credit which have far greater effect in producing collapses. To protect the convertibility of the Bank of England note, was the leading purpose of the act. If the act had been of a really *preventive* character—if it could have prevented undue advances of capital by bankers and joint-stock banks, there would have been no necessity to bring into action those *correctives* which were devised to rectify an adverse exchange, which those advances were far more instrumental in producing than the overissues of the Bank of England. If by an external or internal drain of gold the bank was rapidly losing its treasure, to produce an influx at least equal to the efflux, the paper currency was contracted, either by raising the rate of discount or by the sale of exchequer bills. The violence of this action on the currency, by rendering it of higher value, induced the return of the gold for investment in the English funds or the purchase of English commodities. If the source of the scarcity of money was hoarding, accompanied by a panic, the corrective was expansion, and not contraction, for there had been a vacuum produced by hoarding. Sir Robert Peel's act, therefore, brought into conflict two principles adapted to opposite states of the currency—the state of overabundance that requires reduction of currency, and that of deficiency that requires an increased supply. It is possible to reconcile the two principles, to wit, that a mixed currency should vary as would a metallic currency if paper had formed

no part of it, if the measure of issue were the wants of the
population, but not that which regulates the currency of England on an entirely arbitrary principle—to wit, the sum due the
Bank by the government.   In the absence of any *preventive*
check—any self-regulating power—the use of a violent *corrective* became absolutely necessary.

Everything seems to depend on the proper interpretation to
be given to the principle enunciated in the bullion report of
1810, that *the whole currency should vary in its amount and
value exactly as a metallic currency would do were the paper
currency withdrawn and coin substituted in its stead.*   Now,
let us suppose the currency, exclusively of gold and silver coin,
to the amount of thirty millions of pounds, and that a deficiency in the harvest should require the export of five millions
in gold to pay for imported corn.   There being no banks issuing paper money, the gold would be taken from the reserves
of bankers, and from the mass of circulating medium in the
hands of the people.   A contraction necessarily ensues with an
adverse exchange.   Prices fall and the English market becomes
favorable for the purchase of English commodities.   This leads
to a reflux of gold, and the vacuum caused by the previous export of treasure is filled.   This inconvenience would be only
temporary.   It is the loss of so much capital, in the form of one
of the precious metals, and would soon be repaired by the export of commodities.

Now let us suppose a mixed currency, composed partly of
coin and partly of paper, and the efflux of gold to the same
amount, five millions, would the final result of restoring the
gold be different?   Assuredly not.   But the process would be
essentially different, if the Bank of England, which is supposed
to have lost the gold, should raise the rate of discount making
money artificially scarce so as to produce a rapid instead of a
gradual return of the gold.   This would be, not to make the
whole currency vary as would a metallic currency in similar
circumstances, but to do by violent action what would otherwise be accomplished gradually.   The convertibility of the
Bank of England notes is the plea for this sudden contraction
of the currency.   It is evident that this state of things presents

a choice of evils, the suspension of specie payments by the bank, or mercantile bankruptcy proportioned to the extent of the contraction. The choice of the latter alternative would be the sacrifice of means to end; for, for what purpose are banks organized, if not for the support of mercantile credit? It would be better then for the evil to be redressed by permitting commerce to take its natural course, by letting gold flow out without any effort to impede its efflux, and then flow back by the operation of natural causes.

We have thus briefly traced the series of effects that have followed the British attempts to regulate the currency. The conclusion from the survey, brief as it has been, is that after the failure of these attempts there must be something radically defective in the principle of that system in its latest phase, and that the regulation of the currency is a problem still open for practical solution. After the lapse of half a century it is still the opprobrium of British legislation.

Having thus finished our preliminary survey, we are now prepared to enter on the main question, and to discuss it under the two general heads laid down by us at the outset, to wit: *The Regulation of Currency,* and *The Regulation of Credit.* And first, of the Regulation of Currency. There is no problem in monetary science so difficult of solution as this. Volumes upon volumes have been written on the subject, and the problem is no nearer a solution now than it was fifty years ago. It appears to us that the solution lies on the surface. It would seem that if the makers of money, whether coin or paper, would allow the most unlimited freedom not only to the export and import of coin and bullion, but to the public demand for both as currency, there never would be either excess or deficiency. But in almost all countries there are mint regulations that impede this freedom, irrespective of those which protect the standard from debasement. As however our present object is to offer some suggestions on the abuses of the credit system, we will limit our remarks to that branch of the currency that consists in the issue of paper money. If the makers of paper money would issue no more than the amount of gold and silver for which paper is the substitute and representative, pound for pound, or dollar for dollar, the great requisite so anxiously sought would be attained. This condition would of course dispense with banks of circulation, for there could be no profit on circulation if the issuers were limited to dollar for dollar, or pound for pound. There is then some other proportion than that of equality in amount which the public are willing to concede as a compensation for the tax they pay for paper issues, and for the convenience of paper money. What that proportion should be has always been indeterminate. One third in specie and two thirds in paper is a proportion that seems to unite the largest number of suffrages in its favor under a rigid system of specie payments. As far as regards the convertible bank note, this is an adequate security against *excess*, if the community are protected against *discredit*. But it is not the bank note which is the great source of abuse of private credit. Credit assumes so many forms—bills of exchange, checks, book entries, etc.—that the issues of banks in the form of notes, constitute but a small proportion of the mass of private credit, while the abuse of public credit, in the form of government paper seems to be the paramount evil against which we are called upon to provide safeguards.

The great desideratum in countries that employ a mixed currency, it appears to us, is, a *preventive* check that would at the same time be self-regulative. The ordinary checks against the excessive action of banks are too slow in their operation. They are in the nature of *correctives*, instead of *preventives*. They are brought into play after the evil to be corrected has reached a certain height, and requires a force to be imparted much greater than the irregularity by which the evil has been produced. When the Bank of England loses five millions of gold, the effect of overtrading, to bring about an influx of gold, a contraction of the currency to the extent, perhaps, of seven or ten millions would be necessary; but if, by regarding the indications of an adverse foreign exchange produced by excess of paper money, and by exercising prudence, no more currency be issued than will keep the foreign exchange at par, or the currency at an equality of value with other currencies, no inducement will be presented to those who make a profit by an export of specie. It is inconceivable that the harmony of Nature's laws should be preserved, not only in the realms of physical creation, but in social arrangements generally, and yet fail in the single case of providing a circulating medium that will preserve steadiness of value—that will prevent those ruinous fluctuations that cause the rupture of all industrial relations. We are satisfied that such a principle of harmony extending to so necessary an element of prosperity as the medium of exchange, does exist. We have no difficulty in confiding in the great law of demand and supply in all departments of production and industry and values that are exchangeable. Why should currency form an exception? We leave to the operation of the principle of public demand the supply of coined money. The law of increase of population regulates the increase of gold and silver *as currency:* why not of that which is their substitute and representative? It is here, if anywhere, we must look for that which is so much desired; to wit, the principle by which currency may be regulated. The whole analogy of Nature shows that the source of this principle must be sought in population and the rate of its increase.

The first point of inquiry is, the measure of issue and rate of increase. We propose the amount of population as the measure of issue, and the rate of increase of the one, as the rate for the increase of the other. The population when the census of 1870 is taken will be, in round numbers, 42,000,000. According to the enumeration of 1860, our numbers were 31,443,322. The paper currency of the United States in 1860 was $207,102,477; specie $83,604,528;[8] total $290,667,005, which is so near ten dollars *per capita*, that we will assume that figure as representing the ratio of currency to population. In this ratio the

[8] These figures are copied from the Census Report of 1860. We think the estimate of specie too small, but have not felt ourselves at liberty to alter it. Large quantities of the precious metals, in the form of coin, were hoarded during the war, which the resumption of specie payments, whenever that takes place, will bring to light. The special Commissioner of the Revenue, Mr. Welles, in his Third Annual Report, 1868, estimates that between 1865 and 1868, 1,000,000 of emigrants have arrived in the United States, and that they have 'brought with them the average amount of eighty dollars per head in specie or its equivalent,' which, according to this computation, must have added to the specie of the country $80,000,000.

quantity of circulating medium is in excess about seventy-five per cent. The Secretary of the Treasury's statement of the debt of the United States not paying interest (legal tender) on the 1st of July, 1868, was, including fractional currency, $388,768,674.75, in round numbers $400,000,000, and the amount of the notes of the National banks $300,000,000; total paper currency $700,000,000.

Mr. Kennedy, Superintendent of the Census, has recently published an able preliminary report of the Eighth Census, in which he compares the different decades since 1790, and draws the conclusion that the rate per cent. of increase from 1850 to 1860, was 35.46, and from 1840 to 1850, 35.87. If, therefore we assume the rate of decennial increase at $33\frac{1}{3}$ per cent., it will be as near an approximation as it is possible to attain. On this principle of calculation, and assuming ten dollars *per capita*, our currency, both paper and specie, should not, in 1870, exceed $420,000,000, and in 1880 (increase $33\frac{1}{3}$ per cent.) exceed $560,000,000, our population then being 56,000,000.

Mr. Welles seems inclined to reject the principle of population as the basis of calculation for an increase of the currency, and appears to think that the amount of circulating medium depends, to adopt his phrase, on 'wealth and mobility.' This phrase we do not profess to comprehend. If it refers by wealth to rate of increase of property, real and personal, in the United States, we would inquire, in what category he would place the immense territorial possessions acquired by the United States within the last twenty-five years? If he refers by the expression *mobility* to the movement of commodities, when put into a form for commercial exchange, we can understand that when the mineral treasures, which are the products of those possessions, are put into a form to be exchanged for other products, they should be estimated as contributing elements of national wealth, and as forming the basis for an increase of currency; but until they are put into such a form by a fresh application of capital and labor, they do not contribute to those components of wealth which should constitute the basis of currency. Looking to the increase of wealth, and adopting Mr. Kennedy's statement in his *Preliminary Report*, that the rate of increase of real and personal property in the United States in the decade from 1850 to 1860, one of the most prosperous in the history of this country, was 126½ per cent., and admitting that bank notes circulate four times within the year, the rate of increase of population would supply as large a quantity of paper money, under the rule we have suggested, ten dollars per head, as would be commensurate to the general wants. The Commissioner of the Revenue computes the proportional quantity of circulating medium for the United States, (coin and paper,) at $11.50 per head for the whole population, but seems willing to accept $10 *per capita*. It is remarkable that we have arrived at the same result by a different process, in limiting the increase of currency to the same rate by which the population is augmented.

We would suggest the adoption of a system recommended by the late distinguished author and legislator, David Ricardo. When the question was discussed in England in 1832, whether the Bank of England should not be divested of its monopoly, and the profit derived from its circulation transferred to the State, he proposed the establishment of a National bank, under the administration of commissioners, to whom should be entrusted the privilege of issuing paper money with the other usual banking privileges. We are inclined to favor that part of his scheme that would confide the important and responsible trust of making and issuing paper money *exclusively* to a Board of Commissioners, to consist of not more than three persons, rendered, by the tenure of their office, independent of Executive or Legislative control, except as to original appointment, and irremovable except for breach of trust. The advantages of such a board would be threefold: 1. Its functions would be exclusively directed to supplying the country with a circulating medium on a well regulated principle. 2. It would have no power to issue currency for public expenditure, making such expenditure the measure of issue; but, on the contrary, it would save taxation, thus getting rid of that curse and opprobrium of nations, an irredeemable paper currency. 3. It would have no mercantile sympathies of which, during periods of speculation and overtrading, bank credits are the instrument.

As part of such a scheme, and a necessary part, would be the establishment of banks of deposit and discount, each with adequate capital, affording all reasonable facilities of credit, which would, in gathering together the scattered means of those who prefer leisure to work, unite those means into large aggregates by which the productive power of the country would be developed and extended.

Again, as a part of the same scheme and an extension of the deposit system, we would suggest that the Superintendent of the Mint be authorized to receive deposits of gold and silver coin and bullion in sums not less than $1,000, for which he would give receipts or certificates that could be used as means of remittance as substitutes for domestic bills of exchange, saving the expense of remitting specie, and avoiding the risk attendant on the failure of parties on which bills may be drawn, as the receipts or certificates will rest on that which possesses intrinsic value.

The collapse of the State Bank system, from the destruction of their capital, and the prohibitory clauses of the National Bank law, have led to the necessity for adopting a system of banking equal to the wants of the South, and adapted to its peculiar circumstances. The imposition of a tax of ten per cent. on the circulation of all banks in the United States except the National Banks, will compel a resort to banks of deposit and discount. The first difficulty would appear to be the want of capital. This is more an apparent, than a real, want.

There is only wanting the inducement which will draw the hoards that accumulate, from the want of investment, into active employment; and this will be found in a device which has proved efficacious in Europe. A small rate of interest on deposits has attracted to the Scotch banks more than one hundred millions of dollars at one time, and it constitutes the basis of the business of the joint stock and many of the private banks in England, which are not banks of circulation. An interest of two or three per cent. will be an effectual motive to numerous small capitalists whose surplus gains are dormant from the absence of convenient modes of investment. They are now compelled to keep these surplus sums in private repositories,

exposed to risk in the midst of a disorganized society, from the
want of a bank of deposit in their neighborhood. Let such
but appear organized by men of integrity and capacity, and we
are unable to perceive any difficulty in their formation. At
the present time they are peculiarly necessary. The earnings
of the planter found in the investment of slave property a too
ready means of placing those earnings in what he conceived to
be a safe lodgment. With what vain expectations time has
shown.

It will, no doubt, be said that if banks are driven to the
necessity of banking exclusively on their capitals and deposits,
without depending at all on the profits of their circulation, to
which the deprivation of their function of issue would force
them, they would require large deposits to render banking
profitable. This would be a desirable result if it withdrew
from banking some portion of the capital that now finds its
way inordinately into that channel of investment, to the prejudice of other forms of enterprise, particularly manufacturing
pursuits. But if there is no other mode of obtaining that
important desideratum—steadiness in the value of the currency
where it is a mixed one, partly coin and partly paper, this
must be one of the conditions of the secure enjoyment of one of
the triumphs of civilization—the invention of paper money.
The practical conclusion, then, from this view is, the adoption
of some other system by which those fluctuations in the value
of the circulating medium, and in the value of all property,
shall be avoided. If the issue of paper money in the proportion of three, to one in specie, or any higher proportion to liabilities, or even to circulation, has the effect of rendering society
liable to periodical revulsions, the system of restriction ought
to be abandoned, and that of freedom substituted. Some self-
acting principle ought to be devised. There is considerable
delusion with regard to paper money as issued by banks. It
will, no doubt, startle many of our readers to learn, that every
increase beyond what would have been the amount in circulation if it had been exclusively metallic, causes an advance in the
foreign exchange, which is, in its final effect, a tax on the community—as much so as an increase in the duties on imports—

the importer being compelled to get it back from the consumer, if the equality or profit is to be preserved. It is a law of currency, that unless the level of value is preserved in a country that substitutes paper for gold or silver, a derangement of the foreign exchange follows, and although profit may inure to the issuers, it is at the expense of all other classes of the community. Let us imagine ourselves at the commencement of the reign of William the Third, when bank notes were for the first time introduced. Let us suppose that the directors of the Bank of England have determined to substitute paper for gold and silver coin to the extent of one-half of the whole amount of the circulating medium, that amount being, in gold and silver, one hundred and fifty millions sterling. As long as the notes substituted for the coin do not exceed the amount that would have been in circulation if the currency had been exclusively metallic, no disturbance is produced; the level of value between English and foreign currencies is not altered. The foreign exchange, provided there is no other cause in operation to disturb the exchange, remains at par. But let the Bank of England, with a view to profit, determine to alter the proportions that have kept the currency of England at a level with the currencies of other countries, by adding to the fifty millions of notes supposed to be in circulation, fifty millions more, making the entire circulation two hundred millions, instead of one hundred and fifty millions; rendering fifty millions of gold unnecessary as currency. There follows, necessarily, an adverse exchange. A profit is made by the export of gold, which is fifty millions in excess of the wants of the country; in other words, there is a premium on the foreign exchange in proportion to the excess. The premium is a tax on the other classes of the community, the same as an increase of the duties on importation is a tax on the consumers. The practical conclusion is obvious,—all increase of circulating medium beyond what would have been the amount of the circulation if it had been exclusively metallic, is a gain to the issuers of paper money, and a loss to the community, in proportion to the excess.[9] The final inference

[9] The following passage from the *Principles of Political Economy*, by John Stuart Mill, affords confirmation of this view: 'An issue of notes is a manifest gain to the issuers, who, until the notes are returned for payment, obtain the use

from this view is, that if banks of circulation are to keep a reserve of specie as large as to equal the notes they issue, there will be no profit on their circulation. This establishes the distinction between *capital* and *currency*, on which our system is founded. The distinction is not new, but its application claims the merit of novelty. It is the true basis of the separation, imperfectly accomplished, between the issue and banking departments of the Bank of England.

If the distinction between capital and currency is sound, of which there can be no doubt, it affords ground for the separation of the function of issue from that of discount, limiting the latter to the use of capital exclusively, including in that term the aggregate employed by individual bankers and the sums subscribed by those associations called joint stock banks, and the deposits lodged with bankers and banking institutions. This is capital. Currency admits of being separated and placed under distinct management. We have suggested a Board of Commissioners as a body in which, being properly constituted, the function of making and issuing paper money might be safely reposed, as governed in its exercise by a principle that will secure steadiness and stability to the circulating medium consisting of paper.

The principal source of evil in our day is *excessive credit* in the form of bills of exchange, checks drawn against deposits and ledger entries, and not bank notes. This is the hydra we have to contend against. It will be borne in mind, that the scheme of currency, of which the above is an outline, is, in one of its aspects, of a *tentative* character. The feature that regulates the quantity or amount of currency by so much *per capita*, will be one of trial or experiment. It is possible that

of them as if they were a real capital; and so long as the notes are no permanent addition to the currency, but merely supersede gold or silver *to the same amount*, the gain of the issuer is a loss to no one; it is obtained by saving to the community the more costly material. But if there is no gold or silver to be superseded —if the notes are added to the currency, instead of being substituted for the metallic part of it—all holders of currency lose, by the depreciation of its value, the exact equivalent to what the issuer gains. A tax is virtually levied on them for this benefit. It will be objected by some, that gains are also made by the producers and dealers, who, by means of the increased issue, are accommodated with loans. Their's, however, is not an additional gain, but a portion of that which is reaped by the issuer, at the expense of all possessors of money. The profits arising from the contribution levied upon the public, he does not keep to himself, but divides with his customers.'

ten dollars per head may be too much, or it may be too little. Twelve dollars per head may not be too high a figure, or eight dollars per head may not be too low a figure. But after the trial or experiment is made, it will be a *fixed*, *unalterable* relation. The increase of the currency will then be in proportion to the *aggregate* increase of the population. If a population of 42,000,000 at ten dollars per head will allow $420,000,000 of currency in 1870, it follows that, in 1880, the population (since it increases at the rate of 33⅓ per cent. in every decade) being 56,000,000, the currency will amount to $560,000,000. By thus making the *per capita* a *fixed* and *permanent* relation, and the increase an *aggregate* increase, an element of steadiness and stability will be communicated to the circulating medium, which it could not receive by any other mode. It will be impossible for it to fluctuate—to be less or more than is required for the wants of the community. It will be under the influence of the great law of demand and supply. The *fixity* in the rate *per capita* is an essential element of the system. The great source of the present moneyed derangements—fluctuation—will be entirely removed. The functions of those who will have the administration of the currency will be entirely *automatic*. They will be guided by an inflexible rule or principle, namely, the increase of population. The only source of instruction and of guidance will be the tables of population.

The deposit and discount banks will be dealers exclusively in capital; in other words, distributors of capital. The Board of Commissioners will be dealers exclusively in currency. The banks of deposit and discount will be agents or intermediaries between the lenders of capital and the borrowers. They will gather into large aggregates those portions of capital which, in the hands of the owners, are lying unproductive, and distribute them to those who will employ them productively, nourishing industry, stimulating enterprise, and ministering to the wants of the mercantile public.

To show that we have not *invented* a distinction to sustain a theory, we copy the following remarks from Tooke's *History of Prices*, a standard authority: 'Totally unacquainted as the authors of the new system [the system of banking and currency adopted under Sir Robert Peel's act of 1844] were, ignorant of the distinction between capital and currency when applied to the distinct functions of the precious metals when serving in the shape of coin for internal purposes, and of capital when transmitted abroad in liquidation of an adverse balance of trade, still more striking, if possible, has been their disregard of that distinction in our internal exchanges.'

The subjoined remarks by Mr. Kinnear, are taken from his tract entitled, *Crisis and the Currency*, published in London in 1867—a very able production: 'Money is employed to perform two operations essentially distinct, the confounding of which is another source of error in the currency theory, [the theory adopted by the framers of Sir Robert Peel's act.] As a medium of exchange between dealers and dealers, it is the instrument by which transfers of *capital* are effected; that is, the exchange of a certain amount of capital in money, for an equal amount of capital in commodities. But money employed in the payment of wages, and in purchases and trade between dealers and consumers, is not capital, but *income*—that portion of the income of the community which is devoted to daily expenditure. It circulates in daily use, and is that alone which can, with strict propriety, be termed currency. Advances of capital depend entirely on banks and other possessors of capital, for borrowers are always to be found. *But the amount of the currency depends on the wants of the community,* among whom the money circulates for the purposes of daily expenditure. By currency, I therefore understand that amount in bank notes and coin which is circulating in the hands of the community for the purposes of expenditure in directing the payment of wages. The importance of this distinction will appear obvious from the following passage in Col. Torrens' letter to Lord Melbourne: "If the circulation were purely metallic, an adverse exchange, causing an export of the metals to any given amount, would occasion a contraction of the circulation to the same amount. If the currency of the metropolis consisted of gold, an adverse exchange, causing an export of gold to the amount of one million pounds, would withdraw from the circulation one million of sovereigns." The fallacy involved in this, which appears a self-evident proposition to Col. Torrens, arises from the misapplication of terms. It is self-evident, on the contrary, that an exportation of one million in gold would not withdraw a single sovereign from the circulation, unless all the gold in the country above the amount circulating as currency had been previously exported.'

The question arises, if the system we have suggested should be adopted, How is the new currency to find its way to the public? as the function of discounting mercantile paper would be limited exclusively to the banks of deposit and discount, and it would be no part of their function to issue paper money. The notes issued by the Board of Currency would find their way to the public through the disbursements of the Government. The drafts of the Secretary of the Treasury, under such a system, quarterly or monthly, as may be most convenient, to carry into effect the appropriations of Congress, would, of course, be paid from the issues created by the Board of Currency limited by the amount authorized by law to be issued in the ratio of the increase of population.

The system of banking and currency we have suggested being founded on the distinction between capital and currency, leads necessarily to the separation of the functions of issuing paper money from that of banking proper. The separation is in form that which prevails in the Bank of England, which is divided into two departments, that of issue and that of banking. Our Board of Currency corresponds with the former. Our system of deposit and discount banks with the latter. There is, however, this difference. Under the system we propose, the separation is *virtual.* Under the British system, it is *nominal.* The issue department of the Bank of England has no original power. It is acted on exclusively by the public. Its sole function is to receive gold for notes and notes for gold.[10] The office of the Directors is a sinecure, and may,

[10] It is difficult to perceive the reason of the policy of compelling the Bank of England to purchase all the gold offered to it at a higher than might be the market price. It is evident that the dealers in gold bullion will take the whole supply they may receive to the Bank, if they are able to obtain a higher price than the market affords. It is one of those interferences with the freedom of trade in the precious metals from which nothing but evil can result. If the bank did not purchase when there was a large influx, that influx would be distributed throughout the various countries of Europe, instead of being concentrated, and finally accumulated, in the vaults of the Bank of England. It was these accumulations of treasure that induced the Bank to reduce, at times, the rate of discount to avoid the loss of interest on so much dead stock, and it was this reduction in the rate of discount that led to specu'ation.

in the language of Mr. Gilbart, in his *Practical Treatise on Banking*, 'as well be filled by twenty-four broomsticks.' The banking department exercises all the banking power. It discounts bills of exchange, receives deposits, and makes advances on Exchequer bills. If the separation of the departments had been complete, it would have led to the adoption of Mr. Ricardo's or some similar plan of transferring the privilege of issuing paper money from the Bank of England to a body independent of all control or influence by the government. The plan suggested by us makes a still more effectual separation; for Mr. Ricardo would have clothed his Commissioners with certain banking powers. Under the system we recommend, there would simply be the making and issuing a certain quantity of paper money, not limited by an arbitrary principle, as in the case of the Bank of England and the National banks, but regulated by a principle that adds to the currency in proportion to the increase of population, thus making the wants of the public the measure of issue. There would be no banking powers, in the ordinary sense of the term; the function of the Board would be automatic, as much so as that of the issue department of the Bank of England.

We have stated that the basis of our system is the distinction between capital and currency. The Board of Currency would be dealers in currency exclusively. The deposit and discount banks would be dealers in capital; in other words, distributors of capital; intermediaries between lenders and borrowers.

In fact, the distinction is so subtle as to require an effort of abstraction to comprehend its full force. We speak of capital in the sense of currency, as often as in the sense in which it is *realized* as material objects. When capital in currency, or to adopt the familiar phrase, moneyed capital, is borrowed, it may be sought as a purchasing power to affect the transfer of property either for temporary use, or for permanent investment. The merchant who obtains an advance from a bank, obtains it for the purchase of commodities which are parted with in exchange for other commodities. The manufacturer borrows a portion of the capital he employs in his business, to purchase the things that become fixed capital, such as buildings and machinery; the other components of his capital, such as raw materials and money for the wages of his workmen, become circulating capital; and this alone can, with strict propriety, be called currency. The capitalist who purchases stock in a bank, an insurance company, or any other joint stock association, or in the public funds, is compelled to employ the same agent as the merchant or the manufacturer, although he purchases for permanent investment. But when the term capital is used, in the sense of currency, it is not used in the strict technical sense. Strictly speaking, it is the *power* conferred by the possession of currency, and not currency itself, which is capital; the power, namely, over all those things which the borrower has acquired or wishes to acquire, and for which he has to pay a price in proportion to what he can make by its use; in other words, a rate of interest in conformity with the rate of profit. There is, thus, a real distinction between the instrument or agent that conveys the power, and the power itself—between the material objects that constitute capital, and the currency which conveys the power to acquire those objects.

There is much more importance attached to the bank note currency than we are disposed to admit, when it is recollected that if the public is secured by the solvency of specie-paying banks, a *permanent* over-issue of notes is impossible. The mistake made by the framers of Sir Robert Peel's act of 1844 was, that they attached undue importance to bank notes, and not sufficient importance to other forms of credit, such as bills of exchange, checks drawn against deposits, and book debts, whose agency in the expansion of credit beyond its due limits is unquestionable. The disproportion between the note currency in England and bills of exchange, is surprising to those who have looked at the facts. According to a table published in Tooke's *History of Prices*, (Vol. VI., p. 585,) the general conclusion drawn was, that in 1854 the average amount of bills of exchange, inland and foreign, in circulation *at one time*, in England and Wales, was about 150,000,000 sterling, or more than four times the amount of bank notes of all descriptions. This conveys an inadequate idea of the general inflation of credit in periods of prosperity. Mr. Bosanquet's tract entitled, *Metal-*

lic, Paper, and Credit, Currency, published in 1842, contains a detailed statement estimating the amount of bills, checks, &c., at £18,000,000, daily, which would make the annual aggregate £6,570,000,000; which agrees very nearly with the statement in Mr. Tooke's work. The highest estimate we have ever seen of the entire note circulation of Great Britain is a little less than £40,000,000. The relative disproportion is remarkable. Bills of exchange are excessively multiplied during periods when a low rate of interest increases the facilities of credit; and it is a prevalent delusion that if they have for their basis real transactions, they cannot be excessive. The agency of bank notes in *producing* speculation, is a doctrine no longer tenable. That they *prolong* it is, we think, evident. In the reasoning and conclusions of Mr. John Stuart Mill on this subject, there must be general concurrence. He divides the market into two periods, which he calls 'the *quiescent* and *expectant* periods; the first in which commercial affairs are regularly progressive, in which there is no speculative excitement; the last in which speculation takes place from the supposed deficiency of one or more staple productions of commerce. Speculators then enter the market, and, either by their own capital or advances from banks, make purchase of the commodity or commodities of which there is expected to be a scarcity.' This is called by Mr. Mill 'the *expectant* state of the market. It is to enable holders to retain their stocks that banks of issue do mischief. They nourish and prolong speculation by their advances, although they may have had no agency in originating it. Expedients may be contrived to check this tendency in banks of issue to prolong speculation.' [11] It was a period of twenty years before that principle first formally enunciated in the Bullion Report of 1810, that the Bank of England should regulate its issues by the state of the foreign exchange, became a part of the practice of that bank. It slumbered in that document until about the year 1830, for

[11] Principles of Political Economy, Vol. II., p. 219.—We can add our personal experience in confirmation of the truth of this statement. Residing for many years in a city having a large export trade in cotton, and where there was much bank capital, we have known this staple to be held for a considerable period at speculative prices,—the holders receiving advances at Board of Directors where their influence has enabled them to obtain unusual facilities of credit.

it was only when the British Legislature modified the usury
law that the Bank was able, by raising its rate of discount, to
check the efflux of its gold. Before this, the only rule by
which it regulated its issues was, the amount of bullion in its
coffers and the solvency of the borrowers. A comprehensive
survey of the field, embracing, not only the state of the foreign
exchange, but the probability of a favorable or unfavorable
harvest, and the state of the loan market, were considerations
that formed no part of its administration of the currency. Not
that the principle enunciated by the Bullion Committee, proved
sound and reliable. On the contrary, it proved the source of
fluctuation. For there are a great variety of causes that affect
the foreign exchange. 1. The debasement of the coin, which
has precisely the same effect on the exchange as a depreciation
of the paper currency. 2. The excess of imports beyond exports. 3. Large foreign loans placed on the money market.
4. A deficiency of the harvest, compelling an export of gold in
payment of imported corn. 5. Political events, which sometimes have a considerable influence on the foreign exchange.
It is seldom that more than two of these act in conjunction,
and are classed among the causes that influence the *real* exchange, which has a limit in the expense of transmitting specie
from the debtor to the creditor country. As there is only one
cause that affects the *nominal* exchange, (if the coin is of
standard weight and fineness,) namely, the cost of the freight
and insurance of specie from the debtor to the creditor country,
the *premium* is easily ascertained. That the currency ought
to be regulated by the state of the foreign exchange, cannot
then, with truth, be affirmed. The proposition assumed an
axiomatic form in the Bullion Report, and was acted on by the
Directors of the Bank of England from the year 1830, according to the evidence of several of them. But a moment's
reflection will show that such a rule acted on must give rise to
constant fluctuations in the value of money and in prices. That
the foreign exchange would be a correct index of the value of
the currency as compared with foreign currencies, if there were
no other causes by which it could be influenced, except the
state of the coinage and the amount and value of the paper

money which is a substitute for and representative of the metals, there can be no doubt. But as above shown, there are various causes by which the foreign exchange may be affected. It would therefore be to confound the *real* with the *nominal* exchange, to adopt, as a rule for the regulation of the currency, the state of the foreign exchange generally.

The influence of public banks in England, taking into view her whole system of credit, is comparatively limited. The joint stock and private banks have very large capitals as well as deposits, and their agency in the undue extension of credit in periods of speculation and overtrading must not be overlooked. It is only occasionally that the Bank of England engages in the business of discounting commercial paper, and those are periods of great monetary pressure. Its over-issues are manifested in the purchase of exchequer bills, and public securities, and, at times, in other questionable investments.

But it is not in this direction we must look for the worst abuses of the paper system through bank credits of any kind. The establishment of a system that will remove from government the necessity and the temptation to issue irredeemable paper money, would be an unmixed good; and if combined with a plan for the regulation of credit, if only tolerably successful, would lessen, if it did not remove, the evil of the periodical recurrence of those crises that shake society to its centre.

The Scotch banks would seem to form an exception to our principle of the separation of the functions of issue and discount, as they unite both functions. But the exception is more apparent than real. They deal mainly in capital and very subordinately in currency. The capitals of the Scotch banks are very large, frequently from £500,000 to £1,000,000 and £1,500,000, while their deposits are £25,000,000 to £30,000,000. Their circulation is rarely in the aggregate more than £3,500,000.

Since the above remarks were penned, we have seen in the *New York Herald* of May 26, a letter from its Vienna correspondent, giving an historical account, in brief, of the Austrian currency, which sheds much light on this branch of our subject. It was the earliest issue of irredeemable paper money in European annals. The first issue made, in 1762, was for sums amounting to 12,000,000 florins to defray the expenses of the seven years' war with Frederick of Prussia. Being issued in moderation it did not depreciate. There was no discount on it when exchanged for silver, that metal being then the standard. But as the expenses growing out of the wars produced by the French Revolution augmented, so did the paper currency of Austria. It was not made a legal tender except in payment of the taxes, for which it was receivable, and hence its designation of taxation currency.

The writer of the letter makes several divisions of his subject, but two principal divisions are all that are necessary ; to wit, the period anterior to 1800, and the period from that time till 1866. As long as the Austrian government used this perilous instrument with moderation, and kept the privilege of issue in its own hands, it was beneficial to the State. But in 1815 it chartered the Austrian Privileged Bank for twenty-five years, the bank consenting to pay its own notes, and those of the government in specie, for which purpose a loan was effected by the government. In 1860 the renewal of war increased the public expenditure, and a second suspension took place with great depreciation of the notes both of the bank and of the government. In 1848 the charter of the bank was renewed for another twenty-five years. In 1866 there was final resumption.

Two conditions arise out of this state of facts. 1. That a paper currency issued by the State, although irredeemable, will preserve its value if limited. 2. That if not issued in amount exceeding the gold and silver coin for which it is a substitute, it will supersede the necessity of specie payments. This is the correct theoretical principle, but it is owing to the circumstance that no means have yet been found to give effect to this theoretical principle, that specie payments have become practically indispensable. As long as the Austrian government issued paper notes in moderation they were in value equal to silver, but when expensive wars compelled it to issue them in excess, they fell in value considerably below the standard.

Another principle is exemplified by this Austrian example. As long as the State reserved to itself the privilege of issuing paper money, the profits from the circulation accrued to it. These profits it afterwards transferred to the Austrian bank to the extent of the issue it permitted, which was about 300,000,000 florins, the government issue being at the same time to an equal amount. Now the surrender of the benefit of an issue of three hundred millions of florins to a corporation was a sacrifice to that extent of the national interests; for during the time that resumption was preparing, it called for 300,000,000 florins of Austrian commodities to pay for imported silver, while the expense of the loan effected to enable the bank to resume was an uncompensated loss.

We need not point out how well this Austrian example illustrates our own practice, in which the profits of $300,000,000 in notes are surrendered to the National Banks. Nor need we adduce further argument to prove that if Congress would adopt a stable principle of issue, such as that of the increase of population, the evils of an irredeemable paper currency would be avoided, while there would be a saving to the United States of the expense of a metallic circulation, with the exception of a limited reserve of coin.

It has been imagined that the sum we have named as the measure of issue would be inadequate to the national wants. The increase of wealth has been suggested as not an excessive measure for the increase of paper currency in the United States. Those who make this suggestion appear to be oblivious of one important fact. Steam and electricity have given an impetus to the *circulation* of money scarcely conceivable except to those who have watched the operations. They have at least doubled, if not trebled, its rapidity. Credits that formerly extended to 60 and 90 days, are now abridged to less than an average of 30 days. So far from an increase in the volume of paper money in the ratio of the increase in population not being sufficient, we apprehend it may prove redundant.

Having now finished what we have to say on the first branch of our subject, we proceed to the consideration of the second, namely, *The Regulation of Credit.*

The system of currency and banking we have suggested requires the conversion of the National Banks into banks of deposit and discount exclusively, in other words, the relinquishment by those banks of the profits of their circulation. That this would be a real sacrifice to a majority of those banks we do not believe. Some of the most prosperous institutions do not issue notes. Mr. Gilbart, in his work on *Practical Banking*, mentions three in Liverpool. There is one at least in New York, the Bank of Commerce. Where capital centres the funds are always ample, in the shape of deposits, for every commercial want. Circulation forms the main resource of inland banks. The organization of a system of *preventive* checks presents difficulties hard to surmount. The most formidable is, the prevalent notion that any system which runs counter to self-interest would be impracticable in the execution, and would not be adhered to. Without systematic and organized efforts, the action of the banks in carrying into effect a system of preventive checks would be desultory and irregular. We would suggest for this purpose a check which for the want of a better name we would call *a graduated rate of discount and term of credit*. In making this suggestion we are influenced by no spirit of innovation. Those who are familiar with the practice of banks will at once recognize it as a restraining influence. Among the first questions put to a borrower who is an applicant for accommodation, is, For what term will the loan be required? and one of its most ordinary conditions, especially during a money pressure, is the shortness of the period allowed the borrower; while one of the most usual checks to speculation is, an advance in the rate of discount. The combination of the two is the only system of defence to banks during a period of speculation, short of positive refusal to lend.[12] In the speculative year, 1857, when the Bank of England was rapidly losing its treasure, it raised its rate of discount, by successive steps, from two to ten per cent., and reduced its term of credit from ninety-five to seven days. This expedient did not arrest the panic, but it no doubt limited application for

[12] For example : assuming that six per cent. is the average rate of discount, and sixty days the average term of credit, when credit is given for ninety days. the rate of discount to be increased to seven per cent.; if for one hundred and twenty days to eight per cent., and in the descending scale, when the term of credit is shortened to thirty days, and so on. We believe the principle prevails practically among banks and bankers, of charging a higher rate of discount on paper of a long date than on paper of a short date, but it would, we conceive, be an improvement in banking if it were made a part of the system.

discount. Nothing but a letter of authorization to the Directors to exceed the legal limit of issue, or a knowledge that such a letter would be issued, calmed the agitation.

We are aware of the objection that lies against the attempt during the *furor* of speculation to restrain the tendency to excessive credit. It will be urged that at such periods, those who have embarked in speculation will give the most extravagant rates for money. This is true. But this is assuming an exceptional state of things as furnishing the rule of action universally for all who borrow money. Money is borrowed *ordinarily* not for speculation, but for regular and productive employment. The rate of interest is then governed by the rate of profit—by the wholesome competition of lenders and borrowers. On the contrary, when loans are sought to sustain speculation, to meet engagements that will not bear delay, almost any price will be paid for money. The rate of interest at such periods is not governed by the rate of profit, but by the demand for lendable capital compared with the supply.

It must not, however, be imagined that speculation and overtrading are vices peculiar to countries which have indulged in the dangerous luxury of paper money. Banks exclusively of deposit, in various parts of the continent of Europe, in Hamburg, Amsterdam, Rotterdam, &c., have, at times, been seriously embarrassed, and mercantile failures have been a conspicuous feature of the financial history of those cities. Such banks have experienced, equally with those of England, the ill effects of too extended credit, not through the agency of bank notes, but through that of bills of exchange. Mr. McLeod, in his work entitled, *Theory and Practice of Banking*, remarks: 'The year 1763 is the first of those great eras of commercial distress and prostration, caused by too great an expansion of credit. And these disasters took place where there was no currency at all but what represented bullion—at Hamburg and Amsterdam. The progress of the seven years' war had probably encouraged speculation among the continental merchants, which involved in ruin those connected with them when peace came. A general failure took place at Amsterdam. A much greater number in Hamburg followed immediately. No business was for some time transacted but for ready money. The failures were equally general in many other parts of Germany.' As late down as 1857, a similar state of things occurred at Hamburg, Amsterdam, &c.

Deposit and discount banks get, occasionally, into difficulty by not having an organized system of credit connected with deposits. It is part of our commercial history that, in 1857, the banks in the city of New York suspended specie payments from not being able to pay their depositors, their deposits amounting to $97,000,000.[13] It seems obvious to the most superficial observation that, if there is no correspondence between the periods of call for money lodged with banks (unless specially deposited) and periods of payment by those to whom the deposits are lent, both as to time and amount, difficulty and embarrassment, if not failure, must result. Some general rule regulating these matters between the banks and their customers, substituting conventional arrangements for loose and random practice, is absolutely necessary, especially among Southern banks, as banking on deposits appears to be almost their only resource for organized credit, Congress having imposed a tax of ten per cent. on the circulation of all but National banks,—which amounts to a prohibition.

To secure uniformity under a system of preventive checks, of which a graduated rate of discount and term of credit would form an essential part, we would suggest a convention of the banks which may be parties to such a system, through delegates, who should meet at some central point, to secure organization and the desired uniformity; for without systematic action, there would be failure. The recent action of the insurance companies to affect uniformity, has been attended by complete success. On account of destructive fires in the different cities of the United States, it became absolutely necessary, if they would save their capitals from annihilation, that these companies should unite on some system of prevention. Accordingly, an invitation was sent to the various insurance companies in the United States, and a meeting was held in the city of New York, the result of which was, the formation of a

[13] Colwell's Ways and Means of Payment.

National Board, having under its supervision the rates, or tariff, of insurance, and all other matters connected with or affecting the interests of underwriting. Now, what is there in the nature of banking so peculiar as to forbid the formation of a similar board representing the interests of banks? whose office it would be to watch the indications of a rise of the spirit of speculation, and sound the alarm to those who control the operations of the banks, and thus, by a timely check, arrest speculation in its earliest stages. Shall we surrender all chance of such improvement in the administration of banks as may prevent the periodical recurrence of speculation and over-trading, attended by crises, revulsion, panics, and bankruptcy, inflicting social evils which are an opprobrium to civilization? The public of Great Britain and the United States have witnessed for the last half century abortive attempts, by the application of *correctives,* to cure the evils of abuse of credit arising from its undue extension. It is high time that other remedies should be tried. We venture to submit the following:

1. That a Board of Currency be constituted to consist of three Commissioners, rendered independent of other departments of the Government, not removeable except for breach of trust, on impeachment and conviction, who shall be clothed with the power exclusively of making paper money, and of issuing such sums quarterly as may be necessary for the public service, on drafts or orders from the Secretary of the Treasury, not exceeding the rate of increase of population. That to support the credit of the notes thus issued, $100,000,000 in gold be set aside as a reserve of any surplus in the Treasury from duties on imports, and that the notes thus issued shall be receivable for all dues to the Government, payable on demand, and no note shall be issued of a lower denomination than ten dollars. The advantage of such a system of issue would be twofold. (1.) It would preclude the possibility of creating irredeemable paper money under the plea of public necessity. (2.) It when other arrangements are perfected, furnish a sum sufficient to defray the entire public expenditure, and a surplus, in all probability, of $100,000,000, in lieu of taxation.

2. The formation of banks of deposit and discount which,

under a system of open competition combining, in the highest possible degree, freedom with security, by making the parties associating for the purpose suable, as in the case of an ordinary partnership, shall, while acting as distributors of capital, and intermediaries between lender and borrower, supply abundant resources of lendable capital for all legitimate mercantile purposes.

3. That authority be given to the Superintendent of the Mint to receive deposits of gold or silver in bullion or coin, in sums not less than $1,000, charging thereon a warehouse rent, and giving therefor receipts or certificates, which shall answer as means of remittance, and, to a certain extent, supersede domestic bills of exchange, thus saving the expense and risk of remitting specie, and avoiding the hazard from the failure of parties on whom bills may be drawn, as the receipts or certificates will be based on that which has intrinsic value—gold or silver.

We have suggested the possibility of so regulating credit by concert among the banks, as to furnish all the funds required for the legitimate purposes of trade, through banks of deposit. The Southern banks are prevented from exercising the functions of banks of circulation by the banking law of the United States, which imposes a tax of ten per cent. on all bank notes issued under State authority. As the large majority of Southern banks hold charters from the States in which they are situated, they are virtually deprived of the function of banks of circulation. With regard to the suggestion thrown out that the Southern banks may regulate credit by a concerted movement, we find some support to such an idea in Colwell's *Ways and Means of Payment*, a work that unites sound theory of banking with a large experience of the various processes of credit. The difficulty to be overcome consists in settlements of the domestic exchange. Mr. Colwell says: 'Foreign exchange, which, like domestic exchange, is only a mode of setting off debts against debts, by the mode of its operation becomes concentrated upon a few points, and in few hands. The foreign exchange of this country is chiefly carried on through New York, and by the agency of a few persons there, because it is scarcely the interest of many to form foreign connections, with a view to so limited a business. The function is therefore small, and the business is transacted with facility, because few are engaged in it. The domestic exchange, on the other hand, involving more than five times the amount, with less difficulty in forming the needful connections, becomes a favorite business with the public banks, a host of private bankers, brokers, and merchants. From this ensues not only much friction, and many complications, in the movement, but a wide field is opened for fictitious operations in exchange. Undue competition of parties thus dealing in exchange, induces them to offer, sometimes, more than the legitimate facilities, and at other times more than reasonable rates, for their agency; at the best it is productive of mischievous and embarrassing rivalry, and is the cover of not a few of the worst abuses of the credit system.'

Mr. Colwell's mode of correcting these abuses of the credit system, is, the establishment of offices of domestic exchange representing whole cities and districts, which by concentrating their debts and credits could settle their mutual claims with the same facility as the clearing houses. He proposes the formation of a capital of $5,000,000 for the accomplishment of this scheme; but as he suggests the remittance of the public funds as one of its functions, and as this forms no part of the system we have proposed, so large a capital would be entirely unnecessary. The banks which may unite in such a system as we have suggested could easily supply the funds to carry into effect something like a central point of redemption—a central *agency* and not a central *institution*—an international clearing house, as far as the States were concerned, whose banks would combine in such a concerted operation.

But our true reliance for an efficient device for the regulation of credit, is on the two agents steam and electricity—on facility of transportation and the shortening of credit. It has been always deemed one of the most difficult problems in social science to restrain and regulate credit. The periodically recurring tendency to excess has become a part of modern history. Cycles of speculation, at nearly regularly recurring periods, had almost led to despair of a remedy or corrective, when fortunately nature furnished the preventive. The two agents, steam and electricity, have brought the most remote parts of the globe into close contact. An order for merchandise or produce is now received in one-tenth the time it formerly required. The limit of foreign credit is now thirty days, when the minimum even a few months since was sixty days. Time is money. Capital is made four times as efficient as it was within the last decade. Nature has thus accomplished what art and contrivance have vainly essayed to effect.

But velocity of movement, and the rapid transmission of thought, are not the most conspicuous results of this change. The material consequences are in close correspondence with the moral and intellectual. The economy of time and the improved processes of credit will yet bring into harmony labor and capital.

We have remarked that the principle of restraint as regards excessive credit was to be sought in a graduated rate of discount, and corresponding term of credit—a principle on which banks have been unconsciously acting from the earliest period of their organization.

The agency of nature has come to equalize the profits of capital and the rate of interest. The value of money tends every hour to this desirable consummation. A loan may be negotiated on the Stock Exchange of London, on the Bourse of Paris, or on the exchange of Hamburg, at a difference less than the expense of remitting specie between these places. The decline in the value of money has kept pace with the reduced term of credit and rate of interest; and it is this reduction of credit that has checked its abuse. When credits were more extended—when the same bill of exchange or promissory note represented a number of commodities, no check could be found in bank regulations in restraint of renewals; but when credits were shortened, and bills were drawn at sight, the preventive check which had been so anxiously and fruitlessly sought, was found. Nature supplied what the ingenuity of man had vainly endeavored to invent.

Having concluded our exposition of the system of currency

and banking suggested by us, it is proper that we should state the probable *modus operandi* of the system.

1. The retiring of the notes of the National Banks, amounting to $300,000,000, and the substitution of the notes to be issued by the proposed Board of Currency, to be called United States Treasury notes. Notice to be given to the National Banks, say, on the 1st of January, 1871, to retire one-third of their notes on the subsequent 1st of April, one-third on the 1st of July, and one-third on the 1st of October. This is readily accomplished. As the notes of the National Banks are paid into the Treasury for taxes and other government dues, the Secretary of the Treasury has only to apprise the respective banks that such an amount of their notes waits redemption, and if not redeemed at a specified time, a cancellation of their bonds to an equal amount will take place. Thus the retiring of them will be insured. This will not be a *contraction* of the currency, but a *substitution* of one species of paper currency for another—a substitution of United States Treasury notes for National Bank notes.

2. The cancellation of the bonds of the United States, (deposited in the Treasury as security for the National Banks' notes,) by applying to this purpose the excess of the new United States Treasury notes beyond the public expenditure, (supposed to amount to $100,000,000,) at whatever rate per month may be deemed expedient, so as to correspond with an equal reduction of the floating debt, (the old legal tender notes,) by which there would be a saving to the Government of interest on $300,000,000 of bonded debt.

3. That authority be given to the Secretary of the Treasury to sell any surplus of gold arising from the duties on imports, in open market, in his discretion as to time and amounts, after payment of the gold interest, but never to keep a larger surplus of gold on hand than would be sufficient to pay one quarter's interest.

By such an arrangement, while the new United States Treasury notes will readily find their way into general circulation, through the various channels of the public expenditure, both the floating and the funded debt will be in process of reduc-

tion, in such proportions as it shall be found expedient to reduce the former—in other words, safe to contract the currency;
at the same time, the public will get rid gradually of a large
mass of irredeemable paper currency. The profit on the circulation amounting to at least $300,000,000, will be a gain to
the government and to the people, instead of a gain to the
banks. Specie payments will, in all probability, be restored
within three years, with a moderate and gradual contraction
of the currency; while the entire annual expenditure of the
Government will be defrayed from a fund adequate to the public service without taxation to the extent of that saving.

The scheme, in its financial aspect, requires a little additional
explanation. The amount of new notes to be issued is estimated at $400,000,000, in the ratio of the increase of population,
which is found to be about 33⅓ per cent. every decade, equivalent to ten dollars *per capita.* We have already said that this
rate *per capita* is a *tentative* experiment. If found to be in due
proportion to the wants of the population, for that is the true
criterion—neither more nor less than will maintain our currency at a level with the currency of foreign countries—the sum
per capita will be unalterable. It will be a fixed relation,
absolutely necessary to secure steadiness. For example, if,
after trial, ten dollars per head is found to be the proper proportion in 1870, the population then being assumed to be
42,000,000, the amount of currency will be $420,000,000. It
follows that, the *aggregate* increase of population being 33⅓
per cent., in 1880 the population will be 56,000,000, and the
currency will amount to $560,000,000. The public expendi-
ture, it is estimated, unless we should have war, will be brought
within $300,000,000.[14] Should this be the case, there will be a
surplus of income over *current* expenditure of $100,000,000,
and, the surplus of gold being also $100,000,000, there will be
a specie reserve of $100,000,000 to protect the new notes, un-
less the present mode of collecting the revenue on imports
should be changed.

The system we have suggested of banking and currency,

---

[14] It will be recollected that the Secretary of the Treasury, in his last Annual Report. stated that the public expenditure admitted of being reduced to $250,000,000.

pre-supposes a return to specie payments. It is proper, therefore, that we offer such views on this subject as would show the probability of that event within a reasonable time, in case of a change of our financial system.

This subject cannot be intelligently discussed unless in connection with the public expenditure and the state of our foreign trade. 1. *The Public Expenditure.* Mr. McCulloch, in his Annual Report for 1868, states that the public expenditure ought to be reduced to $250,000,000. He estimates the revenue from the two principal sources—the customs and the internal revenue at $300,000,000—a saving of $50,000,000, which he would apply to paying off an equal amount of funded debt. 2. *State of our Foreign Trade.* This is an element of great importance, of which little or no notice has been taken in the remarks made on the subject. We cannot at present form an estimate of the crop of 1869–70, but supposing it to yield 2,250,000 bales, and the price for the average of the season to be ten pence in gold, equal to twenty cents currency, the money value would be $225,000,000

The crop of 1868–69 has been estimated at a money
    value of 250,000,000
                                    —————
                                  475,000,000
Add to this the value of Rice, Sugar, Naval Stores,
    Petroleum, Tobacco, &c. . . . 75,000,000
                                    —————
                                $550,000,000

We are reasonable in estimating an aggregate money value in exports of $550,000,000 for the two years 1870, 1871.

3. A no less important element, however, is the aggregate amount of our imports. The balance of commercial debt has been greatly against us since the year 1865. In 1865 and 1866 we imported much more in value than we exported. The cheapness of money stimulated the consumption and importation of foreign fabrics greatly beyond our ability to pay for. We were compelled to send our gold and bonds to redress the balance against us. The contraction of the currency will have the effect, by lessening the consumption of foreign merchandise,

to diminish our importations. Without any formal resolution or act of Congress to reduce the floating debt, the process of such diminution is going on. The year 1870 will witness a large reduction of our imports from Europe. This co-operating with the increased value of our exports, will bring about an equilibrium between our exports and imports, which will be a good *preparation* for resumption. But this cannot take place unless Congress has the moral courage to cancel a large portion of the legal tender notes, or compel the National Banks to retire their currency. One or the other of these curtailments must take place, before we shall be able to resume specie payment. But if Congress will authorize the Secretary of the Treasury to cancel the legal tender notes at the moderate rate of $50,000,000 annually, and, at the same time, reduce the public expenses to an equal extent, the exports being within the next two years brought to an equality with the imports, we may, perhaps, witness a return to cash payments on the first of January, 1872.

The appearance of the report of Mr. Welles, Commissioner of Internal Revenue, enables us to add some illustrations of the subject discussed in the present article. The relation of the paper currency to the wealth and population of the country is too intimate to be overlooked. Mr. Welles estimates the National wealth at twenty-three and a half thousand millions of dollars. We are inclined to accept the correction of this statement by a writer in *Lippincott's Magazine* for February, who rectifies his calculation by adding fifteen hundred millions of dollars, on account of the expense of the war; thus enlarging Mr. Welles's estimate of the National wealth to twenty-five thousand millions.

The same writer exposes a remarkable discrepancy between Mr. Welles's estimate and that of the Secretary of the Treasury with regard to the amount of the National wealth; the latter officer estimating it at fifty thousand millions. The source of this difference is very evident. Mr. Boutwell seems to have assumed that the rate of increase of the National wealth in the decade from 1860 to 1870 was nearly the same as that between 1850 and 1860, making no allowance for the waste of productive resources caused by the war, while Mr. Welles appears to have made such allowance. He computed the increase at 8 per cent. per annum; and as Mr. Kennedy's *Preliminary View of the Eighth Census* estimated the National wealth at sixteen thousand millions of dollars in 1860, the estimate by Mr. Welles of the rate of annual increase, 8 per cent., was eighty millions at the end of the decade, or the aggregate of twenty-five thousand six hundred millions. If the same rate of progress had continued to the present time, it would have presented the large aggregate of nearly forty thousand millions of dollars.

The bearing of these facts on the subject in hand will be seen on reference to the state of the bank note currency and the population in 1860. The population of the United States at that period was 31,445,322, and the quantity of the bank note currency $207,000,000, which was within a fraction of $7 *per capita*. In the same proportion, the population being now (as estimated by Mr. Kennedy) forty-two millions, the aggregate amount of our paper currency ought not to exceed three hundred millions of dollars. It will be borne in mind that the decade from 1850 to 1860 was one of the most prosperous in our annals, and the present age the most fruitful in those inventions by which the use of money is saved or partially superseded. The Clearing House is an eminent example, while the extension and multiplication of railroads operates in the same direction.

We have heard the objection, that the rate at which population increases, although very rapid in the United States, is too slow for the commercial activity and industrial enterprise of the American people. It has been affirmed that the rate of progress of the National wealth or some compound ratio between wealth and population would afford a safer criterion than population alone. Commercial prosperity is subject to the hazards and vicissitudes of war, and much of our apparent wealth has had this unstable basis, while the requirements of the people constitute a power that is self-acting and independent of extrinsic influences. But let any principle of proportion be adopted that may be deemed expedient;—the great *desideratum* is *fixity* of the ratio.   What is required for a stable currency, not open to the influences of credit, is some settled rule that would leave nothing to the discretion of the issuers, but be under the control of a fixed principle, increasing or contracting with the wants of the population, leaving the ratio, when once fixed, unalterable.   Let us suppose eight dollars *per capita* to be the fixed ratio, and forty-two millions, as at present, the amount of population, increasing at the rate of three and a half per cent. per annum or thirty-five per cent. every decade.   The paper currency, on that supposition, would be increasing with the population, and would amount at present to three hundred and thirty-six millions.   At the census of 1880 the population, increasing at the same rate as before, would be fifty-four millions, and the currency would necessarily have augmented from three hundred to four hundred and thirty-two millions ; or if the ratio of ten dollars is preferred, the paper currency would be increased from four hundred and twenty millions in 1870 to five hundred and forty millions in 1880.

It must be obvious to those conversant with the subject, that the scheme of currency and banking, of which the above is an outline, is a combination of a principle first enunciated by the late eminent economist, David Ricardo, and that system of free banking which is the principal characteristic of the Scotch scheme of banking.   Mr. Ricardo was the first to announce that there was no necessary connection between the business of banking proper, which is the lending of money, and the issue of a paper currency ; and he made the basis of his system a total separation of these functions ; but he did not live to give it complete maturity.   A subsequent economist, Col. Torrens, the present Lord Overstone, persuaded Sir Robert Peel to embody the idea in an act of legislation, which was done in 1844, by the separation of the Bank of England into two departments, one of issue and the other of banking ; but, unfortunately, he coupled it with the restriction that the notes issued by the banking department should not exceed £14,000,000, which allowed the Bank to receive any sum on deposit which was liable to *immediate* call for payment in gold, while the same deposits loaned and liable to call from the creditors of the Bank at longer or shorter periods, placed the Bank in such embarrassment that two suspensions of the act became necessary.

It is evident that one of the reforms in banking on sound and safe principles, contemplated under the system above recommended, is a correspondence in *term* of payment as well as *amount*, between the *deposits* of banks and their *loans*, which does not exist at present. For example, depositors should be required to give from thirty to forty-five days' notice; and if this were the established usage, the system of bank credits would conform to its liabilities, credits would be shortened, renewals would not exist, and banks being simply banks of deposit and discount, and not of circulation, the correspondence to which we have referred would prevail, speculation would be lessened, and the great desideratum would be attained of making banks exclusively the distributors of capital.

Mr. Ricardo's plan differs from the above in two important particulars. 1. His Board of Commissioners, consisting of five, were to have the power to increase the paper currency at their discretion. Under the system we propose, the Commissioners of Currency, consisting of three, would have no such discretion. They would be bound to follow a principle that would be self-acting and unalterable, namely, the increase of the paper currency in the ratio of the increase of population. 2. Mr. Ricardo's plan is, that of a species of National bank. Its connection with the Government a certain control and influence over it. Under the plan above proposed, the Board of Currency suggested would form an independent department connected in no other way with the Government, than as the medium of its receipts and disbursements.

The figures we have presented demonstrate that an increase of paper currency in the ratio of the increase of population, will furnish an ample supply of such currency. According to those figures the increase of wealth between 1850 and 1860, the most prosperous period in our annals, was 126½ per cent. The increase in the number of banks and the bank capital, was between 70 and 80 per cent. The increase of the bank loans about 60 per cent. The increase of the population 35 per cent., while *the addition made to the bank note currency was only about* 27 *per cent.*, showing conclusively that the proportion of increase of the currency to population, seven dollars *per capita*, making, in the aggregate, $300,000,000, would supply an ample amount, and proving that paper issues do not augment in the ratio of bank capital, as has been proved in the instance of the Bank of England, and clearly demonstrating further the efficacy of those contrivances for economising the use of money, such as the clearing-house.

In regard to the other branch of the subject, namely, the throwing open to general competition the business of banking, the example of Scotland is conclusive, where all who choose may engage in banking without applying to the legislature for a charter, subject to *unlimited liability*, on the *principles of an ordinary mercantile partnership.*

APPENDIX IV

Supply and Consumption of Cotton

De Bow's Review May 1858

ART. VI.—SUPPLY AND CONSUMPTION OF COTTON,

WITH TABLES ANNEXED OF THE SUPPLY AND CONSUMPTION FOR THE LAST THIRTY YEARS, BY J. N. CARDOZA.

We incline to the opinion that Mr. Cardoza, who is an able writer and statistician, much over-estimates the supply of cotton, and greatly underrates the consumption, but his paper is worthy of preservation.—EDITOR.

GENERAL REMARKS.—We are passing through one of those commercial cycles with which we are destined to be visited at about every decade. One branch of our subject has an intimate relation to the changes which have been thence superinduced. The consumption of cotton having greatly increased, correspondently with the enlargement of productive power, has again receded to the point at which it stood five years since. It would serve to elucidate the subject if the general causes which led to its unparalleled extension and reaction were briefly indicated. The last ten years have been characterised by all the signs of a delusive prosperity. The cotton trade has largely participated in the stimulus, which has been imparted to various branches of commerce. In the recoil which has taken place, more than proportionally to the advance in the raw material, we are perhaps to look for the solution in the speculative character of the trade itself. There is no staple of commerce in which there are such large sums invested, and which, consequently, feel as sensibly the influence of a financial revulsion. It is impossible at this time to determine, even proximately, the degree and duration of that decline, dependent to a great extent on the renewed operation of the causes which have so greatly enlarged the limits of the cotton trade, in common with those other branches of productive industry, which appear to have received a forced and unnatural impulse. These causes may be reduced to three general heads :

1. The increase of gold and re-distribution of both the precious metals.

2. The extension of credit in all enterprises in which it could be made available.

3. The new applications of steam and electricity.

An argumentation of the precious metals will show its effects either by a general rise of prices, or by extending the sphere of commercial transactions. It seems to be admitted that there has been no general advance of prices at all commensurate with the addition that has been made to the stock of gold since the Californian and Australian discoveries, nor has there been such an increased consumption in the arts as could have absorbed any considerable portion of the excess. We are led, necessarily, therefore, to the conclusion, that the enlargement of trade, and the increased number of exchanges, and not the enhancement of prices, have employed the large additions made to the supply of gold within the last ten years.*

To the effect of this addition in stimulating enterprise and exertion in Europe and the United States, is to be conjoined the very considerable accessions of silver in the East, which have operated, also, in supplying a new incentive to production and trade in that division of the globe. The silks and teas of China as well as the cotton of the British East Indies, have been paid for by nearly depleting Western Europe of its silver. The gold of California and Australia has more than replaced the other metal—it has stimulated production and consumption, as well were gold has filled the void caused by exporting the silver, causing a change of the standard, as were no such change has taken place—as well in Great Britain and the United States as in France and Germany. The result, therefore, of this re-distribution of the precious metals, particularly silver, has been the same in kind as if new silver as well as gold mines had been discovered. The combined effect has been that the entire mass of monied capital has, by its greatly increased volume, produced the usual consequence, a fall in the value of money, as the antecedent of speculation. The history of all simply commercial revulsions present the same phase as relates to the originating cause. A plethora of monied capital, compared with its remunerative employment, has invariably led to overaction in trade. The crisis of 1824-'25 in England was preceded by a period of stagna-

---

* In this conclusion we are sustained by the high authority of Mr. Tooke, who in his History of Prices has demonstrated that there has been no general advance of prices as the effect of the California and Australian Discoveries, but that the extension of commerce and the increased number of exchanges have absorbed the additions made to the stock of the precious metals. That future additions at the same rate of increase will be attended by an enhancement of prices generally, with no correspondent increase of trade, can admit of no rational doubt, as that such addition, without a proportional enlargement of the present limits of commerce, must be accompanied by the general depreciation of these metals.

tion in commerce, accompanied by a superabundance of monied resources. The interest of money fell. Speculation and over-trading succeeded. Boundless credit, with its collapse and almost general bankruptcy were the results. The same phenomena were the forerunners of the recent convulsion, antecedently to which money was worth only 1½ to 2 per cent. in all the financial centres of Europe.

That all parts of the world open to such an influence had felt the effects of the great additions made to the metallic treasures of the world, enlarging the limits of general commerce, does not admit of controversy. The natural, as it is the inevitable consequence, was an extension of credit—but to a degree beyond all parallel within an equal period of time. In Great Britain, in the United States, and on the continent of Europe, there was a heaping up of obligations in all the various modes of credit. Every process in the formation of fictitious capital was exhausted. In England it took the form principally of commercial advances and investments in foreign securities. In the United States, of railroad, land, and mercantile speculations. On the continent of Europe it assumes all the shapes of hazardous enterprise, excepting that of jobbing in land, which was peculiar to the United States. It was not the agency of credit, as too generally imagined, in the issue of bank-notes, but the increase and misapplication of capital and deposits employed in banking, constantly enlarging the ever widening circle of credits, created by corporate and individual obligations, which became infinitely multiplied in the diversified form of checks, bills of exchange, promissory notes, certificates of deposit and book debts. The changes in commercial law also imparted to speculative adventure increased stimulation. In England such was the effect of repealing the corn laws and modifying the navigation acts. In the United States the reduced rate of duties, under the act of 1856, excessively augmented importations.

PROBABLE SUPPLY OF 1858.—The supply of cotton is at all times dependent on the weather; but the circumstance of two unfavorable seasons in succession in the United States, is remarkable in the history of the cotton culture. The crop of 1856-7, fell short about 11 per cent. of that of 1855-6 ; that of 1857-8, will, it is fairly estimated, not exceed that of 1856-7. The estimate that assumed some 3,250,000 bales has gradually receded to 3,000,000, and few of the estimates now range higher than 2,900,000 for this year's product.

The usual emigration to the virgin lands of the Southwest would, no doubt, have been followed by the ordinary rate of increase, assisted by improved processes of agriculture, but for the physical checks to cultivation in a backward spring, heavy rains, and premature frosts. But for these hindrances to extended culture, the crop would, no doubt, have reached 3,700,000 to 4,000,000 bales. Opinions vary widely as to the extent of the production. One of the indexes by which we may reach an approximative result, is the extent of the receipts at the shipping ports.

The ability of the planters generally, to hold over for what they may deem more remunerative prices, is unquestionable. The high money value of the staple for the last three years, has enabled many of them to clear off the incumbrances upon their estates ; and the improvement of their pecuniary position is likely to influence their conduct, in this respect, more extensively than usual. These considerations will operate, of course, only within certain limits ; for the fair presumption is that the next crop will be a very full one, and this probability is to be weighed against the hazards of holding, in the prospect of an abundant yield. The receipts have fallen off to date, as compared with last year, to the extent of 479,726 bales ; but the comparison, to be proper, should embrace a period of at least five years. Calculated on this principle, the average annual per centage of increase to the 19th February in each year, from 1851-2 to 1855-6, has been a little more than 58 per cent. estimated according to *quantity* and not *number of bales.* This is exclusive of 1856-7, as the monetary embarrassments of the last three months of 1857 retarded the receipts and rendered that year exceptional. In this ratio, the total receipts ought to reach 2,960,913 bales. Between, however, the quantity and number of bales made this year, there is said to be a wider difference than at almost any preceding season. The amount of unmerchantable cotton was unusually large, owing to the unfavorable weather for maturing the crop. To what extent this will operate in reducing the quantity of merchantable cotton is yet only matter of conjecture. Thus much for the supply from the United States.

The East India receipts in Europe will, of course, be governed by the course of political events in the Oriental countries in which war now prevails. If peace should be shortly made with China, a portion of Surat cotton, which was diverted in 1847 to Western Europe, (which amounts on an average of some five years back, to 150,000 bales,) will take the usual direction to China, which, in connection with the fall of price in the European market, must proportionally lessen the East India export to Europe. Under any circumstances, the European receipts of East India cotton cannot be estimated at a higher figure than 700,000 bales, which is a diminution from last year's receipt of 100,000 bales. On these data we estimated the

supply from the United States at..................... 2,900,000
East Indies... 700,000
Brazil, Egypt, &c..................................... 300,000
——————
3,900,000

PROBABLE CONSUMPTION IN 1858.—The consumption of cotton differs from its production in being influenced solely by moral and not physical causes, such as frosts, floods, drought, &c. These do not affect the demand ; but war, revolution, and financial changes increase or diminish it according to the duration and intensity of their operation. There is this remarkable difference, however, as to the influence of these circumstances, on the production and consumption respectively. A failure in the supply from natural causes, seldom affects it more than from five to ten per cent. in any one season. It has required two successive short crops to reduce the product 12 per cent. from the yield of 1855-6. But the reduction of demand from financial circumstances exclusively, within the short period of two months, from the middle of October to the middle of December, was, in Great Britain, 30 per cent., the price falling in a higher proportion, and in the United States upwards of 50 per cent.

The wars in the East will have a limited, and, perhaps, temporary influence on the demand; but the monetary revulsion which has swept like a whirlwind over Europe and the United States, will have consequences of a more general and permanent character. The limitation and curtailment of credit, and the consequent diminution of purchasing power in the great body of consumers of cotton goods, must affect the demand for the raw material to an extent that will most materially influence its value. Any estimate as to consumption and prices in Europe during the present year, must necessarily be conjectural in a higher degree than in periods in which there are fewer changes in the value of money. These changes constitute more than ever a disturbing element. In a few weeks prices fell with a rapidity that has rarely marked any previous alteration in the relation of demand and supply, and these alterations have not yet worked out all their full consequences.

Independently, however, of any general causes which may influence prices, oscillating above or below a certain point, which must be assumed as that to which they will constantly gravitate; the great object of present anxiety is to know at what standard they will finally settle and adjust themselves. We must, in the absence of any but conjectural data, look to *probabilities*, when these transitory circumstances have spent their force. To what do probabilities lead, then, as relates to the consumption? The under stimulus being measurably withdrawn, which was found in excessive credit, we are bound to bring the consumption within narrower limits, not losing sight of the causes which imparted to it an unusual impulse. These were free trade, cheap money, inventive power and extended intercourse. These causes will continue to operate, but modified by circumstances, such as high price of the raw material, diminished demand for goods and yarn, &c. The motive to produce, as well as the ability to consume, will receive a serious check, at least for the present year. We must be influenced in our calculations by views of moderate improvement and gradual amelioration.

At what point, then, shall we fix our estimate of the consumption, which will be approximative on probable grounds. Opinions vary here much more considerably than as relates to the supply. Should the crop of the United States, of the present year, not exceed 2,900,-000 bales, and not be disproportionately pressed on the market, it is reasonable to conclude that the average price in Europe would be equivalent to 6d. in England for Middling Upland, as that standard of value which would not unduly stimulate or check consumption. This is, however, matter of conjectural inference, as well as the extent of consumption. Opinions differ as regard the British consumption, from 150,000 to 200,000 bales. We presume that it will range between 35 to 37,000 bales weekly. It appears not material whether the highest or lowest figure is adopted, in view of the large excess of the supply over the consumption. We will, for the moment, assume

the consumption in Great Britain to be 36,000 bales weekly, or for
the year, say.................................... 1,900,000 bales
The consumption on the continent of Europe will not
suffer so large a proportional diminution. In Germany, although there was a greater prostration of
commercial confidence than in any other part of Europe in the latter portion of 1847, still owing to the
great increase of manufacturing power in that country, consumption will be better sustained than in
Great Britain or the United States. In France the
diminution will be comparatively limited. We have
deducted from the consumption of the Continent,
therefore, about 15 per cent. from the average of the
last three years................................ 850,000 bales
The consumption of the United States will have been
reduced much more than in any other part of the
world where cotton is extensively consumed. It is
estimated at nearly two-thirds less than last year.
There has been a large destruction of manufacturing
capital and a general closing of factories. The exports to the Northern ports have fallen short of those
of last year to the same time 369,250 bales, six months
of the season having elapsed. For these reasons the
consumption of the United States cannot be supposed to exceed................................. 300,000 bales
                                                    ―――――――
Making the total consumption,................... 3,050,000 bales
Comparing on these data the entire supply with the total consumption for 1858, assuming the stock in Europe to have been 625,000 on the first of January,
1858, (in Great Britain 452,000 and on the Continent 172,500,) the following would appear to be the
result as the probable excess of the supply beyond the
consumption on the 31st December, 1858. Stock in
Europe January 1, 1858...................... 625,000 bales
Supply from the United States.................. 2,900,000 "
  "   East Indies........................... 700,000 "
  "   Brazil, Egypt, &c...................... 300,000 "
                                                    ―――――――
Total Supply,.............................. 4,525,000 "
British Consumption.............. 1,900,000 bales
Continent of Europe.............. 850,000 "
United States .... 300,000 "
                                  ――――――― 3,050,000 bales
                                                    ―――――――
Excess of supply beyond consumption............. 1,475,000 "

So that if the consumption should be increased from one to two
hundred thousand bales, and the supply lessened in the same ratio, the
margin of excess is sufficiently ample to cover any increase on the

one side or diminution on the other, or both combined, that can be supposed.

We annex tables of the consumption and supply for the first thirty years, embracing average periods of five years. The results show that for ten years, between 1827-8 and 1837-8, there was an increased rate of consumption of between 1 and 2 per cent., while in the subsequent period of ten years the consumption diminished from $\frac{2}{3}$ to 4 per cent., the rate of increase being nearly the same for the last as compared with the first period.

Contrary to expectation there has been less variation in the supply than in the consumption, the former not differing more than from $1\frac{678}{1000}$ to $2\frac{918}{1000}$ per cent. between any two periods, but keeping a nearly equal progress in the last period between 1847-8 and 1856-7, inclusive. Another remarkable fact is disclosed by these figures as regards the supply, to wit, that from the first to the second decennial period there has been a progressive decrease in the rate of increase, while in the last decade there has been an increase in that rate.

For these tables we are indebted to a gentleman of this city, to whom we have had to acknowledge similar favors on precious occasions, and for whose accuracy in figures and calculations we can vouch.

CHARLESTON, 1858.

—

CONSUMPTION OF COTTON.

United States.		Europe.		Totals.	Total of periods of five years.	Increase.
1827–28	121,000	1828	1,104,000	1,225,000		
1828–29	119,000	1829	1,219,000	1,288,000		
1829–30	127,000	1830	1,200,000	1,327,000	6,911,000	
1830–31	182,000	1831	1,305,000	1,487,000		2,221,000
1831–32	174,000	1832	1,360,000	1,534,000		or $4\frac{812}{1000}$ p.c. yearly.
1832–33	194,000	1833	1,350,000	1,544,000		
1833–34	196,000	1834	1,410,000	1,604,000		
1834–35	217,000	1835	1,475,000	1,692,000	8,742,000	
1835–36	237,000	1836	1,680,000	1,917,000		3,132,200
1836–37	228,000	1837	1,760,000	1,988,000		or $6\frac{815}{1000}$ p.c. yearly.
1837–88	246,000	1838	2,000,000	2,246,000		
1838–39	276,000	1839	1,708,000	1,984,000		
1839–40	295,000	1840	2,300,000	2,595,000	11,874,000	
1840–41	297,000	1841	2,285,000	2,582,000		1,430,000
1841–42	267,000	1842	2,200,000	2,467,000		or $2\frac{800}{1000}$ p.c. yearly.
1842–43	325,000	1843	2,450,000	2,775,000		
1843–44	347,000	1844	2,500,000	2,847,000		
1844–45	389,000	1845	2,356,000	2,745,000	13,304,000	
1845–46	423,000	1846	2,341,000	2,784,000		2,058,000
1846–47	428,000	1847	1,745,000	2,178,000		or $2\frac{918}{1000}$ p.c. yearly.
1847–48	532,000	1848	2,159,000	2,691,000		
1848–49	518,000	1849	2,477,000	2,995,000		
1849–50	488,000	1850	2,451,000	2,989,000	15,362,000	
1850–51	404,000	1851	2,618,000	3,022,000		4,105,000
1851–52	603,000	1852	3,112,000	3,715,000		or $4\frac{850}{1000}$ p.c. yearly.
1852–53	671,000	1853	3,013,000	3,684,000		
1853–54	610,000	1854	3,116,000	3,726,000		
1854–55	593,000	1855	3,316,000	3,909,000	19,467,000	
1855–56	694,000	1856	3,673,000	4,367,000		
1856–57	702,000	1857	3,079,000	3,781,000		
	10,898,000		64,762,000	75,660,000	75,660,000	

SUPPLY OF COTTON.

Crops of U. S. Cotton.		Imports into Europe from other soils.		Totals.	Totals of periods of five years.	Increase.
1827-28	721,000	1828	444,000	1,165,000		
1828-29	870,000	1829	425,000	1,295,000		
1829-30	977,000	1830	423,000	1,400,000	6,825,000	
1830-31	1,089,000	1831	478,000	1,512,000		2,221,000
1831-32	987,000	1832	466,000	1,456,000		or 5 $\frac{796}{1000}$ p. c. yearly.
1832-33	1,070,000	1833	472,000	1,542,000		
1833-34	1,205,000	1834	371,000	1,576,000		
1834-35	1,254,000	1835	551,000	1,805,000	9,046,000	
1835-36	1,361,000	1836	755,000	2,116,000		2,204,000
1836-37	1,423,000	1837	584,000	2,007,000		or 4 $\frac{456}{1000}$ p. c. yearly.
1837-38	1,801,000	1838	533,000	2,334,000		
1838-39	1,861,000	1839	471,000	2,332,000		
1839-40	2,178,000	1840	473,000	2,651,000	11,250,000	
1840-41	1,635,000	1841	569,000	2,204,000		1,715,000
1841-42	1,664,000	1842	545,000	2,229,000		or 2 $\frac{878}{1000}$ p. c. yearly.
1842-43	2,379,000	1843	509,000	2,888,000		
1843-44	2,030,000	1844	511,000	2,541,000		
1844-45	2,395,000	1845	461,000	2,856,000	12,965,000	
1845-46	2,101,000	1846	319,000	2,420,000		2,684,000
1846-47	1,779,000	1847	481,000	2,260,000		or 3 $\frac{834}{1000}$ p. c. yearly.
1847-48	2,848,000	1848	401,000	2,749,000		
1848-49	2,729,000	1849	538,000	3,267,000		
1849-50	2,097,000	1850	747,000	2,844,000	15,649,000	
1850-51	2,355,000	1851	680,000	3,035,000		4,094,000
1851-52	3,015,000	1852	789,000	3,754,000		or 4 $\frac{757}{1000}$ p. c. yearly.
1852-53	3,263,000	1853	882,000	4,145,000		
1853-54	2,930,000	1854	630,000	3,560,000		
1854-55	2,847,000	1855	783,000	3,630,000	19,743,000	
1855-56	3,529,000	1856	843,000	4,372,000		
1856-57	2,940,000	1857	1,096,000	4,036,000		
	58,303,000		17,175,000	75,478,000	75,478,000	